Scottish Property Law

Scottish Property Law

An Introduction

Angus McAllister MA (Hons), LLB, Solicitor
Senior Lecturer in Law, University of Paisley

T G Guthrie LLB (Hons)
Lecturer in Law, University of Glasgow

Edinburgh
Butterworths
1992

United Kingdom	Butterworths, a Division of Reed Elsevier (UK) Ltd, 4 Hill Street, EDINBURGH EH2 3JZ and Halsbury House, 35 Chancery Lane, LONDON WC2A 1EL
Australia	Butterworths, a Division of Reed International Books Australia Pty Ltd, CHATSWOOD, New South Wales
Canada	Butterworths Canada Ltd, MARKHAM, Ontario
Hong Kong	Butterworths Asia (Hong Kong), HONG KONG
India	Butterworths Asia, NEW DELHI
Ireland	Butterworth (Ireland) Ltd, DUBLIN
Malaysia	Malayan Law Journal Sdn Bhd, KUALA LUMPUR
New Zealand	Butterworths of New Zealand Ltd, WELLINGTON
Singapore	Butterworths Asia, SINGAPORE
South Africa	Butterworth Publishers (Pty) Ltd, DURBAN
USA	Lexis Law Publishing, CHARLOTTESVILLE, Virginia

First published 1992. Reprinted 1993, 1996, 1997, 1999
A CIP Catalogue record for this book is available from the British Library.

ISBN 0 406 00105 7

Typeset by Phoenix Photosetting, Chatham, Kent
Printed and bound in Great Britain by
Redwood Books, Trowbridge, Wiltshire

Visit us at our website: http://butterworthsscotland.com

Preface

This book is intended as an introductory textbook on the law relating to heritable property. The title, therefore, for the sake of convenience, uses the word 'property' in its colloquial rather than its strictly legal sense, in that no attempt has been made to cover the law of moveable property. On the other hand, we have included the main principles of conveyancing as they apply to the sale of heritable property.

It is hoped that the book will provide a basic grounding in the subject, not only for law students, but also for non-legal professionals in the property field. With the latter in mind we have included short sections on the legislation relating to estate agency and the case law on negligence claims against surveyors.

We would like to acknowledge our debt to the writers of the specialist textbooks on the various subjects that we have touched upon: without their work as a foundation, a book of this nature would have been immensely more difficult to write. We would also like to thank Mrs Eileen Mochar, Mr Ray McMaster and Mr Joseph Fitzgerald for their helpful comments on various parts of the book. Responsibility for the final text, of course, remains with the authors.

The law is stated as at 1 January 1992.

Angus McAllister
Thomas G Guthrie

February 1992

Contents

Table of Statutes

List of Cases

Bibliography

Bell	G J Bell *Principles of the Law of Scotland* (10th edn, 1899)
Ersk	J Erskine *An Institute of the Law of Scotland* (8th edn, 1871)
Gloag & Henderson	Gloag and Henderson *Introduction to the Law of Scotland* (9th edn, 1987, Greens)
Gordon	W M Gordon *Scottish Land Law* (1989, Greens)
Halliday	J M Halliday *Conveyancing Law and Practice in Scotland* (Greens) Volume I (1985), Volume II (1986) and Volume III (1987). References are not given for the volume concerned. The chapters run consecutively through the volumes; chapters 1-14 in Vol I, 15-24 in Vol II, and 25-42 in Vol III.
McAllister	A McAllister *Scottish Law of Leases* (1989, Butterworths)
McDonald	A J McDonald *Conveyancing Manual* (4th edn, 1989, T&T Clark)
Rankine	Rankine *Law of Landownership in Scotland* (4th edn, 1909)
Rowan-Robinson	J Rowan-Robinson *Compulsory Purchase and Compensation* (1990, Greens)
Sinclair	J H Sinclair *Handbook of Conveyancing Practice in Scotland* (2nd edn, 1990, Butterworths)
Stair	Viscount Stair *The Institutions of the Law of Scotland* (5th edn, 1832)
Walker	D M Walker *The Law of Prescription and Limitation of Actions in Scotland* (4th edn, 1990)
Young & Rowan-Robinson	E Young and J Rowan-Robinson *Scottish Planning Law and Procedure* (1985, T&T Clark)

List of Abbreviations

AC	Appeal Cases (Law Reports)
All ER	All England Law Reports
Bell's App	SS Bell's Scotch Appeals (House of Lords) 1842–50
D	Dunlop (Court of Session Reports, 2nd Series, 1838–62)
F	Fraser (Court of Session Reports, 5th Series, 1898–1906)
GWD	Green's Weekly Digest
HC	High Court
HL	House of Lords
Hume	Baron Hume's Reports of Decisions, 1781–1822
JLSS	Journal of the Law Society of Scotland
KB	King's Bench (Law Reports)
LR	Law Reports, Exchequer (1865–1875)
M	Macpherson (Court of Session Reports, 3rd Series, 1862–73)
Macq	Macqueen's House of Lords Reports 1851–65
Mor	Morison's Dictionary of Decisions, publ 1811
R	Rettie (Court of Session Reports, 4th Series, 1873–1898)
Rob App	Robinson's Scotch Appeals (House of Lords) 1840–41
S	Shaw (Court of Session Reports, 1st Series, 1821–1838)
Sc J	Scottish Jurist
SCLR	Scottish Civil Law Reports
SLCR	Scottish Land Court Reports
Sh Ct Rep	Sheriff Court Reports
SLR	Scottish Law Reporter
SLT	Scots Law Times
SN	Session Notes
TLR	Times Law Reports
WLR	Weekly Law Reports

1. Basic concepts

1. INTRODUCTION

By the term 'property' we normally mean anything that can be owned. A car, a TV set, a house are all property in this sense. The subject matter of this book, however, is property in a much narrower sense. Here we will be concerned with property in the form of land and buildings, what in England or elsewhere would be known as real property or real estate. The nearest equivalent Scottish term is heritable property, though as we will see shortly, it is not an exact equivalent.

We should also be aware that the term 'property' is commonly understood in other, slightly different ways. We talk about property rights to describe the various legal interests that a person may have in a piece of property, eg the right of an owner, or a tenant, or that of someone who enjoys a servitude right (eg a right of way) over another person's property. We also use the word 'property' to denote ownership itself, the legal right enjoyed by a property owner.

Heritable and moveable property

This is by far the most important way in which different types of property may be classified. The most convenient way to formulate the distinction is that heritable property (also sometimes referred to as heritage) consists of land and anything (including buildings) attached to the land. Heritable property also includes rights over, or connected with, land and buildings, eg the right of a tenant, or a right in security over land or buildings. Moveable property is simply every kind of property other than heritable property, eg a book, a car, or a TV set. It is heritable property in the above sense that will be the subject matter of this book.

Unfortunately this formulation, though we would get by with it, is not strictly accurate. The word 'heritable' does not simply

1

mean 'immoveable'. Historically the term derives from the law of succession as it used to be before radical reforms were made to the system in 1964.[1] Under the old system of succession, heritable property was the property which, after a person's death, passed entirely to the heir, usually the eldest son. Moveable property, on the other hand, was divided equally between all those entitled to succeed to the estate, eg all of the children. Land and buildings always passed to the heir because that was the most valuable property, and it was considered desirable that landed estates should pass to one person and remain intact over the generations, rather than be divided up and eventually fragmented. It is for this reason that the term heritable property tends to get equated with land and buildings and the rights connected with them. However, in strict law, the ambit of the term heritable property extends a little wider than this to include, for example, pensions, annuities, interest-bearing bonds and titles of honour.[2]

Since these additional types of heritable property are not part of our present subject matter it will be convenient, having put the record straight, to stick to our original definition from here on.

The distinction between heritable and moveable property can be of considerable practical importance. For example, when a house is sold, disputes can arise regarding which items (eg carpets, kitchen units etc) are sufficiently attached to the property to become heritable. The answer to this may determine whether the article has been bought along with the house, or whether it still belongs to the seller and can be removed by him. This will be decided by the law of fixtures, which is considered in detail in chapter 6.

In addition to the distinction between heritable and moveable property, there are other ways in which types of property are often classified. One such distinction is between **corporeal** and **incorporeal** property. Corporeal property consists of things that exist in the physical world and can be seen or touched, eg a car or a house, whereas incorporeal property consists of rights, eg company shares, patents, copyright etc. Another distinction is between **fungibles** (things like money or grain which can be replaced by their equivalent) and **nonfungibles** (things with a unique character or value). As these other ways of classifying property have little practical bearing upon our present subject matter, they will not be considered further.[3]

---

1 Succession (Scotland) Act 1964.
2 Gordon *Scottish Land Law* (1989) paras 1–03 to 1–04.
3 For a brief explanation of these terms, together with references for further reading, see Gloag & Henderson *Introduction to the Law of Scotland* (9th edn, 1987) para 36–2

Definition of ownership

There have been many attempts to frame a legal definition in Scots law of ownership (or 'property', in the final sense mentioned above). Probably the best one is that of the institutional writer Erskine, who defined ownership (or property) as 'the right of using and disposing of a subject as our own, except in so far as we are restrained by law or paction'.[1] 'Paction' means 'agreement' or 'contract'; in other words, the restrictions on an owner's rights may be imposed on him by the law or may be incurred voluntarily.

Erskine's definition is a useful one because, as well as being concise, it draws to our attention two fundamental aspects of ownership. First of all, it recognises that, in theory, the right of ownership is unqualified; ownership is still the largest right that a person can have in a thing. However, it also acknowledges that, in practice, there are many restrictions on an owner's rights. We may think that, because something is ours, we can do what we want with it, but it only takes a moment's consideration of many everyday examples to realise that this is not so. The fact that I own a gun does not mean that I am entitled to shoot people. I may own a car, but am not entitled to drive it unless I hold a driving licence. Likewise, an owner of land or a building is not entitled to do anything at all with it just because it is his. If he regularly creates an excessive noise, or in any other way interferes with his neighbours' right to the peaceful enjoyment of their own property, the neighbour or neighbours can take him to court to have the nuisance stopped.[2] If he wants to erect a building, he is subject to the legislation relating to town and country planning, which regulates the use and development of land.[3] He will normally therefore have to apply to the local planning authority (usually the district council) before proceeding. He must also conform to the laws relating to building control, to ensure that any building he may erect is safe and otherwise conforms to proper standards.[4] At the ultimate extreme, under the law relating to compulsory purchase, he may be forcibly deprived of his right of ownership altogether.[5]

An owner may also, of his own free will, further restrict his right

---

1 Erskine *An Institute of the Law of Scotland* (8th edn, 1871) II, 2, 1; for a critical discussion of this and rival definitions, see Rankine *Law of Landownership in Scotland* (4th edn, 1909) ch 5.
2 See ch 4, pt 2 below.
3 See ch 12, pt 2 below.
4 See ch 12, pt 3 below.
5 See ch 18 below.

of ownership by granting subsidiary property rights to others. For example, he may grant a right of way over his land (or some other servitude right) to a neighbouring owner. Or he may deprive himself entirely of the right to occupy his property for a period of time by granting a lease to a tenant.

Real and personal rights

It is part of the basic nature of a legal system, not confined to property law, that some people have rights which can be legally enforced in the courts. Likewise, other people owe legal obligations, also enforceable. This brings us to another fundamental distinction which we must take note of, that between a **real** right (*ius in re*) and a **personal** right (*ius ad rem* or *ius in personam*).

The difference between the two is that a real right can be enforced against anyone in the world, whereas a personal right can only be exacted against a particular person, the one who owes the corresponding obligation.[1] A real right is typically created by the completion of some kind of formality, eg the recording of a title deed in the Register of Sasines.[2] A personal right, on the other hand, may be created by a contract, or even automatically, by operation of the law; under the law of delict, for example, if someone causes harm to another by his negligent actions, the law will impose a personal obligation on him to make reparation to the person whom he has harmed.

The most obvious, and probably the most easily understood, real right is that of ownership: if I own a piece of property I may defend my right against anyone at all, not just against a particular person. And the way by which ownership of heritable property is acquired provides a good example of the distinction between real and personal rights.

As we will see in chapter 15, the first stage in the purchase of heritable property is the completion of a contract (known as missives) between the buyer and seller. At this point ownership is not transferred; in fact there is still no proof that the seller *is* the owner and is legally entitled to sell. There may be a flaw in his title, or he may even be a tenant or some other kind of occupier who is fraudulently attempting to sell the property without having the right to do so. All that has been created by the contract are personal

---

1   See Stair *The Institutions of the Law of Scotland* (5th edn, 1832) I, 1, 22; *Ersk* III, 1, 2.
2   See ch 15 below.

rights and obligations between the parties, including an obligation by the seller, in return for the price, to transfer ownership with a good title to the purchaser. If the seller fails to do so, the purchaser may sue him for breach of contract and claim damages, but he will have no right to the property; his personal right only gives him a right of redress against the seller.

The second stage is for the seller to fulfil his personal obligation by taking the necessary steps to transfer ownership to the purchaser. This involves, among other things, satisfying the purchaser that he has a good title to the property and, finally, signing and handing over a formal document of transfer (usually a deed known as a disposition). This deed is made effective by the purchaser sending it for recording to the Register of Sasines (or, depending on the area in which the property is situated, to be registered in the Land Register for Scotland).[1] Once the title has been recorded (or registered) the purchaser is truly the owner of the property. He now has a real right to it; or, to use the correct technical expression, he is the **infeft proprietor**.[2]

It will be noted that two different registers were mentioned above, the Register of Sasines and the Land Register for Scotland. The Land Register only operates at the moment in certain areas of the country which have become operational for the new system of registration of title. Eventually this system will cover the whole of Scotland and the Land Register will completely replace the Register of Sasines. At the moment, however, the two systems are co-existing side by side. Registration of title will be explained further in chapter 14.

Ownership is the greatest of the real rights which a person may have over heritable property, but it is not the only one. There are a number of subsidiary property rights which are nevertheless real rights in terms of our definition. A good example is the right of a tenant. Since his lease is a contract which he has signed with his landlord, it might be thought that a tenant only had a personal right, but this is not the case. Provided that certain legal conditions are satisfied, a tenant obtains a real right, valid not only against his original landlord, but also against any future owners of the property.[3] This means that if a landlord sells a property before his tenant's lease is due to end, the tenant may stay on, even though he has no contractual relationship with the new owner. His lease

1 See ch 3, pt 2 and ch 14 below.
2 For the formalities regarding transfer of ownership, see chs 15–17 below.
3 Leases Act 1449; see also ch 8, pt 1 below.

has conferred on him not just a personal right, but a real right, valid against the original landlord's **singular successors**.

In relation to property, an important feature of real rights is that they tend to attach to, or go along with, the property itself rather than a particular person, and this is another useful way by which they may be distinguished from personal rights. A common way of expressing it is that a real right **runs with the land**. For example, if a landowner enjoys a servitude right (eg a right of way) across the property of a neighbouring owner, the right will not stay with him, or be extinguished, when he sells the property. Instead it will pass to the new owner and any subsequent owners.[1] Also, if a right in security is created over a piece of heritable property (eg in favour of a building society) that right does not automatically end if the property is sold. And so, when someone buys a property, one of the most important tasks for him (or his lawyer) is to make sure, before parting with his money, that arrangements have been made to pay off and extinguish any security rights; otherwise, the new owner may find that the property is sold off from under him to repay the loan of a previous owner. The building society (or whoever the creditor is) has a real right in security which has attached to the property, irrespective of who owns it.[2]

In relation to heritable securities, a real right is created by the creditor recording the appropriate document (called a standard security) in the Register of Sasines (or registering it in the Land Register as the case may be). A servitude right may also be made real by recording or registering the appropriate deed, though in this case there are alternative possibilities.[3]

Separate tenements[4]

Here the word 'tenement' is being used in a technical legal sense, not in its usual meaning of a block of flats. In the present context it simply means a piece of heritable property that may be separately owned, or be the subject of some other property right. For example, mineral rights are a separate tenement in the sense that they are capable of being (and generally are) in separate ownership from the surface of the land.[5] Also, a number of Crown rights (known

---

1 See ch 9 below.
2 See chs 11 and 16 below.
3 See ch 9 below.
4 *Gordon* ch 10.
5 See ch 4, pt 2 and ch 17 below.

as the *regalia minora*) are separate tenements, not only because they are held separately from the ownership of the land in question, but also because the Crown is entitled to sell them as a separate entity. They include rights to precious metals, to the sea and foreshore, to treasure and lost property and to salmon fishings.[1]

2. TYPES OF LAND TENURE

By 'tenure' we mean the form of right or title under which a person has the right to occupy a piece of property. The types of tenure discussed below are by no means exhaustive, nor are they necessarily mutually exclusive.

Feudal tenure

This is the prevailing form of tenure in Scotland. In theory, it means that all land is held under the Crown as ultimate feudal superior, and it derives historically from the rather surprising fact that the feudal system, long superseded as an economic and social system, has survived, though much changed, as a form of landholding. A feudal right is a perpetual right, and so when one talks of 'owning' a piece of heritable property, it will almost certainly mean that it is held under a feudal title. The history and present status of feudal landholding will be discussed further in chapter 2.

Leasehold tenure

This is not separate from feudal tenure, but co-exists within it. It simply refers to the right of a tenant who has been granted a lease from an owner holding a feudal title. Although a lease, on the face of it, is simply a contract conferring a temporary right of occupancy of someone else's property, it can in some cases confer a right very like ownership. We have already seen that a lease normally confers a real right on a tenant, valid against future owners as well as the original landlord.[2] If a lease is granted for a long enough period (say 99 or 120 years), the tenant's interest, because of his long security of tenure, becomes very similar to that of an owner: he can sell it for a capital sum or, after recording his lease in the

---

1 See ch 5, pt 3 below.
2 Leases Act 1449; see pt 1 above and ch 8, pt 1 below.

Register of Sasines or registering it in the Land Register, raise money on the security of it.

It should be noted that the above applies mainly to commercial and industrial leases (ie leases of shops, offices and factories) and to agricultural leases. In Scotland it is illegal to grant a lease of a dwellinghouse for a period of more than twenty years, for reasons that will be explained later.[1] This contrasts with the situation south of the Border: in England, when one 'buys' a house (or any other type of real property) what is acquired may be either a freehold interest (outright ownership) or a leasehold one (the tenancy under a long lease).

Allodial land[2]

This is separate from feudal tenure, being land which is held free of the Crown or any other feudal superior; it is not strictly speaking a form of tenure at all, as that word implies that the land is being held under another party (eg a superior or landlord). Land which is allodial, or said to be allodial, includes Crown property, certain Church property, land acquired by compulsory purchase and Udal land in Orkney and Shetland. Land said to be allodial refers to certain anomalous kinds of ownership that are, arguably, not really separate from feudal tenure; it is a distinction of mainly theoretical interest that need not bother us further here.

The anomalous status of land acquired by compulsory purchase is probably an unintentional by-product of the wording in the original compulsory purchase legislation.[3]

Udal land in Orkney and Shetland is a survival of Norse law, which was preserved in these islands when they were transferred from Denmark to Scotland in the fifteenth century. Unlike feudal holdings, Udal land does not require a written title or conveyance. Again, this is a distinction that is more theoretical than real in modern times, as there has been considerable encroachment of the feudal system in Orkney and Shetland. Probably the main reason for this is that a written title, recorded in the Register of Sasines, is required before a security right can be created in favour of a building society or any other lender of money over property.[4] Furthermore, when

---

1 Land Tenure Reform (Scotland) Act 1974, s8; see also ch 2, pt 2 below.
2 *Gordon* ch 3.
3 Lands Clauses Consolidation (Scotland) Act 1845, s80 and subsequent legislation; see also ch 18 below.
4 See ch 11.

the area becomes operational for registration of title, all registered titles will have to be in writing and registered in the Land Register.[1] Strictly speaking, the mere use of feudal styles of documentation is not enough to convert udal land to feudal tenure;[2] in practical terms, however, the effect is similar.

3. LEGAL REQUIREMENTS IN PROPERTY TRANSACTIONS

In the course of this book, we will be considering a number of situations where parties enter into contracts or sign other legal documents that relate to heritable property. It will therefore be convenient at this point to take note of certain legal requirements that are necessary in property transactions.

Contractual capacity

A party entering any contract (not just relating to property), or signing a legal document, must have contractual capacity. This means in the case of a person that he must be under no legal disability (eg from age[3] or insanity); in relation to companies or trustees it means that they are acting within the scope of the powers conferred upon them.

The powers of a company are set out in its Memorandum of Association which is lodged in the Register of Companies when the company is formed. The Memorandum sets out the purposes of the company and the powers that it has to act, eg to buy and sell property. Dealings not authorised by the Memorandum are referred to as *ultra vires* transactions (ie beyond their powers) and, historically, such obligations were unenforceable against the company, even though the person dealing with the company had done so in good faith. This situation was modified slightly in 1973, and the current situation is that dealings with companies are not open to challenge on the ground that they are outwith the powers conferred in the Memorandum. This means that a third party is now able to enforce an agreement with a company even if that agreement is not authorised by the company's Memorandum of

1 Land Registration (Scotland) Act 1979, s3(3)(b); see ch 3, part 2 and ch 14 below.
2 *Gordon* para 3–09.
3 Age of Legal Capacity (Scotland) Act 1991.

Association.[1] Similarly, third parties dealing with a company in good faith are protected even where the directors of the company exceed their powers,[2] and there is no requirement upon persons transacting with companies to enquire as to the capacity of the company or its directors.[3]

The powers of trustees will normally also be limited by the terms of the trust which they administer; however, in terms of the Trusts (Scotland) Act 1961[4] a person acting in good faith who purchases property from trustees obtains a title to the property which cannot be challenged on the ground that the trustees exceeded their powers in selling it.

Requirement for writing[5]

In Scotland, contracts and other legal documents relating to heritable property belong to a category known as the *Obligationes Literis*. This means that they must be entered into in writing, they must be signed by the parties concerned and, in addition, certain formalities must be observed. There are three alternative formalities that will suffice:
(1) *An attested document.* This is a formal deed, which is signed by the party or parties concerned on the last page, each before two witnesses, who sign opposite the signature they are witnessing. Formal legal deeds (including title deeds such as dispositions and feu charters) normally take this form. A lease may also take this form, particularly if it is one of importance because of its duration or rental value.
(2) *A holograph document.* This is written entirely in the handwriting of the party concerned and signed by him. Either a contract to sell heritable property (ie missives) or a lease might therefore consist of an offer handwritten and signed by one party followed by an acceptance handwritten and signed by the other. Such a holograph contract would be perfectly valid but, for obvious reasons, professionally drawn up legal agreements do not usually take this form.
(3) *A document adopted as holograph.* This is a variant of (2). The document is not in the handwriting of the party concerned, but

1 Companies Act 1985, s35.
2 Ibid, s35A.
3 Ibid, s35B.
4 Section 2.
5 See Walker *The Law of Contracts and Related Obligations in Scotland* (2nd edn, 1985) para 13.2 et seq; Halliday *Conveyancing Law and Practice* (1985) ch 3; McBryde *The Law of Contract in Scotland* (1987) ch 27.

is handwritten by someone else or, more commonly, printed or typewritten. The party signs it, writing above his signature the words 'adopted as holograph'. This means that he is accepting the document as if it were in his own handwriting and, as a result, it has the same effect as a holograph document. This method is generally used in missives for the sale of property, the offer and acceptance each being adopted as holograph and signed by the respective solicitors for the parties. It is also commonly used for short leases and, in the case of leases for longer periods, as a means of holding the parties contractually bound until such time as a formal document can be drawn up.

A lease for a year or less is in a privileged position and may be entered into either orally or by an informal document. However, this could create difficulties in proving the lease's existence and establishing its terms, and so is not an advisable policy.

A contract relating to heritable property that fails to observe one of these three alternative forms will technically be defective in form. At common law a contract so entered is said to be voidable, ie one which is initially valid, but which may be successfully challenged by either party.[1] However, such a challenge must be made immediately, or the contract will be validated by the actings of the parties. If they ignore the defect and carry on as if the contract were valid (eg in the case of a lease, by the landlord allowing entry and accepting rent and the tenant moving in and paying the rent) it will not be possible for one of them later to back out because of the formal defect. The contract will have been validated under the equitable doctrine of **personal bar**, in the forms known as **rei interventus** and **homologation** (the actings respectively of the party loyal to the contract and the party who wants to back out). However, for personal bar to operate there must be some form of written document, however informal.

4. PRESCRIPTION[2]

The legal concept of prescription looms large in property law and will recur several times in this book, particularly when we consider the transfer of ownership of heritable property[3], and also in connection with servitudes[4], as well as in several other places. For

---

1   See eg *Goldston v Young* (1868) 7 M 188.
2   For a comprehensive coverage of the law on this topic, see Walker *The Law of Prescription and Limitation of Actions in Scotland* (4th edn, 1990).
3   See chs 15–17.
4   See ch 9.

this reason, it will be helpful to give a general introduction to the principle at this point.

Prescription is a means whereby legal rights may be either gained or lost through the passage of time. Broadly speaking, there are two categories of prescription, **positive prescription** and **negative prescription**. In the case of positive prescription, the lapse of time creates rights, and in the case of negative prescription, it extinguishes them.

Prescription has a long history in Scots law, having been introduced by a series of statutes in the sixteenth and seventeenth centuries[1] and amended on a number of occasions thereafter. However, in recent times the doctrine has been subject to extensive re-thinking and revision and its modern formulation is mainly contained in the Prescription and Limitation (Scotland) Act 1973.[2] We will now look briefly at the main categories of prescription that affect property law.

Positive prescription

By this means an interest in heritable property (notably ownership) can be acquired by possession of the property over the requisite period of time. The possession involved may be either **natural possession** (physical occupancy) or **civil possession**, where the person possessing does not occupy the property, but is represented by another who is the actual occupant; the most obvious example of this is the case of a tenant who has natural possession, but occupies on behalf of his landlord who has civil possession. For the purpose of prescription either natural or civil possession may meet the legal requirement under the 1973 Act.

The possession must be for a continuous period and must be held openly, peaceably and without any judicial interruption.[3] 'Openly' simply means that the possession must not occur in a clandestine fashion, so that the person or persons entitled to challenge the possessor are in a position to know that the claim is being made; it is not necessary for prescription to operate to show that the potential challenger actually **did** know of the situation.[4] 'Judicial interruption' means challenge in a court action or arbitration by a person entitled

1   Walker *The Law of Prescription and Limitation of Actions in Scotland* (4th edn, 1990) ch 1.
2   As amended *inter alia* by the Prescription and Limitation (Scotland) Act 1984 and the Prescription and Limitation (Scotland) Act 1987; for a full list of amendments, see *Walker* pp 8-10.
3   Prescription and Limitation (Scotland) Act 1973, ss1(1)(a), 2(1)(a).
4   *Wemyss' Trs v Lord Advocate* (1896) 24 R 216 at 229, per Lord Robertson; 4 SLT 194.

to do so.[1] The use of the word 'peaceably' suggests that the prescriptive period may also be interrupted by non-judicial means, if the person claiming the right is only able to remain in possession by means of force or violence.[2]

Other rights over heritable property that do not involve actual possession may also be created by positive prescription, the most obvious being a servitude right, eg a right of way. The right will be created if it is asserted continuously without challenge for the required period, eg by a landowner regularly taking a short cut over his neighbour's land. Here also the right must be asserted openly, peaceably and without any judicial interruption.[3]

Ten year prescription. By this means, a person may acquire ownership of a piece of heritable property, or any other interest that may be recorded in the Register of Sasines or registered in the Land Register.[4] Other such interests would include the right of a tenant under a long lease, and the right of a creditor under a heritable security; however, since the creation of ownership by this method is the most significant, we shall for the moment confine our discussion to that.

Possession of the property for ten years is not enough by itself to make the possessor the owner; it must be preceded by the recording of a title deed in the claimant's name in the Register of Sasines (or registration in the Land Register, as the case may be). Furthermore, for the ten year prescription to operate, the deed must meet certain requirements. These will be examined in more detail at a later point,[5] but there is one requirement worth considering briefly at this point. This is the provision that the deed must be *ex facie* (on the face of it) valid, ie that it should contain no patent defects (such as a missing clause or unwitnessed signature) that can be detected by examination of the document itself. This could lead to a situation that, at first sight, seems rather surprising. The person one normally expects to sign a deed transferring ownership would of course be the current owner of the property. But suppose that the deed (normally a document called a disposition) were instead signed by someone who had no right to the property at all and, furthermore, knew that he had no right? That rather important fact

---

1   Prescription and Limitation (Scotland) Act 1973, s4.
2   *Walker* p 22.
3   1973 Act, s3.
4   1973 Act, s1(1)(b) (as amended by the Land Registration (Scotland) Act 1979, s10).
5   See ch 16.

could not be detected merely by looking at the document itself. Provided that it had all the required clauses, was properly signed and witnessed etc, it would be *ex facie* valid.

It is even possible for someone to settle on land to which he has no right having got an accomplice (with no more right than him to the property) to sign a disposition purporting to transfer ownership. If he recorded the disposition and possessed the land for ten years without challenge, he would become owner. In the vast majority of cases, of course, such an enterprising, pioneering venture would be thwarted by the arrival of the real owner, long before the ten years was up.

So what is the point of the above example? Simply that prescription can cure the most radical defect in a title: what could be more radical than the fact that at some stage in its history a property was fraudulently acquired by someone who did not own it?

This brings us to the real importance of positive prescription. Not as an aid to carpetbaggers, but as a means of curing any defects in the older title deeds of a property; indeed, to make it unnecessary even to look at such older deeds in order to check for defects. There are many properties still in use that are of a fair age (100 years or more), and ownership of the site on which they are built will of course go back indefinitely. During its life, such a property will have acquired a number of title deeds, notably a disposition representing every time the property has changed hands. It would be impracticable if a flaw in just one of these deeds were to scar the title forever; likewise, it would be impracticable if, every time the property was sold, each one of this growing number of documents had to be minutely examined for such a flaw. There has to be a cutoff point, and this is what the ten year prescription provides. When a purchaser's lawyer is examining the title deeds of the property being bought by his client, he merely looks for the most recent disposition that is more than ten years old. Provided that this deed is *ex facie* valid, he need not look at any earlier ones, unless they are required for some other purpose, eg if they contain burdens on the title. On the other hand, if the property has changed hands within the ten year period, he will have to check each disposition to establish a valid chain of ownership leading up to the current seller. This is what is known as a **prescriptive progress** of title deeds, and is a principal ingredient of a **marketable title** to a property, something we will be discussing in more detail at a later stage.[1]

This shows that, in a normal situation when one buys a property,

1   See ch 16.

the purchaser will get a good title immediately, without having to wait ten years. This, of course, is only what we would expect. In other words, the requirement for ten years possession may be fulfilled by a succession of different occupiers, provided that each change is represented by a valid disposition or other deed of transfer.

It should be noted that the ten year positive prescription is of more importance in relation to the old system of recording deeds in the Register of Sasines; once a title has been registered in the new Land Register for Scotland it is normally subject to a government guarantee, which renders the validating process of prescription unnecessary. However, this guarantee will not be given in the first place if there is not a good title; in such cases the Keeper of the Register will register the title without indemnity (or, if the title is only defective in respect of part of the land, he may register it with partial indemnity). The process of prescription will normally ensure that this state of affairs will not last forever and that the indemnity can be given after ten years has elapsed without the title being challenged.

Twenty year prescription.   As we saw above, the foundation title must appear on the relevant register before the ten year prescription can operate. However, if the relevant deed has been completed and signed and the only requirement lacking is that it has not been recorded (or registered), then prescription may still operate, except that the period will be twenty years.[1] The twenty year prescription also applies to the acquisition of certain other property interests which were excluded from the ten year prescription. These include a tenant's interest under an unrecorded lease, interests in allodial land, servitudes, public rights of way, and rights in salmon fishings and the foreshore where the dispute is with the Crown.[2] In the case of servitudes and public rights of way, no title at all is required.[3]

Negative prescription

As we saw above, negative prescription is where rights and obligations are extinguished rather than created by the passage of time. It is extremely important in relation to contractual obligations and reparation claims, as it sets time limits within which such claims may be made. In relation to property law, it is much less important

---

1   Prescription and Limitation (Scotland) Act 1973, s2.
2   Ibid, ss1(4), 2, 3; see also chs 5 and 9 below.
3   See ch 9, pt 3.

than positive prescription, but it has a few applications that should be briefly noted.

There are two types of negative prescription, the **twenty year prescription** and the **five year prescription**. In the property field, the twenty year negative prescription can operate to wipe out servitude rights, public rights of way, claims under the law of nuisance, and any other property rights that are not specifically declared to be imprescriptible.[1] The five year prescription applies, among other things, to the obligation to pay a periodic sum of money such as rent or feuduty.[2] However, it should be clear what this implies; only those payments which are five years or more in arrears will be extinguished, and those falling due within the five year period can still be legally claimed.

Imprescriptible rights and obligations.   Certain rights and obligations are not subject to the process of negative prescription, and will not be extinguished however much time has elapsed.[3] These include a real right of ownership in land (ie where there is a recorded or registered title) and the right of a lessee under a recorded lease. It also includes the right to take any steps necessary for making up or completing title to any interest in land. This would include, for example, someone who had a title deed but had not yet recorded it; it does **not** include someone who has merely completed Missives, as he has merely a personal right under the law of contract. Such a right can be extinguished by the twenty year negative prescription.[4]

---

1   Prescription and Limitation (Scotland) Act 1973, s8; see also ch 4, pt 2 and ch 9, pt 4 below.
2   Ibid, s6 and Sch 1.
3   Ibid, ss7, 8 and Sch 3.
4   *Macdonald v Scott* 1981 SLT 128.

2. The feudal system

1. HISTORICAL BACKGROUND[1]

General

It must come as a surprise to those studying property law for the first time to discover that, in the late twentieth century, the system of landholding in Scotland is still based upon the feudal system. Even more immediate must be the shock to the purchaser of a dwellinghouse who, under the impression that his crippling outlay has made him the outright owner of his home, consults his title deeds only to find himself described there as a vassal; moreover, some stranger, who has assumed the title of feudal superior, has retained the right to tell the new owner what he can and cannot do with his property. A few years ago the superior would also have had the right regularly to demand money from his vassal and take him to court, or even relieve him of the property entirely, if he refused to pay; this last grievance, at least, has now been remedied.

Most readers will have heard of the feudal system as the prevailing economic system back in the Middle Ages when land, rather than commerce or industry, was the main source of wealth. So all-embracing was its influence, that the feudal system also provided the structure of the social and political system at that time. And, because land played such a central role in the process, it was also, of necessity, a system of landholding. In its economic, social and political aspects, of course, it has long been superseded; however, it still survives to provide the framework for our land tenure. The reader will perhaps be relieved to learn that, over the centuries, it has been adapted and subjected to so many reforms that it is almost unrecognisable. Nevertheless, a brief outline of the historical background is necessary. It will make the mysteries in this area of law that bit easier to penetrate.

---

1 For a fuller account of the historical background, see Gordon *Scottish Land Law* (1989) ch 2 and Halliday *Conveyancing Law and Practice* (1986) ch 16.

The feudal system was developed in Western Europe in the Middle Ages, crossing the channel from France to England along with the Norman Conquest. Thereafter it made its way north to Scotland, where it was introduced by David 1 in the twelfth century. The essence of feudal theory, which the monarch no doubt found irresistable, is that the right to all land in the realm derives from the Crown as ultimate feudal superior. The historical justification for this is that, originally, the king would make grants of land to his most powerful nobles on condition that they provided the military service necessary to maintain his position as monarch. The nobles in turn were entitled to make sub-grants, perhaps to people who would actually work the land, and these new owners would also have to give something in return on a regular basis, such as grain, agricultural services, or some other produce of the soil. In theory there was no limit to the number of times land could be subfeued and this is still true today. (Subfeuing means that an owner makes a grant of land to a new party, while himself still retaining a legal interest in it.) The person making the feudal grant was called the superior, the ultimate superior being the Crown. The person to whom the grant was made was called the vassal. Because of the ability to subfeu, a hierarchical structure was created in which a person could be, in different capacities, simultaneously a superior and a vassal: in relation to the person to whom he had granted the land he was a superior, and in relation to the person who had granted it to him, he was a vassal. The structure could be compared to a pyramid, the peak of which is the Crown as ultimate superior; in between are intermediate owners, sometimes known as mid-superiors; at the base of the pyramid are the vassals who actually occupy the land. The right of the superior is traditionally known as the *dominium directum* (direct ownership) and that of the vassal the *dominium utile* (useful ownership). The term *dominium plenum* (full ownership) is also used to describe a situation where the rights of superior and vassal are combined.

Main characteristics of the feudal system

From this historical sketch we can identify several characteristics of feudal tenure that survive to the present day:

(a) It is generally wrong to consider a person to be the 'owner' of a piece of heritable property in the sense that he or she has all rights to it. It is the nature of feudal tenure that a property may have a number of owners who co-exist simul-taneously, who have the right to certain estates in the land.

Only one of these, the vassal, has the right to occupy the property; however although a superior does not have this right, he has certain other rights which we will note below; moreover, his superior's interest (the *dominium directum*) has other characteristics that identify it as a piece of property that can be owned. It can be bought and sold like any other piece of property and, like the vassal's right, it is perpetual. It is a separate tenement in the sense we noted in chapter 1.[1]

(b) A feudal grant is normally made subject to a number of conditions regarding how the property may be used, and the superior can continue to enforce these conditions, not only against the current vassal, but also against his successors. These are known as real conditions (ie that run with the land) and will be examined further in chapter 10.

(c) The vassal may still have to make some kind of return to the superior. Military service (known as ward holding) was abolished after the Jacobite rebellion of 1745, and other types of payment in kind also gradually disappeared over the centuries. In modern times this return survived in the form of a feuduty, an annual money payment made by the vassal to the superior. Feuduties are now being phased out but, as we will see below, they have not yet quite disappeared.

(d) When a vassal disposes of his property, by sale or otherwise, there are still two ways in which it can be done. Normally he will sign a document known as a disposition, which has the effect of transferring his entire interest to the new owner; the latter will take his place as vassal in the feudal hierarchy and the seller will retain no legal interest at all in the property. This is what happens in the vast majority of cases. However, it is still legally possible for a vassal instead to grant a **feu charter** (or perhaps a variant of this such as a **feu disposition** or **feu contract**). In such a case he is not divesting himself of his entire legal interest in the property, he is splitting it in two. He is creating a new feudal estate of superior and vassal, retaining for himself the right of superior. In other words, he has subfeued: in relation to his existing superior he is still a vassal, but in relation to the new owner he is now a superior. He is still entitled to impose conditions on the land when making the grant to his new vassal, though he can no longer create a feuduty.

(e) In theory, the Crown is still the ultimate superior. In many ways this is a legal fiction, in the sense that it would be impossible

---

1   See ch 1, pt 1 above.

to trace the ownership history of most land back to an actual Crown grant; apart from anything else, the feudal system had been in operation for several centuries before a permanent record was kept of feudal grants by the creation of the Register of Sasines in 1617. However, the Crown's right in all land as ultimate superior is still recognised in the form of certain special Crown rights known as regalia.[1]

The position prior to 1970

Before we look at the most recent reforms (which may not have yet ended), it may be helpful to take stock of the condition of the feudal system as it had evolved by the middle of the twentieth century. As mentioned above, many changes had taken place over the centuries; in particular, from the middle of the nineteenth century onwards, a number of important statutes did much to modernise the system.[2] It would be wrong, therefore, to look upon feudal tenure entirely as an anachronism that had no place in the modern world. In its evolved form it had certain functions and characteristics that were far removed from its original medieval nature.

Feuduties as a form of investment.   About 100 years ago, if the owner of a landed estate was disposing of land for development, he or she would probably have done so by feuing the land and retaining a right of superiority. More than likely no capital sum would change hands, the only monetary return to the superior being the payment by each of the new vassals of an annual feuduty. Since the feuduties were payable in perpetuity, the superior was thereby creating a permanent income out of each property feued. Moreover, this right to an income was something that could be sold to someone else. As we saw above, the superior's right (the *dominium directum*) is as much a right of ownership as that of the vassal. It was possible, therefore, for a person who wanted to invest in feuduties to buy a superiority for a capital payment. Along with the *dominium directum* would pass the right to collect feuduties from the vassal or vassals. It is still legally possible to sell a superiority as a separate estate from that of the vassal; however, with the demise of feuduties, there is little motivation for such a transaction.

The main problem with feuduties as a form of investment was

---

1   See ch 5 below.
2   Eg the Titles to Land Consolidation (Scotland) Act 1868; the Conveyancing (Scotland) Act 1874; the Conveyancing (Scotland) Act 1924.

that, once created, the amount of a feuduty generally remained the same, and so its value in real terms would decline with the process of inflation. 100 years ago this was not a significant factor, but by the middle of the present century feuduties as an investment had become much less attractive and the capital value of superiorities had declined as a result.

Control of land use.   Another significant function of the feudal system in its evolved form was as a means of controlling land use. In modern times, this is properly the territory of the town and country planners and the public authorities which employ them.[1] However, we should remember that the modern system of town and country planning is a comparatively recent phenomenon; it only began to significantly develop in the early years of this century and, in its present form, after the 1939–45 war. However, prior to that there was not exactly a planning free-for-all. If we look at the terms of a typical feu charter of a dwellinghouse,[2] what we will see is not the restrictions of an oppressive feudal overlord serving his own selfish interest; instead we will find conditions preserving the residential amenity of the area by forbidding any commercial use of the property, laying down specifications for the buildings to be erected on the feued site, prohibiting the carrying on of a nuisance etc. As the superior would normally be disposing of a number of plots at the same time, he would do so according to a feuing plan and probably impose similar conditions on all the vassals in the same estate. In certain circumstances, these conditions could be enforced by the vassals against each other as well as by the superior.[3]

Sometimes this informal system of town planning could achieve quite spectacular results, such as the creation of Edinburgh New Town in the late eighteenth century.

The emergence of the modern planning system has largely superseded the need for the feudal system as a system of controlling land use. However, it can still be useful as a supplement to planning powers; for example, local authorities when disposing of land for development may still retain a right of superiority and impose real conditions, perhaps to plug any gaps in their statutory powers. Private developers, though they have less apparent motive, still often do the same.

1   See ch 12, pt 2 below.
2   See the specimen land certificate in the appendix, in which the burdens section details typical conditions found in the feu of a dwellinghouse.
3   See ch 10 below, on the right of *ius quaesitum tertio.*

Disadvantages of the pre-1970 system

Despite the many fundamental changes to the feudal system over the years, it was felt by many that these had not gone far enough. Feuduties were greatly resented, particularly by householders who saw them as a quite unjustified form of unearned income for superiors. No longer were plots of land being disposed of with a feuduty being the only return; rather, it was an additional cost imposed on top of a capital payment.

Moreover, the conditions attached to feudal grants, while they might have served a useful social purpose when first imposed, often became less appropriate with the passage of time. A condition reserving a piece of rural land for agricultural use might seem less reasonable 50 or 100 years later if the land was by then on the edge of a town and forming an obstacle to legitimate development. And conditions originally designed to preserve the residential character of an area might eventually become unnecessary or undesirable. We can see a good example of this in the number of large town houses built in the last century for which there is no longer any market except for subdivision into flats, or for a commercial use, such as an office or hotel; all of these changes are likely to be prohibited in the original feudal grant.

Prior to 1970, such changes of use could normally only take place with the consent of the superior. There were (and are) certain limited situations where a superior might be considered to have lost the right to enforce conditions,[1] but otherwise superiors were virtually in a position to hold would-be developers to ransom. They might not object to particular changes of use, but nevertheless were prepared to use their legal power to extort sizeable capital sums from owners in return for the waiver of conditions. In an age when the income from feuduties was becoming seriously eroded by inflation, this was a useful alternative way for a superior to make some money from his property interest; in modern times, however, it was not a practice that was easy to justify.

2. LEGISLATIVE REFORMS

In the 1960s, several committees met to consider changes to the system and their reports formed the basis of reforming legislation. The one most relevant here was the Halliday Committee, under

1 See ch 10 below.

the chairmanship of Professor JM Halliday, which reported in 1966.[1] On the basis of its recommendations, two statutes were passed: the Conveyancing and Feudal Reform (Scotland) Act 1970 and the Land Tenure Reform (Scotland) Act 1974.

1970 Act

One of the main functions of the 1970 Act was greatly to weaken the power of superiors to hold a landowner to ransom if restrictive conditions in his title stood in the way of a reasonable development. Section 1 of the Act gives power to the Lands Tribunal for Scotland to vary or discharge land obligations, including the real conditions imposed in feudal grants, where the obligation in question is out of date or otherwise unreasonable.[2]

The Lands Tribunal is an administrative tribunal, a quasi-judicial body made up partly of lawyers and partly of surveyors, which has a number of statutory functions in relation to heritable property. With regard to real conditions, it is important to distinguish the jurisdiction of the Lands Tribunal from that of the ordinary courts; the latter have, and always have had, the jurisdiction to *enforce* conditions that are still extant. It is to the court that a superior can go if a vassal acts in contravention of his feu charter. Since 1970, the Lands Tribunal has had the jurisdiction to vary or discharge conditions. It is there that the **vassal** applies if he wants a condition to be modified, or no longer to apply at all.

As well as the right to vary or discharge land obligations, the Lands Tribunal has the power to award compensation to **benefited proprietors**, such as the superior or neighbouring landowners, whose interests were being protected by the imposition of the condition and might therefore suffer loss (such as a loss of amenity) by its removal.

It should also be noted that the real conditions contained in feudal grants are not the only type of land obligations that may be varied or discharged by the Lands Tribunal. Their power also extends to certain other real obligations (ie that run with the land), including servitudes[3] and the obligations in registered leases.[4] Among the

---

1 Report of Committee on Conveyancing Legislation and Practice (Cmnd 3118).
2 For a fuller account of the jurisdiction of the Lands Tribunal and relevant case law, see ch 10 below.
3 See ch 9 below.
4 See ch 8 below.

exclusions are feuduties, but only because they are separately dealt with in the 1974 Act (see below).

The 1970 Act implemented a number of other conveyancing reforms, which we will take account of, where relevant, as we go along. Notable among these was the complete overhauling of the law relating to heritable securities, including the introduction of a new form of security known as a standard security.[1]

The 1974 Act

The other main piece of legislation to implement the recommendations of the Halliday Committee was the Land Tenure Reform (Scotland) Act 1974. This addressed itself to the vexed problem of feuduties by setting up the legal machinery that would eventually eliminate them altogether.[2] It achieved this in several ways, firstly by prohibiting the creation of any new feuduties after the Act came into force, ie 1 September 1974. It dealt with existing feuduties by providing two main situations where the feuduty may be redeemed (ie permanently eliminated) by the payment of a capital sum to the superior, calculated in accordance with a formula laid down in the Act. **Compulsory redemptions** occur when a property changes hands; the seller is obliged to pay off the superior from the sale proceeds, so that the purchaser obtains the property free of feuduty. **Voluntary redemptions** are when the vassal, although he is not selling the property, chooses to get rid of his feuduty by paying off the superior. It is only from the point of view of the vassal that a redemption is either compulsory or voluntary; in neither case does the superior have any choice.

The provisions relating to feuduty redemption also apply to other monetary burdens on land, such as ground annuals. These are similar to feuduties and were developed during a period when it was legally competent for superiors to prohibit a vassal from subfeuing. Vassals got round this by entering a contract of ground annual which, strictly speaking, did not amount to a subfeu, but allowed them when disposing of property to impose conditions and a monetary burden in a very similar way.

It will be seen that the provisions of the 1974 Act have gone a long way to disposing of feuduties entirely. Virtually the only feuduties now left are those payable from properties that have not changed hands since 1974. (There is a minor exception in the case

1 See ch 11 below.
2 For a fuller account of the provisions for feuduty redemption, see ch 10 below.

of unallocated feuduties which will be explained later).[1] And since all of these remaining feuduties must have been created prior to the Act, the process of inflation is gradually seeing to it that the amounts of money involved are becoming progressively less significant as time goes by.

One result of this is that, having either no feuduty to collect or one of so derisory an amount that it is not worth collecting, superiors are dropping out of sight and often cannot be identified. This can create problems in finding the party entitled to grant waivers, and helps justify the further proposals for reform discussed at the end of this chapter.

Long residential leases. The 1974 Act also prohibited the creation of leases of dwellinghouses for a period in excess of twenty years.[2] The reason for this initially rather surprising provision was the need to plug a potential loophole in the provisions for abolition of feuduties. It was feared that developers, denied the right to impose feuduties, might switch to leasehold tenure instead, in a form similar to that prevalent in England; in other words, instead of granting a feudal right subject to a feuduty, they might grant long leases (for possibly 99 or 120 years) in return for a similar capital sum and a similar periodical payment in the form of rent rather than feuduty. The system would therefore have been perpetuated in another form.[3]

3. CONCLUSION

The provisions of the 1970 and 1974 Acts, far reaching though they were, did not complete the proposed reforms to the feudal system. It was originally envisaged by the government that the system be abolished altogether.[4] This has not yet happened, perhaps because the reforms of the 1970s have dealt with the main objections to the system and deprived the matter of political urgency.

There certainly seems little need to perpetuate the system in its present emasculated form. The only real power left to superiors is to impose and later enforce real conditions in their feudal grants. This can still serve a useful purpose; however, as we will see later

---

1 See ch 10 below.
2 Land Tenure Reform (Scotland) Act 1974, s8.
3 For a fuller account of this, see McAllister *Scottish Law of Leases* (1989), pp 63–64.
4 Land Tenure in Scotland – White Paper 1969 (Cmnd 4099); Land Tenure Reform in Scotland – Green Paper 1972.

on, real conditions can be imposed on land without the necessity of creating a new feudal estate, though a superior may find such conditions easier to enforce.[1] It is clear that, though the system may possess some residual advantages, there must be alternative ways of achieving these that do not have 1,000 years of feudal history as a substructure.

The Scottish Law Commission have reached a similar conclusion in a recent discussion paper.[2] Its proposals include the replacement of the feudal system with one of absolute ownership and the redemption of existing feuduties within a prescribed timetable. Two alternative proposals are made for the enforcement of real conditions. However, when (if ever) these proposals will materialise as legislation remains to be seen.

There is one major reform of the 1970s (mentioned in passing in chapter 1) that we have not yet properly considered. The Land Registration (Scotland) Act 1979 introduced a system of registration of title that is presently in the process of radically changing and simplifying the conveyancing system in Scotland. However, since that Act does not directly affect the structure or theory of feudal tenure, we have postponed consideration of it until later.[3]

---

1 See ch 10 below.
2 Scottish Law Commission *Property Law - Abolition of the Feudal System*, Discussion Paper No 93 (July 1991).
3 See ch 14 below.

3. The registers of Scotland

1. INTRODUCTION[1]

In Scotland there is a long tradition, extending over many centuries, for legal deeds to be registered in public registers. These registers catered (and continue to cater) for a wide variety of documents, including wills, trust deeds, all kinds of contracts, and documents conferring state appointments (eg in the Register of the Great Seal). However, the most important and widely used of the registers are those relating to heritable property and rights affecting heritable property, and references to those will crop up frequently throughout the course of this book. It will be useful at this stage, therefore, to provide a brief introduction to the main registers that affect property and property transactions.

Most of the registers we will be discussing are maintained by a state official known as the Keeper of the Registers of Scotland, whose headquarters are situated at Meadowbank House in Edinburgh. (The sole exception to this in our selective list is the Register of Charges, which is kept in the companies' registration office). The process of registration (often also referred to as 'recording') generally involves the register keeping a copy of the document and returning the original to its owner, but sometimes (as with the register known as the Books of Council and Session) it involves the register holding on to the original for safekeeping and issuing a substitute.

Registering a legal document in the appropriate register can achieve several purposes. As we saw above, it can save the deed from being lost by preserving the original. In relation to property transactions, registration provides a formality whereby property rights conferred by the relevant document become legally effective. For example, transfer of ownership of heritable property is completed by the recording of a disposition or feu charter in the Register of Sasines

---

1 For a concise introduction to this topic, see the booklet issued by the Keeper of the Registers of Scotland entitled *The Registers of Scotland* (1989).

(or, in the operational areas, registration of the same deeds in the Land Register); also, many creditors' rights are made effective by the registration of the appropriate document, eg a standard security or an inhibition.[1]

Arguably, the most significant feature of the Scottish registers is that they are open to the public. In this respect alone, Scotland was ahead of many other countries; the English Land Register, for example, was only made fully public a few years ago.[2] This right of public access to the registers is of great importance. First of all, it safeguards the position of the person acquiring rights under the document in question by making these rights a matter of public record. We saw in chapter 1 that a real right in heritable property is created by the recording (or registration) of a disposition or feu charter.[3] As a real right is one that can be defended against anyone in the world, it is appropriate that anyone in the world has the right to check its existence, and this brings us to the second great advantage of public access. Not only does it protect the owner of legal rights, but it helps safeguard the position of another party having legal dealings with that person. In particular, an intending purchaser of heritable property, before committing himself legally, can find out what deeds (including security deeds) appear on the relevant register. He can also find out from the Register of Inhibitions and Adjudications whether there is any legal impediment against the seller himself that would prevent him from transferring his title.

Searches

Much has just been made about public access to the registers, and it is literally true that any private individual may consult them. The normal situation, however, is that the agent of the person involved in the property transaction (seller, purchaser, creditor etc) employs someone to consult the appropriate register and provide a written report of what is found there. As a result, there exist in Edinburgh firms of professional searchers whose main function is to consult the registers and provide such reports. For example, one of the legal obligations of a seller of heritable property is to provide clear searches in the property and personal registers.[4] This is achieved by producing a document compiled by a firm of

1 See chs 11 and 16 below.
2 Land Registration Act 1988.
3 See also ch 15 below.
4 See ch 16 below.

professional searchers, and containing a summary of their findings in these registers in relation to the relevant property and its seller.

2. PROPERTY REGISTERS

Register of Sasines

The Register of Sasines is the largest and, along with the Land Register, arguably the most important of the registers we are considering. It is also, having been established in 1617, one of the oldest surviving registers. It is a register of all deeds relating to heritable property, notably deeds transferring ownership of heritable property (eg dispositions and feu charters) and deeds creating rights in security over heritable property (standard securities). Other deeds that affect property rights may also be recorded there, such as deeds creating servitudes,[1] and leases; in the case of leases, recording in the Register of Sasines is optional and only competent in certain circumstances.[2]

The Register of Sasines is divided into thirty-three divisions, according to the old counties of Scotland as they existed prior to the reorganisation of local government in 1975. It is often known for short as the Property Register, in contrast to the Register of Inhibitions and Adjudications which is known as the Personal Register; this simply reflects the fact that the Register of Sasines records deeds relating to individual pieces of heritable property as such, rather than to their owners. Recording a deed in the Register of Sasines is generally known as 'registration for publication'.

Obtaining a search in the Register of Sasines against a particular piece of heritable property will therefore reveal all deeds relating to that property to appear on the register during the period searched. The title deeds of any property will generally include a document of search, compiled and added to by the professional searchers every time the property was sold, and going back to the first time the property came into being as a separate unit. It will contain a brief summary of all deeds revealed, including the type of deed, the names of the parties, the date of signing and the date of recording in the register. When the property comes to be sold again, the seller, as part of his legal obligation, will instruct professional searchers to extend the document to cover the period from the last sale (ie when the

1 See ch 9 below.
2 See ch 8 below.

seller himself bought the property) up to date. The search document therefore comprises a useful, periodically updated summary of the property's history as revealed in the Register of Sasines.

When a deed is recorded in the Register of Sasines, a copy is kept and the deed is eventually returned to the sender, bearing an official docquet certifying that it has been recorded. It is therefore possible, in return for the appropriate fee, for anyone to obtain from the Keeper a photocopy of any deed appearing on the register. This can take the form of a sasine extract, which is legally equivalent to the original deed,[1] or of a 'quick copy', a simple photocopy taken from the register. This facility is particularly valuable if deeds have become lost or destroyed and have not been registered for preservation in the Books of Council and Session (see below).

The General Register of Sasines is gradually being replaced by the Land Register for Scotland, which fulfils the same functions, subject to a number of fundamental improvements. However, as we will see in due course, the transfer to the new register is necessarily a slow process, and the Register of Sasines is likely to be with us for a number of years to come.

Traditionally the placing of a document on the Register of Sasines was sometimes referred to as recording and sometimes as registration. For the sake of clarity we have been adopting (and will continue to do so throughout the book) the modern practice of using the word 'recording' in relation to the Register of Sasines and 'registration' in relation to the Land Register.

The Land Register for Scotland

The Land Register for Scotland was set up by the Land Registration (Scotland) Act 1979, with the object of introducing into Scotland a system of registration of title. Its purpose is gradually to replace the Register of Sasines with a system that incorporates the virtues of that register, while carrying it forward into a new phase of evolution. The Land Register is more than just a register of individual documents. It registers, as a unity, the group of deeds that comprise the title to an individual property; and if the Keeper is satisfied that the title is a good one, he backs up its validity with a state guarantee. The new system also greatly improves the process of identifying properties by recording them on a series of master Ordnance Survey maps.

1 Conveyancing and Feudal Reform (Scotland) Act 1970, s45.

Registration of title is covered in more detail in chapter 14 below.

3. PERSONAL REGISTER

Register of Inhibitions and Adjudications

The Register of Inhibitions and Adjudications is known as the Personal Register because, unlike the Register of Sasines, which records deeds relating to pieces of heritable property, it registers documents relating to individual persons. This register is important because the effect of such a document appearing on it is to deprive the person concerned of the legal right to sell, grant a security over or otherwise deal with his heritable property. Such a document would normally be registered by a creditor of the person concerned, in an attempt to safeguard the repayment of his debt by preventing the debtor from disposing of his property to third parties.

In order to prevent such a third party from being innocently prejudiced, it is necessary for the purchaser of heritable property (or his agent) to obtain a search in the Register of Inhibitions and Adjudications. This enables him to check that the seller does not suffer from a legal disability that would prevent him from passing on a good title.

The various types of document that can appear on the Personal Register are described in chapter 16.

Entries in the Personal Register are not found very often, though inhibitions have made something of a comeback in recent years.

4. OTHER REGISTERS

Books of Council and Session

This register has two quite different functions: registration for preservation and registration for execution.

Registration for preservation. As the name suggests, the purpose of registration for preservation is to secure valuable legal documents against being lost or destroyed. The deed concerned may be any type of legal document, including deeds relating to heritable property. Registration may take place immediately after the document has been signed, or at any time thereafter. For a fee, the Keeper will keep the document in the safety of his vaults and issue in its place an official photocopy (called an 'extract'). This extract is legally equivalent to the original deed and can be used in court or for any other legal purpose as if it were the original.[1] Also, provided that the requisite fee is paid, any number of extracts may be obtained, which can often be very useful.

Registration for execution.   Preservation of documents is the principal function of the Books of Council and Session. However, if the document contains a consent to registration for execution, this process can be carried out at the same time as registration for preservation.[2] The Keeper holds on to the document in the usual way and issues an extract, but in this case he adds to the extract a warrant for all necessary action to enforce any sums payable (or any other obligation) under the deed, ie to proceed with diligence. Such an extract for execution has the force and effect of a decree of the Court of Session.

This process is known as **summary diligence**, ie it allows a person owed a legal obligation, usually a creditor, to bypass the usual process of first having his right established in court before proceeding with diligence. The reason is that the obligant has consented to the process in advance by signing a deed containing a consent to registration for execution. A clause containing such a consent is standard in many deeds, including leases and standard securities, where it can provide a valuable method of recovering rent or mortgage arrears.

Register of Charges

This is the only one of the registers to be considered by us which is not under the care of the Keeper of the Registers of Scotland. However, it is also kept in Edinburgh, at the Scottish Companies Register.

The Register of Charges is a register of charges against limited companies. Among other things, it is the place for registration of **floating charges**, a type of security traditionally only available in England, but which was introduced into Scotland in 1961.[3] The current legislation is the Companies Act 1985.

A floating charge is so called in contrast to other types of security, such as a standard security, which are fixed charges, ie attached to particular pieces of property. Instead, a floating charge 'floats'

---

1   Writs Execution (Scotland) Act 1877, s5.
2   See Halliday *Conveyancing Law and Practice* (1985) para 4–61.
3   Floating charges are more fully discussed in ch 11 below.

over all the property (heritable and moveable) in the debtor's ownership. A floating charge cannot be granted by an individual, but only by limited companies (or registered friendly societies). Its 'floating' nature means that as long as a company is trading normally, any floating charges granted by it will have no effect, allowing the company to buy and sell property without legal hindrance. However on the occurrence of certain events (eg the appointment of a liquidator) the charge is said to 'crystallise', ie it becomes a fixed charge over all property, heritable and moveable, owned by the company at that time. The effect of this is to give the creditor a preference.

It will be seen that, in normal circumstances, a company's ability to sell its heritable property is not affected by a floating charge. Nevertheless, for reasons that will be explained more fully later, it is normal in property transactions with a limited company for a search in the Register of Charges to be obtained.[1]

1 See ch 17 below.

4. Ownership rights

1. GENERAL

When we looked for a definition of ownership in chapter 1, we settled upon Erskine's definition of ownership as 'the right of using and disposing of a subject as our own, except in so far as we are restrained by law or paction.'[1] The second part of this book will be devoted to the latter half of Erskine's definition, when we examine the various restrictions on a property owner's rights, either imposed by the law or by the owner himself (eg when he grants a lease). The right of an owner to dispose of his interest entirely will be considered in some depth in the final part of the book. This chapter will be devoted to the positive side of property ownership, ie what rights an owner **does** possess after all the above-mentioned restrictions have been taken into account. In other words, what precisely is involved in the right to use a subject as our own.

As we established in chapter 1, the sort of 'subject' we are concerned with here is heritable property, in the slightly restricted sense of land and buildings. Some of the owner's rights we examine below (numbers 1-4) apply generally, to all property ownership, and it is on these that most emphasis will be placed; the remainder, which will be dealt with more briefly, are only of importance to owners of substantial areas of land, and are more likely to occur in a rural context.

The main rights discussed below will be (1) the right to exclusive possession (2) the right to use property (3) the right to freedom from interference by neighbours (4) the right of support (5) rights in water (including fishing rights) and (6) the right to kill game.

Some of these rights, namely numbers (3) and (5) and (to a limited extent) number (4), have traditionally been known as **natural rights** in property. This means that they have arisen *ex lege* ('out of the law'), ie they are automatic attributes or incidents of ownership

---

1 Erskine *An Institute of the Law of Scotland* (8th edn, 1871) II, 2, 1; see also ch 1, pt 1 above.

that do not have to be specially created. However, this traditional classification is slightly misleading: apart from a few limited exceptions that we will mention as we go along, **all** of these rights arise automatically from the fact of ownership.

2. GENERAL RIGHTS

(1) Right to exclusive possession

Here we are talking about natural possession, ie physical occupancy, as opposed to civil possession where the owner is represented by the natural possession of another, such as his tenant. An owner normally has the sole right to occupy his property and has the legal right to defend himself against anyone who encroaches upon this right in any way. This assumes, of course, that our subject matter is a property with only one owner: the special problems of multiple ownership will be discussed in a separate chapter.[1]

Within the boundaries of his land, an owner's right to exclusive possession is, in theory, without limit. Traditionally it is said to extend *a coelo usque ad centrum* (from the sky to the centre of the earth).[2] Thus, if the branch of a neighbour's tree overhangs an owner's garden, the owner is entitled to demand that it be removed as it is an encroachment upon his property.

It only takes a moment's thought to realise that this principle cannot be taken absolutely literally; otherwise, every airline company would be guilty of multiple trespass. This is not so because the general rule has been qualified by statute so as to allow flight over another person's property at a reasonable height.[3]

Another exception to our general rule is in relation to the ownership of and right to work minerals. In theory, the purchaser of land should acquire all mineral rights along with it; this after all is a natural extension of the rule we have just stated. However, it seldom works out this way in practice. All coal automatically belongs to British Coal (formerly the National Coal Board).[4] Petroleum, natural gas and certain precious metals belong to the Crown.[5] And anything worthwhile that may be left after this will be caught up in the standard

---

1 See ch 7 below.
2 See Gordon *Scottish Land Law* (1989) para 4–02.
3 Civil Aviation Act 1982, s76(1).
4 Coal Industry Nationalisation Act 1946; Coal Industry Act 1987; see also ch 17 below.
5 Petroleum (Production) Act 1934; Royal Mines Act 1424; see also ch 5 below.

provision, found in virtually every feudal grant, reserving the minerals and all rights to work them to the superior;[1] this occurs irrespective of whether the land contains, or is likely to contain, any minerals at all.[2] And so, in the vast majority of cases, a purchaser of property will buy no mineral rights whatsoever.

Despite this, unless a contract to purchase heritable property makes an express qualification regarding the minerals position, there is a legal presumption that the minerals will be conveyed along with the rest of the property. This makes it imperative upon the seller of property to make sure that the situation regarding minerals is covered in the missives. Otherwise the purchaser will be entitled to resile from the bargain.[3] And while it is unlikely that the purchaser of a suburban semi-detached will want to back out because he cannot dig a mine in his back garden, this could provide a valid legal pretext if he has changed his mind about the purchase for some other reason.

An owner's right to exclusive possession of his property is also subject to a large number of statutory and other exceptions where certain persons, or more likely the representatives of public bodies, may have a power of entry in the public interest. There are far too many of these to mention in detail; they include, for example, the right to enter a property to prevent the commission of a crime, or the right of local authorities to enter properties for the sake of public health.[4]

Trespass.   This is where an owner's right to exclusive possession has been encroached upon by the temporary presence on his property of a person or persons who have no right to be there. It is sometimes said that there is no law of trespass in Scotland. This is not strictly correct, and probably derives from the fact that trespass as such is not a crime (unless some crime is committed in the process, such as breaking and entering upon a dwellinghouse); thus the traditional sign 'trespassers will be prosecuted' is not a threat that could be actually carried out and could only operate as a bluff.

However, an owner is entitled to ask a trespasser to leave his

---

1   For an example of a minerals reservation clause, see the burdens section of the specimen land certificate in the Appendix.

2   See ch 17 below.

3   See eg *Campbell v McCutcheon* 1963 SC 505, 1963 SLT 290; see also ch 15 below.

4   See eg the Burgh Police (Scotland) Act 1892, s118 (as amended by the Local Government (Scotland) Act 1973, Sch 28); see also *Gordon* paras 13–14 and 13–15.

property, and may back this right up with the use of reasonable force, particularly if the trespass is in a dwellinghouse.[1] A trespasser may also incur consequences under the civil law. Trespass as such is not a civil wrong, but if any damage to the property occurs, the trespasser may be sued by the owner for damages. Also, if the trespass is a regular occurrence, or there is any other good reason to believe that it might be repeated, the owner may obtain an interdict from the court to prevent a recurrence; however, the court will only grant an interdict if the trespass is substantial and not trivial, eg where a pet lamb strayed on to unfenced land.[2]

The legal remedies for trespass are available not only to an owner, but to anyone else, such as a tenant, to whom the owner has legally transferred his right to exclusive possession.[3]

Unlawful possession. This is where the encroachment is not temporary (as with trespass), but the property has in fact been occupied by someone having no right to do so. In such a case the owner may take a civil court action to evict the occupant or occupants. There are several variants of this action, depending on how the unlawful possessor came to occupy the property;[4] for example, an action of ejection, where the unlawful possession was taken by violence, or an action of removing, where the possessor claims to be there by right. In all cases the purpose is the same: the eviction of the unlawful possessor or possessors from the property. If there seems any likelihood of the property being re-occupied this eviction action may be accompanied, or followed later, by an interdict, to prohibit the unlawful occupier from returning. In this context, these court actions are often referred to as **possessory remedies**.

As in the case of trespass, these remedies are available also to persons other than owners who have a legal right to possess a property, eg to a tenant. In the unusual situation of there being two parties with a competing claim to the same property, the possessory remedies will be available, at least on a provisional basis, to the party in occupation, if he has been in possession for seven years or more.[5] At the end of the day, however, the party with the better title will win.

---

1 *Bell v Shand* (1870) 7 SLR 267 at 268–269, per Lord Ardmillan; *Gordon* para 13–10.
2 *Winans v Macrae* (1885) 12 R 1051.
3 *Merry & Cuninghame v Aitken* (1895) 22 R 247; 2 SLT 423.
4 See *Gordon* paras 14–22 to 14–28.
5 *Gordon* 14–11 to 14–14; see also *Colquhoun v Paton* (1859) 21 D 996 at 1001, per Lord Cowan.

Bona fide possession.[1] A situation could arise, though nowadays it is probably not very common, where someone occupies a property in the genuine, though mistaken, belief that he has the legal right to do so. The law makes a distinction between the position of such a **bona fide possessor** and that of a **mala fide possessor**, ie a possessor in bad faith who knew all along that he had no right to occupy. Either can be evicted by the person (whether the owner, tenant or otherwise) who really has the legal right to possess. However, the possessor in good faith is entitled to certain rights which are denied to the mala fide possessor. He can keep the fruits from the property, ie any profit earned by him from the property during his period of occupation (such as rents from tenants, or the profit from goods manufactured on the premises). If he has made any improvements to the property, he is entitled to be paid the amount that they have added to the value of the property; this last right arises out of the principle of **recompense** (from the area of law known as quasi-contract), an equitable principle under which one person is not entitled to gain from another person's loss.

The mala fide possessor, on the other hand, may be liable for **violent profits**, a form of penal damages, which would normally mean that he would have to account for all profit made by him from the property during his period of occupancy. In other words, unlike the bona fide possessor, the mala fide possessor forfeits his right to the fruits. Nor does he have a right of recompense in respect of any improvements he may have carried out to the property.

We saw in chapter 1 that, by the process of positive prescription, it was possible for someone who had no right to a property to acquire ownership, provided that he had a recorded title followed by ten years unchallenged possession. It should be made clear at this point that, for prescription to operate, it is irrelevant whether the possession was in good or bad faith.

(2) Right to use property

It is also implicit in our definition of ownership that the property owner has the right, not only to exclusive possession of his property, but also to use it as he wishes, for his own profit, pleasure or otherwise. We have already noted that this right is subject to many legal restrictions, such as the need for planning consent to carry out any development, and we will be considering these restrictions in detail

1 See Gloag & Henderson *Introduction to the Law of Scotland* (9th edn, 1987) paras 39-11 and 39-12.

in due course. Having established that, there is not a great deal to be said about an owner's positive right to use his property; it is what is left after all the qualifications, legal and voluntary, have been taken into account.

However, there is one particular aspect that should be considered here, as it should be taken in conjunction with, and as a prelude to, the next owner's right that we are to consider. This is the right to freedom from interference in the enjoyment of one's property. When examining an owner's rights, we have to take account of the fact that he has neighbours, whether occupiers of the same building or adjoining landowners. If any one owner was allowed an absolutely unlimited right to use his property as he pleased, this would have repercussions on his neighbours. Any owner's use of his property, therefore, must be balanced against his neighbours' right to enjoy their own property in peace and generally free from interference. Likewise, as against his neighbours, he himself has the same right, and that is what we will consider in the next section.

(3) Freedom from interference by neighbours

There are three main categories of harmful action by a neighbour to which a property owner may take legal exception. These are nuisance, malicious action and non-natural use of property. Although our present context is the law of property, we should be aware that these principles may also be considered under the law of delict: they are all forms of legal wrong for which the injured party may seek reparation in the civil courts.

Nuisance. A useful definition of common law nuisance is given by Bell in his *Principles*:[1]

'Whatever obstructs the public means of commerce and intercourse, whether in highways or navigable rivers; whatever is noxious or unsafe, or renders life uncomfortable to the public generally, or to the neighbourhood; whatever is intolerably offensive to individuals, in their dwelling-houses, or inconsistent with the comfort of life, whether by stench (as the boiling of whale blubber), by noise (as a smithy in an upper floor), or by indecency (as a brothel next door).'

There may be more modern examples of offensive practices, but this still gives the general idea. However, a point to note at the outset is that Bell's definition extends beyond the reciprocal rights and obligations of neighbouring property owners and involves the public at large. Thus, in our previous section, the right of an owner

1 Bell *Principles of the Law of Scotland* 974.

to use his property as he pleases is restricted by his obligation to refrain from carrying on a nuisance that would interfere not only with his neighbours, but also with members of the public. Likewise, where an owner's right to enjoy his property is being interfered with, his redress is not limited to nuisances perpetrated by a neighbouring owner; a member of the public may also be liable, eg where the owner of a traction engine was held liable for nuisance when sparks from his vehicle caused damage to property adjoining the road.[1] However, most examples of nuisance arise between nearby property owners or their tenants under the area of law known as the **law of the neighbourhood**.

The most normal sources of nuisance are noise, vibration, fumes etc. In *Webster v Lord Advocate*,[2] the owner of a flat adjoining the esplanade of Edinburgh Castle raised an action of nuisance in respect of the annual military tattoo and, more particularly, the noise caused by the erection and dismantling of the scaffolding for the seating, a process which continued throughout a considerable portion of the year. It was held that the latter did amount to a nuisance, though the interdict was suspended for six months to allow the organisers to find quieter methods of carrying out the work, so that the event could continue.

However, the boundaries of nuisance extend beyond such normal causes, and potential nuisances are virtually unlimited in number, provided that material harm, discomfort or inconvenience is caused. In *Lord Advocate v The Reo Stakis Organisation Ltd*,[3] piling operations during the building of a hotel extension caused subsidence damage to an adjoining building, and this was held to be a nuisance.

A nuisance is something that happens on a regular basis, and there can be no liability for a one-off occurrence.[4] Also, it is irrelevant that the nuisance was known to exist before the complaining owner bought his property, and it is no defence to the perpetrator to say that the party complaining willingly moved into the area where the nuisance already existed.[5] However, failure to object over a period of time may bar an owner from taking action against nuisance under the principle of **acquiescence**,[6] and his right of action and that of any future owners of his property will be extinguished by the

---

1 *Slater v McLellan* 1924 SC 854; 1924 SLT 634.
2 1985 SC 173; 1984 SLT 13; 1985 SLT 361.
3 1980 SC 203, 1981 SC 104.
4 *Gray v Dunlop* 1954 SLT (Sh Ct) 75, (1954) 70 Sh Ct Rep 270.
5 *Fleming v Hislop* (1886) 13 R (HL) 43 at 49, per Lord Halsbury; 23 SLR 491.
6 See ch 9, pt 4 and ch 10 below, where this principle is discussed in relation to servitudes and real conditions respectively.

long negative prescription if the nuisance has continued unchallenged for twenty years or more.[1]

The common law of nuisance is generally reinforced by a standard clause in feu charters, prohibiting vassals from carrying out defined activities that would amount to a nuisance.[2] Where such a clause exists it will therefore give a right of action to the superior, as well as to other parties entitled to enforce real conditions.[3]

The main legal remedy for nuisance is a court action of interdict, to restrain the offending party from carrying on the nuisance in future. Damages also may be claimed, if the nuisance has had a detrimental effect on the pursuer's health or the value of his property.

What we have been discussing so far is nuisance at common law. However, there are also a large number of **statutory nuisances**, where a similar type of liability is imposed by statute.[4] In most cases these are enforced by local authorities (generally district councils) under their environmental health powers, and they reinforce and extend the boundaries of common law nuisance, covering eg overcrowding, refuse disposal, noise and vibration and air pollution. The principal Scottish statute is the Public Health (Scotland) Act 1897, although it has been superseded on many particular issues by more modern UK legislation, notably the Control of Pollution Act 1974. In England, the law relating to statutory nuisance has been integrated by the Environmental Protection Act 1990, though Scotland has been excepted from these particular provisions; however that Act otherwise applies to the whole of the UK and includes, amongst other things, important measures relating to waste disposal, air pollution, litter and radioactive substances.

Statute may also intervene to permit something that would amount to a nuisance at common law because the activity is considered to be in the public interest. Thus a number of public bodies and others whose activities are regulated by statute are given immunity from nuisance, eg airline companies or local authorities in respect of roads and motorways. However, although no interdict can be obtained in such cases, a property owner may be able to claim compensation where the use of the public works in question causes a depreciation in the value of his property.[5] The physical factors that can give

---

1 Prescription and Limitation (Scotland) Act 1973, ss7, 8.
2 For an example of such a clause see the burdens section of the specimen land certificate in the Appendix.
3 See eg *Mannofield Residents Property Co Ltd v Thomson* 1983 SLT (Sh Ct) 71.
4 *Gordon* paras 26-36 to 26-59.
5 Land Compensation (Scotland) Act 1973, Pt I.

rise to a claim are statutorily defined (eg noise, vibration, fumes),[1] but they bear a close resemblance to the usual grounds of nuisance at common law.

Malicious action.   Another exception to the rule that an owner may use his property as he pleases is that he is not entitled to do something with it which does not benefit himself, but is carried out purely from malice or spite in order to do harm to his neighbour. Such an action is said to be *in aemulationem vicini,* ie purely from a malicious motive.

This principle has no equivalent in English law, where the motive of the person involved is considered to be irrelevant. Even in Scotland, it is not encountered very often. It is rare for someone to act purely from spite in a situation where he does not derive some benefit himself, and the existence of such benefit would defeat a claim under this principle. Even if it does occur, it is likely that a claim of nuisance could be made instead. Successful claims under the doctrine therefore tend to be rather old, and include situations where a fair was held immediately beside the property of a neighbour,[2] and also a situation where a man erected a building deliberately beside his neighbour's boundary, rather than elsewhere on his land, purely in order to block his neighbour's light.[3]

Non-natural use of property.   This is where an owner brings an innovation into his land, which escapes and causes damage to neighbouring property. Traditional examples of this are flooding caused by the bursting of a dam or the diversion of a stream or river.[4] A more modern example is damage caused by weedkiller.[5] If it can be established that the owner of the offending property failed to take the necessary precautions to prevent the damage, he will be liable in damages.

Strict liability.   It was previously thought that the liability of a property owner for nuisance and non-natural use was strict in each case. Strict liability is where the mere existence of the phenomonon causing the harm (eg the nuisance or non-natural use) is enough

---

1   Land Compensation (Scotland) Act 1973 s1.
2   *Falconer v Glenbervie* 1642 Mor 4146; *Farquarson v Earl of Aboyn* 1679 Mor 4147.
3   *Ross v Baird* (1829) 7 S 361.
4   *Kerr v Earl of Orkney* (1857) 20 D 298; *Caledonian Railway Co v Greenock Corporation* 1917 SC (HL) 56.
5   *D McIntyre & Son v Soutar* 1980 SLT (Sh Ct) 115.

to establish liability without negligence or other fault having to be proved. In relation to non-natural use, this is still the case in England.[1] However, it has now been established in Scotland that (with the possible exception of the diversion of a stream or river)[2] there is no strict liability in such cases, and that there can be no claim of damages unless *culpa* (blame) can be proved.[3]

(4) Right of support[4]

Land normally requires support, not only from below, but also from the land surrounding it. However, the surrounding land may be the property of another owner; also, as we saw earlier, if there are any minerals beneath the land in question, they are likely to be in separate ownership. The question therefore arises whether a property owner has the legal right to demand the necessary support for his land (and, even more importantly, for his buildings) from surrounding landowners and the owners of any minerals beneath him. The answer is that in some cases there is a natural right of support, ie a right that arises automatically *ex lege* ('out of law'). In all other cases a right of support may be implied from the circumstances of the case; and, as we will see shortly, there are actually very few situations where such a right will not be implied.

Disputes about rights of support most commonly arise where minerals are being excavated beneath the land. The person working the minerals may be the superior or, more likely, someone who has acquired the mineral rights from him. If the mineral in question is coal, then the party in question will of course be British Coal; in that case, however, statute rather than common law is likely to rule the matter. Mineral reservation clauses and the nature of minerals are discussed later in the book.[5]

Natural right of support. A natural right of support exists in only one situation, namely where the land is in its natural state, ie without buildings. Here the situation is perfectly clear: the owner of the surface has an automatic right of support for his land unless he

1 *Rylands v Fletcher* (1866) LR 1 Ex 265, (1868) LR 3 (HL) 330.
2 *Caledonian Railway Co v Greenock Corporation, supra.*
3 *RHM Bakeries (Scotland) Ltd v Strathclyde Regional Council* 1985 SLT 214.
4 *Gordon* para 6–80 et seq; Halliday *Conveyancing Law and Practice* (1986) para 19–05 et seq. For examples of a mineral reservation clause and a clause imposing an obligation to erect buildings (both referred to below) see the burdens section of the specimen land certificate in the Appendix.
5 See ch 17 below.

has given it up. Since a right of support is most crucial when there are buildings on the ground, this natural right is therefore of limited value. Nevertheless there are some situations where it could be useful, eg if farmland was being affected by subsidence.

Implied right of support.[1]   Where there are buildings on the ground, a right of support is most essential, and yet in this situation there is no natural right. However, in the following situations a right of support may be implied:

(a)   Where the buildings were already erected at the time of the reservation of minerals.[2] Obviously in this case the superior (or whoever made the reservation) knew about the buildings and that subsequent working of the minerals might deprive the building or buildings of support.

(b)   Where the feu charter or other deed reserving the minerals also imposed an obligation to erect a building or buildings.[3] This is a very common situation, which will probably account for the existence of an implied right of support in most cases. We have already seen that there is a standard provision in feudal grants for the minerals to be reserved to the superior. It is also virtually standard for the superior to include real conditions obliging the vassal to erect and thereafter maintain a building or buildings on the land. It would be quite unfair and inconsistent of the superior to impose such a condition without giving the necessary support to such a building or buildings. And so, in this situation, a right of support will be implied.

(c)   Where the erection of buildings would have been reasonably contemplated at the time of the reservation of minerals to the superior,[4] eg where the land has been sold to a builder.

(d)   Where a servitude right of support has been created by positive prescription.[5] This is not, strictly speaking, an implied right of support, but it is convenient to include it with the others. In most cases it is likely that an implied right of support will have been created in one of the above three ways, but if not, a servitude right of support will have been created after the building or buildings have existed for twenty years.

1   *Halliday* paras 19-05 to 19-07.
2   *Caledonian Railway Co v Sprot* (1856) 2 Macq 449.
3   *North British Railway Co v Turners Ltd* (1904) 6 F 900, 12 SLT 176.
4   *Neill's Trs v William Dixon Ltd* (1880) 7 R 741, 17 SLR 496.
5   Prescription and Limitation (Scotland) Act 1973, s3; see also ch 9, pt 3 below.

It should be noted that the above implied rights of support can be contracted out of, ie they can be lost if the superior in his feudal grant expressly reserves the right to withdraw support.[1] It is not common to find this, but it is very important when property is being bought for the purchaser or his agent to check that such a provision does not exist in the title; obviously it could have grave implications for the surface owner, especially if there happen to be valuable minerals in the ground.

Right of damages. Where a right of support exists and subsidence occurs, it is an actionable wrong, giving the surface owner a right of damages in respect of any damage caused to his property.

Statutes relating to minerals and support. There are several important statutes relating to minerals and support, including the following:
Mines (Working Facilities and Support) Act 1966. This Act enables parties, including British Coal, who want to work minerals to apply to the Court of Session (via the Secretary of State for Industry) for compulsory powers to work them and to withdraw support from the surface. The application is decided on the basis of national interest and, as regards withdrawal of support, the comparative values of the minerals and surface buildings will be taken into account.
Coal Mining (Subsidence) Act 1991. This Act repeals and re-enacts with amendments the Coal Mining (Subsidence) Act 1957. It imposes on British Coal the liability to carry out remedial work in respect of damage caused to land or buildings by subsidence from 'lawful coal-mining operations'. It also covers damage to 'structures or works, on in or over land', eg sewers, pipes, drains etc.[2] In certain situations British Coal have the discretion to pay compensation instead, eg where the owner undertakes the remedial work himself, or the cost of the work is excessive.[3]

It should be noted that the Act is worded in a way that does not confine claims to damage caused by the coal workings of British Coal themselves. This is very useful, as damage can still occur from old private coal workings that pre-date the nationalisation of coal in 1938.

1 See ch 17 below.
2 Coal Mining (Subsidence) Act 1991, s1.
3 Ibid, ss8, 10.

Other situations involving rights of support.   We have concentrated on the situation regarding minerals because that is where questions of rights of support most commonly arise in practice. It should be noted, however, that similar questions could also arise between adjacent owners, eg by a neighbour digging or quarrying right up to the edge of his property: in such a case he is bound to stop his excavations at such a distance from his boundary as to leave sufficient support for the adjoining land.

3. LANDOWNER'S RIGHTS

(5) Rights in water[1]

The position here varies according to whether or not the water is in a definite channel, such as a stream, river or loch.

Where water is not in a definite channel, it may be appropriated by the owner of the land in which it is situated, eg by sinking a well. However, where it is flowing in a stream or non-tidal river, the position is more complex.

In the latter cases, each owner through whose land the river or stream flows owns the portion of the bed (or alveus) that is situated within his land; where the river or stream forms the boundary between different properties, this runs along the centre line of the bed. The owners on either side are generally known as riparian proprietors.

As far as use of the water is concerned, all the owners through whose land the river or stream flows, and all riparian proprietors, are said to have a **common interest** in the water as a whole. This is a difficult concept which will be dealt with further at a later stage.[2] In the present context, it means that each of the various owners concerned is limited in his use of the water by the interest of the others in it. He may withdraw water for what are said to be primary purposes, such as for drinking, watering cattle or other domestic purposes, even if the supply of water is thereby exhausted. He may not use it for other purposes, eg irrigation or manufacturing, unless this can be done without affecting the interest of the other owners. If a riparian owner diverts a stream or river, the owner opposite may object; however, an owner further downstream has no cause for complaint provided that the stream or river is back on course before it enters his property.

1   *Rankine Law of Landownership in Scotland* (4th edn, 1909) ch 29; *Gordon* ch 7.
2   See ch 7, pt 4 below.

An inland loch, if it is entirely within the land of one owner, belongs entirely to that owner. Where it is bounded by more than one property, each owner owns the segment of the bed opposite his land out to an imaginary centre point; in such cases the water itself is owned jointly for all the owners to use. Where a stream flows out of a loch, the use of the water by the owner or owners is limited by the common interest of the owners downstream.

Sea lochs and tidal rivers are subject to the same rules as the sea and, because of the interest of the Crown in such cases, will be dealt with in the next chapter. It is worth noting at this point, however, that in such cases there is a public right of navigation. There may also be a public right of navigation in a non-tidal river, but only if the river is navigable and the right has been established by public use over a period of forty years or more.[1]

Pollution. There are extensive statutory provisions regarding pollution, which largely replace the common law on the matter.[2] It is not within our scope to do more than note the existence of such provisions in passing.

Fishing rights. In the case of lochs, streams and non-tidal rivers, these belong to the landowners concerned, even if, in the case of a river, there is a public right of navigation. Where the river or stream forms a boundary, each riparian proprietor is allowed to fish out to the centre line. Salmon fishing is in a special category; that (along with fishing in the sea, sea lochs and tidal rivers) is affected by Crown rights and will be dealt with in the next chapter.

(6) Right to kill game

The right to kill game is an incident of landownership, ie belonging to the owner of the land on which the game is found, and this right remains with the owner even where the land is tenanted, unless the tenant's lease contains a specific provision otherwise. This means that the right cannot be sold as a separate piece of property. However, it can be made the subject of a lease, either along with occupation of the property as a whole, or as a separate subject, and leases of

1 *Wills' Trs v Cairngorm Canoeing and Sailing School Ltd* 1976 SC (HL) 30, 1976 SLT 162.
2 Rivers (Prevention of Pollution)(Scotland) Acts 1951 and 1965; Control of Pollution Act 1974.

shooting rights and other uses of land not involving complete occupation are well established in Scots law.[1].

There are a number of (mainly old) statutes regulating the killing of game.[2] These do not completely agree on a definition of game, but hare, pheasants, partridge and grouse are commonly included. The killing of wildlife, by landowners or anyone else, is also regulated by the statutory provisions relating to wildlife conservation.[3]

As detailed consideration of this topic would be incidental to the main purpose of this book, any reader wishing to pursue it further is referred to other authorities.[4]

1 See Paton & Cameron *The Law of Landlord and Tenant in Scotland* (1967) pp 73–84.
2 Eg the Game (Scotland) Act 1772; the Ground Game Act 1880.
3 Wildlife and Countryside Act 1981 (as amended by the Wildlife and Countryside (Amendment) Act 1985).
4 *Gloag & Henderson* para 39-17; *Gordon* ch 9.

5. Crown rights

1. GENERAL

Traditionally a great number of rights were vested in the Crown, in the capacity of monarch (as opposed to his or her personal property). These royal rights are generally known as **regalia**. Many of them have survived to the present day and many of them relate to landownership. In this chapter we will briefly consider some of the more important ones.

Crown rights can be divided into two quite separate classes, known as the **regalia majora** (the greater royal rights) and the **regalia minora** (the lesser royal rights). The difference is that the regalia majora are held by the Crown in trust for the public, and are therefore inalienable, ie the Crown does not have the legal right to dispose of them by sale or otherwise. This effectively means that the regalia majora are public rights which may be exercised by anyone. The regalia minora, on the other hand, although initially belonging automatically to the Crown, may be alienated by the Crown, ie disposed of to another party by sale or otherwise. A public body, known as the Crown Estate Commissioners, is responsible for managing the regalia minora on behalf of the monarch.

A number of the regalia relate to the sea and other water rights, and for this reason what follows should be read in conjunction with the appropriate section of the preceding chapter. An example that illustrates both types of royal right is the foreshore, ie the section of beach lying between the high and low water marks of the ordinary spring tides. The foreshore is part of both the regalia majora and regalia minora, unlike most of the other royal rights which come under one or the other. It belongs to the former category in the sense that the Crown holds the foreshore in trust for the public rights of navigation, recreation and fishing. Otherwise it forms part of the regalia minora, and can be sold by the Crown, most likely to the adjoining landowner. This means that, for the most part, while the owner of the foreshore (the Crown or otherwise) has the same rights in it as any other landowner, the public's rights must be respected. The public will therefore always have the right (for example) of navigation, fishing or swimming etc.

2. REGALIA MAJORA[1]

The main surviving regalia majora are the Crown's rights in the **sea and seabed** within territorial waters, in the **foreshore** (as mentioned above), and in the water and bed of **tidal navigable rivers**. The Crown also has a right in highways, but this has been rendered largely academic by the legislation relating to roads;[2] in other words, the public's right to use roads mainly derives from the statutory road authorities (in most cases the regional councils) rather than through the Crown under the regalia majora.

Territorial waters formerly extended three miles from the shore, but now the limit is twelve miles.[3] The legal position regarding the sea and seabed within that limit, for the foreshore and for tidal navigable rivers, is the same, ie they are owned by the Crown in trust for the public rights of navigation, fishing and probably also recreation. These rights are inalienable, ie the public cannot be deprived of them by any act of the Crown, although they can be (and have been in some cases) removed by Act of Parliament.[4]

3. REGALIA MINORA

The following are the main categories of the regalia minora. For a full list, the reader is referred to other authorities.[5]

Precious metals

Gold and silver mines, no matter where they are situated, and also lead mines where the lead is sufficiently fine for the production of silver, belong to the Crown.[6] However, the owner of the land in which the mine is situated may require the Crown to make a

1 Gordon *Scottish Land Law* (1989) para 27–06.
2 Roads (Scotland) Act 1984.
3 Territorial Sea Act 1987, s1(1)(a).
4 Gloag & Henderson *Introduction to the Law of Scotland* (9th edn, 1987) paras 39–2 to 39–5.
5 *Gordon* para 27–07.
6 Royal Mines Act 1424.

grant to him of the precious metals, in return for a payment known as a royalty.[1]

Sea and foreshore[2]

As we saw above, these come under both the regalia majora and the regalia minora. In the latter capacity, the Crown owns the sea and seabed (including lochs open to the sea), as well as the foreshore adjoining the sea and tidal navigable rivers. It is doubtful whether the seabed can be sold or otherwise alienated, but the foreshore can be alienated, generally to the proprietor of the land adjoining. The adjoining proprietor can also acquire the foreshore by prescription, provided that his title is habile to include it (ie if the title description is such that it includes, or possibly could include, the foreshore).[3]

Treasure and lost property[4]

It might be thought that treasure, or any other long lost property found on land, would belong to the landowner. However, it in fact belongs to the Crown. In theory the Crown may dispose of such finds, but normally it keeps them for itself.

Salmon fishings[5]

Salmon fishings are a separate heritable right (ie a separate tenement)[6] and belong initially to the Crown under the regalia minora. They can, however, be sold either to the riparian proprietors or anyone else. There is extensive statutory regulation of salmon fishing relating, among other things, to the close season and permitted fishing methods.[7]

---

1 Mines and Metals Act 1592; see also *Gordon* paras 6–13 to 6–14.
2 *Gloag & Henderson* paras 39–3 to 39–4; *Gordon* paras 4–24 to 4–26, 7–02 et seq.
3 Prescription and Limitation (Scotland) Act 1973, s1(1),(4); see also ch 1, pt 4 above.
4 *Gordon* paras 10–34 to 10–37; *Lord Advocate v University of Aberdeen* 1963 SC 533, 1963 SLT 361.
5 *Gloag & Henderson* para 39–8; *Gordon* para 8–41 et seq.
6 See ch 1, pt 1 above.
7 See eg Freshwater and Salmon Fisheries (Scotland) Act 1976; Salmon Act 1986.

6. Fixtures

1. NATURE OF FIXTURES[1]

In relation to heritable property, it is natural to think primarily of buildings such as houses, factories, shops or offices, these being the parts of the property that have the most value. Except in the case of large tracts of land, such as agricultural land, the actual site would be considered of secondary importance. In strict law, however, what is owned is land and anything attached to the land, even if what is attached, such as a building, is more valuable than the land itself. Questions relating to fixtures arise when there is some dubiety about an article that is attached to the land: has it become sufficiently attached to be considered part of the heritable property, or is it still a moveable item? As we will see below, there are a number of situations where the answer to this question is vital in order to settle disputes between parties with competing interests.

The best known definition of a fixture was that laid down by Lord Chelmsford in the case of *Brand's Trs v Brand's Trs*.[2] The substance of his definition is that a fixture is anything attached to the land, ie that is fastened or connected with it, not in mere juxtaposition with the soil. There are two Latin phrases commonly used in the definition of fixtures: *Quicquid plantatur solo, solo cedit* ('Whatever is annexed to the soil, becomes part of the soil') and *Inaedificatum solo, solo cedit* ('A thing built on the ground goes with the ground'). There is no hard and fast rule for determining whether an item is a fixture or not, but as we will see below, a number of guidelines have been established for determining such questions, and in many cases there are authoritative court decisions regarding certain types of article.

---

1 For general accounts of this topic, see Gordon *Scottish Land Law* (1989) ch 5; Halliday *Conveyancing Law and Practice* (1986) paras 15–35 to 15–40; Gloag & Henderson *Introduction to the Law of Scotland* (9th edn, 1987) para 36–5.
2 (1876) 3 R (HL) 16, 13 SLR 744.

2. RELATIONSHIP OF THE PARTIES

There are a number of categories of person between whom disputes regarding fixtures can arise. These usually occur where the person who owns the heritable property is different from the one who has a right to the moveables on it.

(1) Seller and purchaser

When, for example, a house is sold, what will transfer to the purchaser's ownership is normally the heritable property, ie the land and anything attached to it. This will naturally include the house itself, but what of subsidiary items such as central heating systems, kitchen units, light fittings, fireplaces, venetian blinds or fitted carpets? Can the seller take these with him or will he have to leave them for the purchaser because they form part of the heritable property? It is normal (and desirable) to expressly state in the sale contract (ie in the missives) which items are to be included and which excluded. In the absence of any such agreement, however, any dispute can only be resolved by determining whether or not the item in question is a fixture.

(2) Landlord and tenant

If a tenant makes additions to the leased subjects during the currency of his lease, the question may arise at the end of his tenancy whether he has the right to remove such items or whether they have become part of the heritable property and now belong to the landlord. If such additions substantially improve the property or are valuable articles in their own right (such as items of heavy machinery in a factory), the question of whether or not they are fixtures could be crucial: if they are, does it mean that the landlord will have the value of his property considerably increased at the tenant's expense?

(3) Liferenter and fiar

A liferent is where a person has the right to use property for his or her lifetime (or other limited period). At the end of the liferent (usually on the death of the liferenter) the property passes to another person (known as the fiar) who is said to have the right of fee. The property in question need not be heritable property, but very often is. A typical example would be where a husband in his will leaves his house to his wife in liferent (allowing her to occupy it for the remainder of her life) and to his children in fee. Disputes regarding fixtures could arise either during the liferenter's lifetime (eg if the liferenter wanted to sell an item that the fiar thought should remain with the house), or after the liferenter's death, if the person due to inherit the liferenter's moveable property was someone other than the fiar.

(4) Heritable creditor and general creditors

A heritable creditor is someone who has granted a loan secured over heritable property (usually by means of a deed known as a standard security).[1] If the debtor defaults in the repayment of his loan, the heritable creditor has the right to sell the property to realise his security. Questions may therefore arise as to what items are fixtures and included in his security as part of the property. If the debtor is bankrupt, the dispute may be between the heritable creditor and other, unsecured creditors who have the right to claim against the debtor's moveable property.

(5) Heir and executor

Prior to the passing of the Succession (Scotland) Act 1964, if a person died intestate (ie without leaving a will) his heritable property passed to his heir-at-law (usually the eldest son), and his moveable property was divided among all the persons entitled to succeed to the moveable estate, probably all of the children. The executor was the person appointed to administer the moveable estate and divide it among those entitled to it. Disputes could therefore arise as fixtures would be the property of the heir and moveable items would pass to the executor. The 1964 Act abolished this distinction and lumped heritable and moveable property together for the purpose of succession, so that all property now passes to the executor for general distribution.

There are still, however, some situations where disputes about fixtures may arise. For example, the surviving wife or husband and surviving children have the right to claim a proportion of the moveable estate as legal rights, whatever the terms of the deceased's will; these are the rights of *ius relictae* (wife), *ius relicti* (husband)

---

1 See ch 11 below.

and *legitim* (children). The 1964 Act made no alteration to this and such legal rights can still only be claimed against the moveable, and not the heritable, estate. Whether or not an item is a fixture can therefore determine whether or not it can be included in a legal rights claim.

Also, a person may still under his will leave his heritable property and his moveable property to different people, and disputes about fixtures could therefore arise in such a situation.

(6) Owner and assessor

When a property is valued for the purpose of levying local rates, it is only the heritable property which will be included in the rateable value. If a valuable item has been added to the property, whether or not it is a fixture may make a difference to the value that is reached.

3. DETERMINATION OF FIXTURES

What a fixture is

There is no hard and fast rule for determining this. The fact that a particular article is in fact fixed to the soil or a building will not necessarily answer the question.[1] The following considerations are also relevant:

(a) Can the article be removed without either being destroyed itself as a separate entity or damaging the soil or building to which it is attached? If the answer is 'yes' the article is probably not a fixture.[2]

(b) What was the purpose of the annexation? Was the article intended to be attached permanently, quasi-permanently or only temporarily? If the intention was a permanent attachment, the article is more likely to be a fixture than in the other two cases.[3]

(c) Was the building or land to which it is annexed specially adapted to its use? If the answer is 'yes' the article is probably a fixture.[4]

---

1 *Scottish Discount Co v Blin* 1985 SC 216, 1986 SLT 123 (overruling *Cliffplant Ltd v Kinnaird*, 1981 SC 9, 1980 SLT 2); see also *TSB Scotland v Jas Mills (Montrose) (In Receivership)* 1991 GWD 39–2406.
2 *Dowall v Miln* (1874) 1 R 1180, 11 SLR 673.
3 *Scottish Discount Co v Blin, supra.*
4 *Christie v Smith's Executrix* 1949 SC 572, 1950 SLT 31.

(d) To what extent would the use and enjoyment of the building or soil be affected by the removal? The less it would be affected, the less likely it is that the article is a fixture.[1]

(e) How heavy is the article? Generally speaking, articles which are attached by their own weight alone are considered to be moveables. However, if the article is particularly heavy, it may be considered to be a fixture. For example, in the case of *Christie v Smith's Executrix*,[2] a two ton summerhouse which rested by its own weight on a prepared site was held to be a fixture. The fact that its removal by the seller left a gap in the garden wall helped to confirm the position, ie rule (c) above was also applied.

In some cases, of course, one of the above considerations on its own may be conclusive, such as the degree of attachment.

Particular articles

(a) *Articles fixed to the soil*.[3] Generally speaking, all things planted in the soil with the intention that they grow there become part of the soil (although in certain cases the planter (eg a tenant) may be allowed to remove them). Into this category fall trees, shrubs and turf. In the case of growing crops such as wheat, barley etc, (which do not grow naturally but are the products of cultivation) there is some doubt as to whether they are fixtures or whether they are moveable.

Buildings sunk into the ground are fixtures, although a building merely resting on its own weight is not unless the weight is considerable.[4] Wire fences are also fixtures.[5]

(b) *Articles attached to a dwellinghouse*.[6] The following are generally considered to be fixtures: doors and windows, tiles, fireplaces, grates, chandeliers, picture rods, built-in cupboards and wardrobes, built-in kitchen units, the rollers of blinds, and cables (including electric light flex down to the bulb holder).

---

1 *Fisher v Dixon* (1843) 5 D 775, (1845) 4 Bell's App 286.
2 1949 SC 572, 1950 SLT 31; see also *Oman v Ritchie* (1940) 56 Sh Ct Rep 216, 1941 SLT (Sh Ct) 13.
3 See *Gordon* paras 5-38 to 5-40.
4 See *Christie v Smith's Executrix, supra.*
5 *Graham v Lamont* (1875) 2 R 438, 12 SLR 327.
6 See *Halliday* para 15-37; *Gordon* para 5-27.

The following are not considered to be fixtures: carpets (even though fitted), lino, pictures and mirrors (even if screwed to the wall).[1]

Some of these (and earlier) points are illustrated in the case of *Nisbet v Mitchell-Innes*.[2] In a dispute between the seller and purchaser of a house and grounds, the following were held to be heritable fixtures: tile hearths laid on and cemented to the hearthstone and enclosed by an iron hoop fastened by iron pins soldered into the hearth-stone by melted lead. The items held to be moveable included grates, lustres and gas brackets, picture rods, and a mirror used as a sliding shutter, which could be removed without injuring the structure; also included were ornamental stone lions and fire clay vases attached to stone pedestals by stucco and cement.

(c) *Machinery.* In accordance with the principles discussed above, factory machinery strongly built in, or specially adapted to the particular premises, is a fixture,[3] but machinery merely resting on the building, unless of very exceptional size and weight, is not. Machinery that qualifies as a trade fixture may be removed by a tenant or liferenter (see below).

(d) *Constructive fixtures.*[4] Certain articles, besides those which become fixtures by annexation to land or buildings, may become fixtures by what is known as *constructive annexation*. These are articles which, although not themselves physically attached, are accessories to a piece of heritable property. Examples of constructive fixtures are the keys of a house, the bell of a factory and the loose parts which are necessary for the use of fixed machinery;[5] the last is qualified by the rule that the machine parts must have been constructed to form part of the particular machine and not be capable of being used without adaptation to other machines of the same kind.

4. RIGHT TO REMOVE FIXTURES

The general rule is that no-one other than the owner of a piece of heritable property has the right to remove a fixture from it. There

1 *Cochrane v Stevenson* (1891) 18 R 1208, 28 SLR 848.
2 (1880) 7 R 575, 17 SLR 438.
3 *Scottish Discount Co v Blin* 1985 SC 216, 1986 SLT 123.
4 *Gordon* para 5–11
5 *Dixon v Fisher* (1843) 5 D 775.

are, however, some exceptions to this and the situation may vary depending upon the relationship between the parties to the dispute. The following two main categories of exception should be noted:

(1) Removal by contract

The person removing the fixture may have a contractual agreement with the owner of the heritable property which allows him to detach the fixture. For example, as mentioned above, when a house is being sold it is common for those items included and those not included in the sale to be expressly stated in the missives; a seller may therefore have the right to take away a fixture if it is expressly stated in the contract as not being included. Similarly, a tenant may enter a contractual agreement with his landlord allowing him to take away certain fixtures at the end of his lease.

The fact that comparatively few of the decided cases on fixtures are modern ones perhaps testifies to the number of parties who have learned the wisdom of avoiding such disputes by means of a contractual agreement.

It is important to note, however, that contracts only create personal rights and obligations, ie they normally only bind the parties to the contract.[1] If the property changes ownership, for example, a contractual right of (say) a tenant to remove a fixture will not generally bind the original landlord's singular successor (eg a purchaser or a heritable creditor who has realised his security).

The English case of *Hobson v Gorringe*,[2] illustrates this point. King, the owner of a sawmill, bought an engine on hire-purchase from the plaintiff (Hobson). The terms of the contract stated that the engine would not become King's property until all the instalments had been paid and that on the default of any instalment it was to be removable by the plaintiff. The engine was so attached to the property as to become a fixture. King did not complete his payments and subsequently went bankrupt. The defendant (Gorringe), to whom King had granted a mortgage over the sawmill (in Scotland he would be termed a heritable creditor), was held entitled to the engine because it was a fixture, and because he had not been a party to the hire-purchase contract and was not aware of it.

There is a possible exception to this rule in the case of landlord and tenant since, under the Leases Act 1449, the terms of a lease

1 See ch 1, pt 1 above.
2 (1897) 1 Ch 182.

can be binding upon the landlord's singular successors.[1] This could only apply, however, if the agreement for the removal of the fixture was a term of the lease itself and not the subject of a separate contract between the landlord and the tenant.

(2) Trade and ornamental fixtures

These are exceptions to the general rule which apply in the case of landlord and tenant and liferent and fee respectively.[2] The law here discriminates in favour of tenants and liferenters in a way which it does not with regard to the other categories of party mentioned above. The reason is that they only have a temporary right to the heritable property and it would be unfair if a fixture provided and paid for by the tenant or liferenter could accrue to the landlord or fiar free of charge.

The two categories of fixture to which this principle applies are fixtures attached by the tenant or liferenter for the purpose of his trade (eg large machines in a factory) and articles which have been annexed for ornament or for the better enjoyment of the article itself. This only applies if the articles can be removed without material injury to the heritable property and without themselves being destroyed in the process or losing their essential character or value. However, it will not prevent a machine being removable merely because to do so would require it being taken to pieces, provided that it can be put together again in the same form in another place.

It is important to note that the above principles do not make trade or ornamental fixtures moveable items. They remain **heritable** items, which the tenant or liferenter has the right to remove. This becomes clear if the dispute is with a third party; eg in a contest about a trade fixture between a landlord and the tenant's creditor, the landlord was held to be entitled to the item.[3]

The above principles are illustrated by the following cases:

(a)   *Spyer v Phillipson*.[4] A tenant on a twenty-one year lease of a suite of rooms installed some antique panelling with chimney-piece and fireplaces to match, worth in total £5,000. To effect this, considerable structural alterations had to be done to the premises and the tenant spent £20,000 altogether. The tenant

---

1   See ch 8, pt 1 below.
2   For the general principle relating to trade fixtures, see *Brand's Trs v Brand's Trs*, (1876) 3 R(HL) 16, 13 SLR 744.
3   *Miller v Muirhead* (1894) 21 R 658, 1 SLT 578.
4   (1931) 2 Ch 183.

died a few years before the end of the lease and there was a contest between the landlord and the tenant's executors over the ownership of the panelling and the executors' right to remove it. The court held that the tenant had installed the fixtures for his better enjoyment of the premises and with that end in view, not for the purpose of beautifying the premises for the benefit of the landlord. The tenant (or his executors) therefore had the right to remove the fixtures, provided that any damage done by the removal was made good.

(b) *D'Eyncourt v Gregory.*[1] In this case it was decided that ornamental statues, vases and garden seats, though merely resting on the ground by their own weight, could not be removed by a life tenant or his representatives if they formed part of the architectural design of the house and grounds.

(c) *Leigh v Taylor.*[2] Here it was decided that tapestries fixed to the walls of a house for decoration were removable by a liferenter on the grounds that he had put them up with the sole purpose of enjoying them himself.

(d) *Syme v Harvey.*[3] The tenants of a nursery garden were held entitled, at the end of their lease, to remove greenhouses, forcing pits and hotbed frames added by them for the purpose of their trade.

5. AGRICULTURAL FIXTURES

This is also a case of a tenant being able to remove fixtures which he has supplied, but it is a special case which should be considered separately. Under the Agricultural Holdings Act, farm tenants are given security of tenure and, where that is denied, a tenant can be compensated for any improvements he has made to the farm holding.[4] In the latter case, a tenant may also remove any fixture or fixtures added by him, provided that the fixture is not an improvement for which compensation has been claimed.[5] The tenant must give the landlord a month's notice of his intention to remove the fixture and make good any damage caused by its removal. The

---

1 (1866) LR 34 Eq 382.
2 [1902] AC 157.
3 (1861) 24 D 202, 34 Sol Jo 98; see also *Lloyds Bowmaker Ltd v William Cook Engineering (Evanton) Ltd* 1988 SCLR 676.
4 See ch 8, pt 4 below.
5 Agricultural Holdings (Scotland) Act 1991, s18.

landlord has the option of purchasing the fixture at the value it would be worth to an incoming tenant.

For the purpose of the above, a fixture is defined as any 'engine, machinery, fencing or other fixture' affixed to a holding by a tenant, as well as any building erected by him.[1] In considering, therefore, whether an item is a fixture for the above purpose, regard should be had to this definition rather than to the general criteria discussed earlier in the chapter.

---

1 Ibid, s18(1).

7. Common rights

1. INTRODUCTION[1]

So far we have been looking at ownership as an exclusive right enjoyed by one person, which is the easiest way to deal with concepts where common rights are not an issue. But there are many situations where a property may have more than one owner. And even where it has not, there are many instances (eg in a block of flats) where the interests of individual owners cannot be regarded in isolation from the interests of their immediate neighbours.

There are several legal forms which such common rights may take; unfortunately the distinctions between them are not always clear or easy to formulate, and there has been much confusion in this area, either in the law itself, or in the minds of those trying to understand it. In our attempt to shed some light on this murky scene, we will first look at the three main forms in which common rights are generally separately identified, namely common property, joint property and common interest. In addition, we will take a separate look at properties (such as blocks of flats) which are in multiple ownership. Finally, we will take a brief look at two other concepts that have grown to prominence in recent years, timesharing (usually of holiday homes), and shared ownership agreements.

2. COMMON PROPERTY

This simply means that a single piece of heritable property has more than one owner; the same applies to joint property, but that is best regarded as an exception to the usual rules regarding common property, and will be dealt with separately below.

An essential characteristic of common property is that each common owner has a separate title to part of the property; this does not necessarily mean that the property is divisible into separate

1 See Gordon *Scottish Land Law* (1989) ch 15.

parts, although it may be. It means that each owner is free to dispose of his share separately, either *inter vivos* or *mortis causa*; in other words, he may sell or otherwise dispose of his share during his lifetime, or he may leave it to someone in his will. The recipient need not be his co-owner, or one of them, but may be a third party.

All co-owners have a right to an equal say in the management and control of the common property. One owner therefore, may not unilaterally act in a way that affects the legal rights of the other owner or owners. For example, in the case of *WVS Office Premises v Currie*[1], one co-owner, without the other's consent, purported to create a servitude right over a common passage in favour of a third party. It was held that he was not entitled to do so. There is an exception to this general rule in the case of essential rebuilding or repair work; in such a case, one co-owner is entitled to have the work carried out without the consent of the others.[2] However, this assumes that there is no contractual arrangement to the contrary; in the case of flatted property, as we will see below, there generally is such an arrangement, and instructing and charging the cost of repairs will normally be the responsibility of a common factor or manager.

Another essential feature of common property is that one owner may insist, even against the wishes of the others, that the property be divided, so that each can have exclusive ownership of a separate portion.[3] Often this is impractical, in which case a single owner may force the sale of the entire property and the division of the proceeds among the co-owners.[4] We must also make an exception here in the case of flatted property and other property in multiple owner-occupation. We will see below that things like the roof or common passage and stairs are generally common property, and it would obviously be inappropriate for a single owner to force a division or sale of such parts; the rationale is that in such situations the common property is not owned as a separate item, but is an accessory to other pieces of property (eg individual flats) that are owned exclusively.

3. JOINT PROPERTY

Joint property is also a situation where more than one person owns the same piece of property. The essential difference between joint

1 1969 SC 170, 1969 SLT 254.
2 *Deans v Woolfson* 1922 SC 221, 1922 SLT 165.
3 *Brock v Hamilton* (1852) 19 D 701.
4 *Brock v Hamilton, supra.*

property and common property is that, unlike the common owner, the joint owner cannot sell his share separately or leave it to a third party in his will. Nor can he normally force a division of the property, or a sale and division of the proceeds. The right of joint owners is said to be *pro indiviso* (indivisible).

In some instances, joint ownership arises naturally, because of the nature of the situation. Trustees, for example, are joint owners of trust property; since they own, not in their own right, but on behalf of others, it would be quite inappropriate for them to have the same powers as co-owners, such as the ability to sell their share separately. The same principle applies to the members of clubs in relation to club property. The new member acquires a *pro indiviso* share of such property when he joins, and his share accresces to the other members when his membership ceases; like the trustee, he cannot deal with his share separately.

In other cases, joint property may exist because it has been made clear in the title conferring ownership that this is what is intended. For example, a husband and wife may take title to their house in *pro indiviso* shares, thus creating joint ownership. Their shares would be inseparable, and when one of them died, his or her share would automatically go to the other. However, the same could be achieved by common ownership if they left mutual wills, and in the event of them splitting up prior to being parted by death, common ownership would make it easier for one party to extricate his or her share without the other's consent.

4. COMMON INTEREST

It is with this concept that most confusion tends to arise, particularly in relation to the distinction between common interest and common property. Enlightenment is not made easier by the fact that they often occur together. The essence of the distinction is that in the case of common property, as we saw above, two or more people actually own the same piece of property. In the case of common interest this is not necessarily so. It is true that common owners may also have a common interest in the same property. But common interest in a property may also occur in a situation where one person owns it exclusively, and the other person or persons who share the common interest do not own it at all. In other words, the criteria for determining whether or not common interest exists are quite independent of whether or not there is common ownership. For example, the walls of a ground floor flat may belong exclusively to the flat owner, but all the other owners share a common interest in it, because it supports their property.

The above example provides an essential clue in determining the real nature of common interest. It occurs in situations where separate properties are in sufficiently close conjunction that what one owner does with his property affects the interest of his neighbours. The neighbours therefore have a common interest which allows them to have some control over any actions that may affect them.

We already saw in chapter 4 that the riparian proprietors of a river or stream all have a common interest in the water. This meant that, among other things, if one owner diverted the stream, or exhausted the water supply by using it for secondary purposes like irrigation or manufacturing, the other owners could stop him. Perhaps the most typical example of common interest, however, is in the case of flatted properties, or other properties in multiple owner-occupation; it is there that what one owner does to his property is most likely to affect the others.

There are two main aspects to the rights and duties arising among the owners who share a common interest. These take a negative and a positive form respectively. The first is the right of the other proprietors to prevent a particular owner from doing something to his property that would affect the interest of the others; for example, the upper proprietors in a block of flats could interdict the ground floor proprietor from knocking down a supporting wall. The other aspect is a positive right of the other proprietors to insist on a particular owner doing repairs to his property that are necessary to protect their interest; to develop our example above, even if the ground floor owner does nothing actively to damage the supporting wall, he can be compelled by the others to repair it if his failure to do so is threatening their support.

However, this duty of repair by a proprietor with a common interest is not an absolute duty; he is only liable if he fails to exert due care, ie if he acts negligently. In *Thomson v St Cuthbert's Co-operative Association Ltd*[1] a cast-iron beam situated on the underside of the ceiling in a ground floor flat provided support for the upper flats. The beam fractured without warning and the owner of an upper flat brought an action against the ground floor owner for the cost of repairs rendered necessary by this loss of support. It was held that the duty of support was not an absolute one, and that in the absence of proof of negligence on the part of the ground floor proprietor, he could not be liable.

1   1959 SLT 54.

This decision has been criticised on the basis that it leaves common interest providing no remedy over and above that which would generally be available under the law of delict where negligence has occurred.[1] It is argued that the doctrine of common interest as traditionally developed sets up a special regime over and above the general law of negligence, which would make such a duty of support an absolute one. However, until and unless it is overruled, we must take *Thomson* as stating the present position.

To return to the negative aspect of common interest, ie the right of other proprietors to object to an action of one proprietor that affects their interest, this right of objection only arises if the infringement is substantial. In *McCallum v Gunn*[2] two properties shared a common passage, and one of the proprietors sought to interdict the other from allowing one of her employees to leave a bicycle parked in the passage. It was held that it was necessary to prove substantial obstruction of the passage and that this had not been done. In *Gill v Mitchell*[3] the back gardens of two dwellinghouses were separated by a mutual wall, half of which belonged to each of the neighbouring proprietors. One owner sought to interdict the other from using his half of the mutual wall to support an extension to his dwellinghouse. It was held that there was no encroachment of common interest as no significant harm would result from the operation.

It should be noted in that last example that the wall in question was not common property, but that each owner owned the half on his side. This provides a useful contrast between common property and common interest: if the wall had been common property, the other owner would have had the right to object, because he would have been co-owner of the part of the wall against which the extension was resting. However, because that half of the wall was wholly owned by the proprietor erecting the extension, the only right of objection was under common interest, and that failed because the infringement was not sufficiently substantial.

5. LAW OF THE TENEMENT

At common law, there are certain rules, evolved over many centuries, that govern the common rights of the various owners in blocks of

---

1   'Common Interest' by Kenneth G C Reid, (1983) JLSS 428.
2   1955 SLT (Sh Ct) 85.
3   1980 SLT (Sh Ct) 48.

flats and other buildings in multiple ownership. These rules are known as the law of the tenement. Before stating them, however, it should be pointed out that they can be superseded by the provisions in the title deeds of the properties in question, and generally are. The law of the tenement, therefore, will only apply in those rare cases where provision for common rights has not been laid down in the titles, or, where it has, to plug any gap in such provision.

Under the law of the tenement, the owners of the lower storeys must provide support for the upper storeys and the owner of the top floor must provide cover for the properties below. The roof belongs to the owner or owners on the top floor, and each is obliged to repair and refrain from injuring the portion above his house. A garret may not be converted to an attic storey without the consent of the other owners. The solum (ie the site) on which the building is erected and ground at the back and front are presumed to belong to the owner or owners on the ground floor; however the other owners have a common interest which would allow them to prevent encroachment on their light, or any other infringement of their interest. The external walls belong to each owner so far as they enclose his property, but again the other owners have a common interest in them and can prevent them from being interfered with in a way that would endanger the building; the same applies to gables, though they are actually owned in common by the owners whose houses they separate. The floor and ceiling of each property are divided by an imaginary line through the middle of the joists, and are also protected from substantial interference by the common interest of the other owners. The common passages and stairs are the common property of all owners who are provided with an access by them.

It will be seen that in the majority of these cases the principle of common interest lies behind the rules: this is rendered inevitable by the close conjunction of the various properties in the same building.

In practice, the common rights of flat owners are virtually never left to rest on the common law of the tenement. The position will of course vary according to the provisions in the titles of different buildings, but a general pattern is evident. In particular, the roof is usually made the common property of all owners, rather than the top floor proprietors, and all owners have to contribute to its upkeep. Any ground at the back will generally also be made common property; alternatively, if the area is large enough, there may be a portion of common property (such as a drying green) and a number of separate plots allocated to individual proprietors.

These common provisions are generally contained in a deed of conditions which will be recorded in the Register of Sasines (or registered in the Land Register) and referred to in the dispositions relating to each individual flat.[1] Alternatively, they are sometimes repeated at length in the disposition by which each flat is first split off into separate ownership from the rest of the building; this often happened in older blocks of flats that were originally in one ownership with the individual flats leased to tenants, but later were sold off to owner-occupiers as they became vacant.

There is therefore something of a divergence between the traditional law of the tenement and modern practice. This has been recognised by the Scottish Law Commission, who have recently published proposals for legislation to introduce a new law of the tenement more suited to current requirements.[2] So far, however, no legislation on this has been forthcoming.

Statutory powers of local authorities. It is inevitable in situations where a number of owners are involved in a property that difficulties may sometimes be experienced in getting everyone's consent to the carrying out of necessary work to the common parts. Buildings may therefore suffer from neglect, or even be rendered dangerous, because a minority of owners, or even one individual, have refused to co-operate. In such cases, local authorities have the power to step in and remedy the situation. Under the Civic Government (Scotland) Act 1982, local authorities are given power to compel repairs, install and connect pipes and drains and provide lighting for common stairs, passages and courts. A duty is imposed on occupiers of common property (whether the owners or not) regarding cleaning and decorating of the common parts, and on common owners of open spaces and boundary walls and fences to maintain them so as to be free of danger or nuisance to the public; all of these duties can be enforced by the appropriate local authority.

Where a property is in serious disrepair and possibly requiring emergency action, the local authority's powers are reinforced by the Housing (Scotland) Act 1987.[3]

In most cases the appropriate local authority is the district or islands council, except in the regions of Highland, Borders, and Dumfries and Galloway where the regional council is responsible.

1 Conveyancing (Scotland) Act 1874, s32; see also ch 10 below.
2 Scottish Law Commission *Law of Tenement* Discussion Paper No 91 (December 1990).
3 Section 108; See also the Building (Scotland) Acts 1959 and 1970.

6. TIMESHARING

Timeshare schemes are a modern development whereby members of the public are invited to 'buy' a share in a holiday home, possibly a chalet in a particular resort. This appears superficially to resemble common ownership except that the timeshare owner has the right to occupy the property exclusively, but only for a particular period (perhaps lasting a week or a fortnight) in each year. His right is generally stated to be in perpetuity and is a marketable asset, ie he can sell it at a later date and possibly make a capital gain.

Such an arrangement, and the way it is marketed, may give the timeshare owner the impression that what he is acquiring is a real right in heritable property. However, this is not generally the case. Usually the title to the property remains in the name of the company setting up the scheme, or perhaps that of a trustee (such as a bank) specially appointed for the purpose. The timeshare owner, therefore, will not have a real right in the property, in the form of a title recorded in the Register of Sasines or registered in the Land Register; he will have a personal right under a contract with the timeshare company. The value of his 'perpetual' interest, therefore, is somewhat dependent on the standing of that company, though the holding of the title in the name of an independent trustee could afford some kind of protection.

Such schemes are also dependent on the timeshare company, or their successor or appointee, playing a continuing role in managing the scheme, so that repairs and other maintenance, transfer of timeshares etc can be dealt with. The future market value of a timeshare may well depend upon the efficiency of such a management arrangement.

It is possible that, with a little legal ingenuity, an arrangement could be reached that would give the timeshare owner something more in the nature of a heritable title. For example, it has been suggested that it could take the form of a lease.[1] It is also feasible that some form of joint or common ownership could be granted; however, this would probably require some backup agreement giving each timeshare owner an exclusive right to possession for his part of the year, and the formalities for transfer to a new owner might well prove cumbersome. In any event, these are not the solutions normally adopted in practice, and it is up to the would-be timeshare owner or his advisers to investigate the real legal nature of any particular scheme to see what protections are offered.

1 *Gordon* paras 15–08 and 19–13.

The Timeshare Bill, which is presently before Parliament, will, if it becomes law, introduce a fourteen day 'cooling-off' period during which the purchaser of a timeshare may withdraw from the agreement.

7. SHARED OWNERSHIP AGREEMENTS

This is a hybrid between a tenancy and a right of ownership. It is an arrangement whereby people who cannot afford to take the full plunge into owner-occupation of their homes are provided with a useful halfway stage between tenancy and ownership. The person involved is partly a tenant, but also has an 'equity share' in the property, ie as well as paying a periodic rent he has paid a capital sum and remains entitled to a percentage of the house's value. He may have the right to increase his equity share over the course of time, and if he terminates the arrangement he may well make a capital gain on the disposal of the equity share, thereby receiving a useful leg up towards home ownership.

A shared ownership agreement is defined in the Housing Associations Act 1985,[1] as

'a lease
(a)   granted on payment of a premium calculated by reference to a percentage of the value of the house or dwelling or of the cost of providing it, or

(b)   under which the tenant (or his personal representatives) will or may be entitled to a sum calculated by reference directly or indirectly to the value of the house or dwelling.'

The property interest acquired by such an agreement is therefore that of a tenant, the equity sharing element being written into the terms of the lease.

Shared ownership agreements as so defined do not qualify as assured tenancies under the Housing (Scotland) Act 1988.[2] This means that they are not protected by the security of tenure provisions applying to assured tenancies; presumably it is felt that enough protection is given by the special nature and terms of this hybrid form of agreement.

1   Section 106(1).
2   Schedule 4; see also McAllister *Scottish Law of Leases* (1989) p 192.

8. Leases

1. NATURE OF LEASES

A lease is a contract by which a person, known as a tenant, is allowed to occupy someone else's heritable property for a finite period.[1] In return for this he pays to the person granting this right (ie his landlord) a periodical payment known as rent. It is therefore an essential part of the normal concept of a lease that ownership remains with the landlord and that, at some stage, possession reverts to him. In strict theory this need not be so, as in the old case of *Carruthers v Irvine*[2] where a lease was stated to endure 'perpetually and continually as long as the grass groweth up and the water runneth down'. Such a perpetual lease, however, is really an anachronism and extremely rare. A lease will generally have a definite date of expiry, although its duration may be extremely long, eg 99 or even 999 years.

Form of lease

A lease is a contract relating to heritable property. This means that, as we saw in chapter 1, it must be in writing and be either holograph, adopted as holograph or attested. We also saw that, at common law, there was an exception in the case of leases for a year or less, which could be entered orally.[3]

Essential elements in leases

Having looked at the form of leases, let us now look at their content. Lease documents typically contain a number of terms, and can

---

1 For a more detailed general account of leases, see McAllister, *Scottish Law of Leases* (1989), from which this chapter has been adapted.
2 (1717) Mor 15195.
3 See ch 1, pt 3 above on the legal requirements for contracts relating to heritable property; for a fuller account with particular regard to leases, see *McAllister*, ch 2, pt 1.

sometimes run to a considerable length. However, to constitute a valid lease at common law only four essential elements need be present:

(1) *The parties.* It is fundamental that a lease must have both a landlord and a tenant. Not only must they be named, but they must also be designed (ie properly identified) usually by the addition of an address.

(2) *The subjects.* It is equally fundamental that there must be some property that is being leased. Furthermore, the subjects of let must be properly identified. Sometimes the postal address may be all that is necessary, except in the case of flatted properties where several subjects may share the same address. It is usually better, however, to describe the property at greater length and to provide a plan, particularly if the lease is to be recorded in the Register of Sasines or registered in the Land Register.[1]

(3) *Rent.* Without the two above elements we would arguably have nothing that could be called a contract at all. On the other hand, it is possible to create a legally binding contract allowing a person to occupy a property rent-free. However, such a contract would not be a lease, but merely a licence.[2] This means that it would not enjoy the benefit of any of the special rules relating to leases, notably the provisions of the Leases Act 1449.[3]

(4) *Duration.* The period of the lease should be stated. However, if it is omitted for any reason (usually by accident), a duration of one year is implied at common law.[4]

Types of lease

There are several different ways by which leases may be categorised, none of them mutually exclusive. There is a traditional distinction between **urban leases** (where the subjects of let are a building) and **rural leases** (where the subjects of let are land), and this distinction can still be important in some cases.

---

1 See the section on recorded leases below.
2 *Mann v Houston* 1957 SLT 89.
3 See below.
4 *Gray v Edinburgh University* 1962 SC 157, 1962 SLT 173; see also *Cinema Bingo Club v Ward* 1976 SLT (Sh Ct) 90.

Two important categories of lease are **commercial leases** (leases of shops, offices and other commercial premises) and **industrial leases** (leases of factories). Commercial and industrial leases in Scotland (unlike their English counterparts) are almost free of statutory regulation. The rights and obligations of the parties are therefore mainly determined by the terms of the lease contract, with the common law filling in any gaps. (There is a minor exception to this in the form of the Tenancy of Shops (Scotland) Act 1949, under which a sheriff may grant a shop tenant an extension of up to one year.)

In contrast, the two other main categories of lease, **agricultural leases** and **residential leases**, are both extensively regulated by statute.[1]

Scots law also traditionally recognises certain types of lease where the tenant does not have an exclusive right to occupy the property, but the right to use it for certain purposes only. These special types include mineral leases and leases of salmon fishings and other sporting rights.[2]

Leases as conferring a property right

We said above that a lease is a contract. While this is true, a lease can often confer upon a tenant a right that is more substantial than the mere personal right usually conferred under a contract. In many cases the tenant acquires something more akin to a right in property. There are three main factors that contribute to this, namely (a) the ability of a lease to confer a real right upon a tenant valid against the landlord's singular successors (b) the long security of tenure that a tenant may enjoy under some leases and (c) the ability to record a lease in the Register of Sasines (or register it in the Land Register).

(a) *Tenant's real right.*   If a lease were like any other contract, we would expect the tenant merely to have a personal right against the original landlord. This would mean that in the event of the landlord selling the property the new owner, having no contract with any existing tenants, would have no need to recognise their rights and could evict them prior to the end of their leases. However, this is not generally so. Under an old Scots Act, the **Leases Act 1449**, a tenant is given a real right valid not only against the original

---

1   See pt 4 below.
2   See Paton & Cameron, *The Law of Landlord and Tenant in Scotland* (1967) pp 73–84.

landlord but also against the original landlord's singular successors. This means that anyone who succeeds the original landlord as owner will be obliged to recognise the rights of any sitting tenant and allow him to remain until the end of his lease and at the same rent. Six conditions have to be fulfilled before the Act can apply, ie (1) the lease, if for more than a year, must be in writing; (2) the subjects of the lease must be land; (3) there must be a specific, continuing rent. The payment of a lump sum, or grassum, in the absence of a continuing rent, is not enough to satisfy this condition;[1] (4) there must be an ish, ie a term of expiry of the lease: (5) the tenant must have entered into possession. This can be satisfied either by natural possession (where the tenant physically occupies the property) or civil possession (where he is represented in his possession by another, eg a subtenant) and (6) the landlord, if he is the owner of the property, must be infeft (ie have a title recorded or registered in the Register of Sasines or Land Register).

(b) *Security of tenure.* The length of a lease can vary enormously, from a month or less to over a century. It is common for commercial and industrial leases to be fairly long, eg twenty or thirty years or more. The tenant's right under a lease of this length, since it confers a significant period of tenure, acquires a capital value and becomes a marketable asset, ie a tenant can charge a substantial sum of money in return for transferring his right to another tenant. Also, in the case of agricultural and residential leases, even if the term of the lease is comparatively short, the tenant is often given a statutory right to security of tenure beyond his contractual termination date.

(c) *Recorded leases.* If certain conditions are fulfilled, a lease may be recorded in the Register of Sasines or (in areas operational for registration of title) registered in the Land Register for Scotland.[2] For this to be possible a lease must (a) be probative (ie an attested document) and (b) have a duration in excess of twenty years.[3]

Recording (or registering) a lease takes a tenant a stage further in the acquisition of a property right. It confers a real right valid against the landlord's singular successors even where the conditions of the Leases Act 1449 have not been fulfilled. Also, it allows

---

1 *Mann v Houston* 1957 SLT 89.
2 See ch 14 below.
3 Registration of Leases (Scotland) Act 1957, s1 (as amended by the Land Tenure Reform (Scotland) Act 1974, Sch 6, para 1); Land Registration (Scotland) Act 1979, s29(1).

the tenant's interest under a lease to be used as security for a loan, ie it can be made the subject of a heritable security in the form of a standard security.[1]

2. RIGHTS AND REMEDIES OF THE PARTIES

At common law, both landlord and tenant have a number of implied rights against each other, and in the event of either party failing to perform the corresponding obligations, these rights are backed up by certain legal remedies. However, these implied terms can be contracted out of and often are, and so in determining the legal position in any particular case the common law should always be considered in conjunction with the terms of the actual lease contract.

It should also be kept in mind that, in the case of farm leases and leases of dwellinghouses, these rights are often altered or in some cases superseded by statute.[2]

Landlord's implied rights

The landlord's implied rights (which of course correspond to the tenant's obligations) are as follows:

(1) That the tenant should enter into possession, occupy and use the subjects.[3] Failure by the tenant in this obligation is a material breach of contract which would justify the landlord in rescinding from the lease.[4]

(2) That the property should be used only for the purpose for which it was let. A tenant in breach of this obligation is said to invert the possession, and the landlord may raise an action of interdict to have the unauthorised use stopped.[5] Although implied at common law, this obligation of the tenant is invariably written into leases (and generally elaborated upon) in a clause known as the use clause.

(3) That the tenant should take reasonable care of the property.[6] This is not a repairing obligation on the part of the tenant. It is a negative duty, which requires him to refrain from being negligent in his treatment of the property, and it exists independently of whether repairs are an obligation of the landlord or the tenant.

---

1   See ch 11 below.
2   See pt 4 below.
3   *Graham and Black v Stevenson* (1792) *Hume* 781.
4   *Blair Trust Co v Gilbert* 1940 SLT 322, 1941 SN 2.
5   *Leck v Merryflats Patent Brick Co* (1868) 5 SLR 619; *Bayley v Addison* (1901) 8 SLT 379.
6   *Mickel v McCoard* 1913 SC 896, 1913 1 SLT 463.

(4) That the tenant should pay the rent when it becomes due. Although implied, this is usually (not surprisingly) written into the lease.

(5) That the tenant should plenish the subjects. This means that the tenant is obliged to stock the subjects of let with sufficient moveable property to provide security for the rent. This is to enable the landlord, if required, to recover any rent arrears by means of his right of hypothec (see below).

Tenant's implied rights

(1) To be placed in full possession of the subjects let and to be allowed to remain there for the duration of the lease. Failure in this obligation by the landlord would entitle the tenant to damages in the form of an abatement of rent; failure to a material extent, might allow the tenant to rescind.

Once the tenant is in the property, the landlord must not do anything that would deprive, or partially deprive, the tenant of possession, as to do so would be to derogate from his grant to the tenant.[1]

(2) To be given subjects that are reasonably fit for the purpose for which they are let. This means that the property must be in a tenantable and habitable condition, not that it is fit for a particular type of business.[2] If the condition of the property makes it substantially unsuitable, this will be a material breach of contract, entitling the tenant to rescind.[3] This implied obligation of the landlord only applies to leases of buildings or other artificial structures, and not to leases of land, ie to urban rather than rural leases.

(3) To have repairs carried out by the landlord. Once the tenant has moved into premises that are in a tenantable and habitable condition, he is entitled to insist that they remain so. This includes, but is not confined to, an obligation on the landlord's part to keep the premises wind and watertight so as to be proof against the ordinary attacks of the elements.[4]

There are two major exceptions to the landlord's repairing obligation, ie (a) where the damage is caused by *damnum fatale* (act

1 *Huber v Ross* 1912 SC 898, 1912 1 SLT 399; *Lomond Roads Cycling Club v Dunbarton County Council* 1967 SLT (Sh Ct) 35.
2 *Glebe Sugar Refining Co v Paterson* (1900) 2 F 615, (1900) 7 SLT 374.
3 *Kippen v Oppenheim* (1847) 10 D 242.
4 *Wolfson v Forrester* 1910 SC 675, 1910 1 SLT 318; see also *Gunn v National Coal Board* 1982 SLT 526.

of God), eg a flood or a hurricane,[1] and (b) where it is caused by the action of a third party or parties.[2]

The landlord's obligation does not arise until the tenant has drawn the need for the repair to his attention; the landlord is therefore not in breach of contract merely because the repair has become necessary, but only after he has been notified and has failed to act.[3]

The landlord's repairing obligation is one which is very often contracted out of, particularly in commercial and industrial leases where the tenant's FRI (full repairing and insuring) lease is very common.

(4) To assign or sublet. An assignation is where a tenant transfers his interest in a lease to another person (called the assignee), who thereafter takes his place as tenant under the original contract. In the case of a sublease, the tenant creates a second lease between him and the subtenant, but his relationship with the landlord is unchanged and he remains directly liable to him for payment of the rent and performance of all other obligations under the original lease.

At common law, a tenant is allowed to assign or sublet most kinds of lease without the landlord's consent. There are one or two exceptions to this, eg in agricultural leases of extraordinary duration or furnished lets of dwellinghouses. Otherwise, the tenant's only obligation to the landlord is that an assignation be intimated to him.[4]

However, this common law right of a tenant is invariably contracted out of in the lease document. It is in a landlord's obvious interest to keep control of who occupies his property, and virtually all leases contain a clause requiring his consent to any assignations or sublets.

Legal remedies of the parties

Standard breach of contract remedies. Under the law of contract, there are standard legal remedies available against the defaulting party, and these can be used in a landlord and tenant situation. They include specific implement and interdict (where the object is to compel compliance with the contract), court action for debt

---

1 Rankine *Leases* (3rd edn, 1916) p 242; *Sandeman v Duncan's Trs* (1897) 4 SLT 336, 5 SLT 21.
2 *Allan v Roberton's Trs* (1891) 18 R 932, 1891 28 SLR 726; *North British Storage and Transit Co v Steele's Trs* 1920 SC 194, 1920 1 SLT 115.
3 *Wolfson v Forrester* 1910 SC 675, 1910 1 SLT 318.
4 See *McAllister* ch 5, pt 1.

(where one party owes the other money), rescission, ie backing out of the contract (where the defaulting party has committed a material breach), damages (where the party not in default has suffered a loss as a result of the breach) and (where a landlord is in breach) retention of his rent by a tenant.

The last of these is probably the simplest and most effective weapon a tenant has over his landlord and, although deriving from the general law of contract, is well established in a landlord and tenant context.[1] The tenant's right of retention, however, is only a right in security, and he must pay the rent in full when the landlord remedies his breach.

Landlord's additional remedies. As well as the standard breach of contract remedies, a landlord has certain additional remedies which exist by virtue of the special nature of the lease contract:

Irritancy. Irritancy means forfeiture and refers to a landlord's right to terminate a lease prematurely because of the tenant's breach of contract. There are two types of irritancy:

Legal irritancy ie implied by law. In other words, it is available whether or not there is any mention of irritancy in the lease contract. There is only one type of legal irritancy at common law, ie for non-payment of rent for two years. If a landlord raises a court action to establish a legal irritancy the tenant, at any time before the action has been concluded and the landlord has obtained an extract decree from the court, has a legal right to purge (ie cancel) the irritancy by paying the arrears in full.

As very few landlords will be willing to wait two years for the payment of arrears, legal irritancies are not used very often.

In the case of farm leases, there is a statutory legal irritancy where the tenant is six months in arrears.[2]

Conventional irritancy. This is a much more useful remedy for a landlord, and somewhat controversial in recent years. A conventional irritancy is so called because it exists by convention, or agreement. In other words, a ground of conventional irritancy only exists if it is contained in an irritancy clause in the lease document. The possible grounds of conventional irritancy are unlimited; those commonly found in leases include rent arrears for very short periods (eg twenty-one days), bankruptcy or liquidation of the tenant, and unauthorised assignation or subletting. It is also

---

1 *McDonald v Kydd* (1901) 3 F 923, (1901) 9 SLT 114; *John Haig and Co Ltd v Boswall-Preston* 1915 SC 339, 1915 1 SLT 26; *Fingland & Mitchell v Howie* 1926 SC 319, 1926 SLT 283.
2 Agricultural Holdings (Scotland) Act 1991, s20.

common for irritancy clauses, after giving a list of specific breaches, to finish with a general statement that any other breach of the lease will also be a ground of irritancy.

The controversy regarding conventional irritancies arose from the fact that, traditionally, a tenant had no right (as he had with legal irritancies) to purge the irritancy by remedying the breach in time. Any landlords or tenants who might have forgotten this were forcibly reminded in the celebrated case of *Dorchester Studios v Stone*,[1] where a tenant was evicted for having barely exceeded the twenty-one day limit in his irritancy clause.

The matter was at least partially remedied by section 4 of the Law Reform (Miscellaneous Provisions)(Scotland) Act 1985 which, in the case of monetary irritancies, requires that the tenant must be given fourteen days to pay the arrears before the irritancy can be enforced. In the case of non-monetary breaches, the court may only enforce the irritancy in cases where it feels that a fair and reasonable landlord would do so.[2] These provisions of the 1985 Act only apply to commercial and industrial leases.[3]

Even prior to the 1985 Act, a tenant had a possible defence to an irritancy action if he could satisfy the court that the landlord was acting oppressively, ie misusing his powers of irritancy; in practice, this has proved a difficult defence to establish.

Hypothec.   The landlord's right of hypothec is probably his most effective remedy for ensuring the payment of rent. It is a 'tacit' or 'legal' right, ie like a legal irritancy it is implied by law and does not need to be specifically provided for in the lease contract.

The landlord's hypothec is a right in security over those moveable items known as the *invecta et illata* ('things brought in and carried in'). This generally includes all moveable items that happen to be on the leased premises; certain items are specifically excluded, eg money, or the tenant's clothes.

One of the great advantages of the landlord's hypothec is that (unlike other forms of diligence) the landlord can include items that belong, not only to the tenant, but also to third parties, including items on hire or hire purchase. For example, in the case of *Dundee*

1   1975 SC (HL) 56, 1975 SLT 153; see also *HMV Fields Properties Ltd v Skirt 'n' Slack Centre of London Ltd* 1982 SLT 477; *HMV Fields Properties Ltd v Tandem Shoes Ltd* 1983 SLT 114; *What Every Woman Wants (1971) Ltd v Wholesale Paint & Wallpaper Co Ltd* 1984 SLT 133.
2   Law Reform (Miscellaneous Provisions) (Scotland) Act 1985, s5.
3   Ibid, s7.

Corporation v Marr,[1] the landlords were entitled to include a jukebox on hire to the tenant.

Other advantages of the landlord's hypothec are that (also unlike other forms of diligence) it is not affected by the bankruptcy or liquidation of the tenant, and that it can be enforced very quickly, allowing the landlord to jump the queue of creditors; the reason for the latter point is that in the procedure in an action of sequestration for rent (the court action to enforce the right of hypothec) the moveables are attached at the beginning of the action, rather than after a decree has been obtained.

The landlord's right of hypothec only covers the current year's rent and not prior arrears;[2] for the latter, another remedy (such as court action for debt) must be sought.

The right of hypothec does not apply to ground let for agriculture or pasture exceeding two acres.[3] In other words, most agricultural leases are exempt.

Summary diligence. If the lease document contains a consent to registration for execution, rent arrears may be recovered without the necessity for court action.[4] This could be useful for rental payments in respect of which the landlord's right of hypothec has been lost.

3. TERMINATION OF LEASES

Premature terminations

There are a number of ways by which a lease may end prior to the termination date (known as the ish) specified in the lease document. For example, the lease may contain a break clause, allowing either the landlord or the tenant, or perhaps both, to terminate at some stated intermediate date during the lease's currency. Also, a landlord may allow a tenant to renounce his lease if the tenant wants out for some reason, though most landlords would be more likely to

---

1 1971 SC 96, also reported as *Ditchburn Organisation (Sales) Ltd v Dundee Corporation* 1979 SLT 218; see also *Scottish & Newcastle Breweries Ltd v Edinburgh District Council* 1971 SLT (Notes) 11; *Rossleigh Ltd v Leader Cars Ltd* 1987 SLT 355.
2 For the way in which this is calculated, see *McAllister* p 44.
3 Hypothec Abolition (Scotland) Act 1880, s1.
4 See ch 3, pt 4 above.

hold the tenant bound until he can find another tenant to assign to. Bankruptcy, liquidation or death of a tenant is also likely (though it is not inevitable) to bring a lease to an end.

Another way by which a lease may end prematurely is under the doctrine of frustration by supervening impossibility. This can either take the form of *rei interitus* (where the subjects of let are totally destroyed) or, more likely, by constructive total destruction, where they are so badly damaged that they can no longer be used for the purpose of the let.[1] The most likely cause of such destruction is fire. Provided that the cause of the damage is accidental and not the fault of one of the parties, the effect is to terminate the lease without liability of either party. It is common in commercial and industrial leases for frustration to be contracted out of, so that the landlord avoids a possible interruption to his rental income.

As we noted above, a lease may also be terminated by irritancy or by rescission.

Termination at the ish

One would expect a lease containing a specific termination date to automatically come to an end at that date. However, that is not so. If neither party intimates his intention to terminate the lease by sending a notice to quit, the lease is automatically renewed for a further period by the principle of *tacit relocation* (silent renewal). The period of renewal will be one year, unless the lease was for less than a year, in which case it will be renewed for the same period as the original let. At the end of the renewed period, the lease will be extended yet again unless a notice to quit is sent, and this process can continue indefinitely.

With the exception of its duration, a lease so renewed will be on the same terms and conditions as the original lease. This means that, even where a landlord does not want a tenant out, it is in his interest to timeously send a notice to quit so that he can negotiate a new lease at a revised rent; otherwise the tenant will be able to hold him to the old rent for a further year.

The period required for a notice to quit may be stated in the lease. However, statutory minimum periods of notice are set out in the Sheriff Courts (Scotland) Act 1907. The required period of notice varies according to the type and length of lease, but in most cases it is forty days. In the case of agricultural holdings,

---

1 *Duff v Fleming* (1870) 8 M 769, (1870) 7 SLR 480; *Cantors Properties (Scotland) Ltd v Swears & Wells Ltd* 1978 SC 310, 1980 SLT 165.

the minimum period of notice is one year (the maximum being two years).[1]

If a lease has a duration of less than four months, the period of notice is one third of the duration of the let. In the case of dwellinghouses, this is subject to a statutory minimum period of twenty-eight days.[2]

If a landlord wants possession of the subjects of let at the termination date, and the tenant fails to remove himself, he cannot be evicted without a court decree.

4. STATUTORY CONTROL OF LEASES

Agricultural holdings

Since the late nineteenth century, there has been evolving a series of statutes, known collectively as the Agricultural Holdings Acts. These have just been the subject of a long overdue consolidation, and the current law is now contained in the Agricultural Holdings (Scotland) Act 1991. There is parallel and substantially similar legislation for England.

The Act applies to leases of land used for agriculture as part of a trade or business. The basic purpose of the legislation is to encourage the tenants of farms to farm well by allowing them in many cases the right to stay on after the termination date of their leases and, when this is not possible, to be compensated for any improvements they have made to the holdings. There is no space here to go into the provisions in any detail, but the following is an outline of the main points:

(1) *Regulation of lease terms.* There are a number of provisions regulating lease terms, including the tenant's right to have a written lease, the maintenance by the landlord of fixed equipment supplied by him, and the provision of rent reviews during any period of statutory extension.

(2) *Security of tenure.* If a farm tenant receives a notice to quit at the end of the lease, he has the right to apply to the Scottish Land Court, who have power to grant him an indefinite extension. There are several circumstances where the tenant is denied the right

---

1 Agricultural Holdings (Scotland) Act 1991, s21.
2 Rent (Scotland) Act 1984, s112.

to appeal to the Land Court, eg where the landlord has planning permission for a non-agricultural use, or in certain situations (bad farming, breach of contract etc) where the tenant is at fault in some way.

(3) *Compensation rights.*   Where a tenant is denied an extension, he is entitled to receive compensation for the value of any improvements he has made to the holding. He can also claim between one and two years rent as compensation for disturbance (though this is denied in some situations where the removal was his own fault). Where the landlord requires the land for a use other than agriculture, he can be paid a sum (four years rent) for re-organisation of his affairs.

(4) *Succession to holdings.*   In some cases an agricultural tenancy can be inherited by a near relative of the original tenant.

The special nature of crofts and other small landholdings in Scotland is recognised in a separate series of statutes dealing with such holdings.

Residential leases: the private sector

Since early in the present century, leases of dwellinghouses from private landlords have been subject to extensive statutory regulation.[1] This has involved giving the tenant indefinite security of tenure and also controlling or regulating the level of rent the landlord can charge. As this was blamed for discouraging private investment in the provision of houses for let, the most recent legislation has been designed to reverse this trend.

Regulated tenancies.   Tenancies of dwellinghouses which began prior to 2 January 1989 mostly still qualify as regulated tenancies under the former system. This allows the tenant indefinite security of tenure and the right to have a fair rent fixed by a local rent officer, irrespective of the figure in the lease document. There are a number of grounds for removal of the tenant by court order, including specified breaches of contract or the requirement of the property by the landlord for his own occupation.

---

1   The current law is contained in the Rent (Scotland) Act 1984 (as amended by the Housing (Scotland) Act 1988); see also *McAllister* ch 13.

Assured tenancies. Tenancies entered into from 2 January 1989 are generally classified as assured tenancies. The tenant no longer has the right to have a fair rent fixed, but is required to pay a market rent. There are similar security of tenure provisions to those in regulated tenancies, though with additional grounds of removal, eg persistent rent arrears or the requirement of the property by the landlord for redevelopment. Much of this protection is eroded, however, by the landlord's power to enter into a **short assured tenancy** (also at a market rent) where the tenant's security of tenure can be as little as six months.

Residential tenancies: the public sector[1]

Secure tenancies. Public sector tenants (eg the tenants of local authorities) also have a right to indefinite security of tenure. The provisions, including grounds of removal, are separate, though broadly similar, to those applying to private sector tenancies.

Right to buy. A secure tenant may have the right to buy his house from the public sector landlord. The provisions regarding this are briefly considered in a later chapter.[2]

---

1 The current law is largely consolidated in the Housing (Scotland) Act 1987; see also *McAllister* ch 14.
2 See ch 15, pt 4 below.

9. Servitudes

1. NATURE OF SERVITUDES[1]

A servitude is defined by Bell in his *Principles* as a 'burden on land or houses, imposed by agreement – express or implied – in favour of the owners of other tenements; whereby the owner of the burdened or "servient" tenement, and his heirs and singular successors in the subject, must submit to certain uses to be exercised by the owner of the other or "dominant" tenement, or must suffer restraint in his own use and occupation of the property.'[2]

We will find this definition a little more helpful if we first explain some of the terms used in it. As we saw in chapter 1, the word 'tenement' is used in a technical sense, ie a piece of (or interest in) heritable property.[3] An 'heir' is someone who inherits property and a 'singular successor' is someone who acquires ownership of heritable property by a means other than inheritance, eg by purchasing it. A servitude is therefore a right which an owner of property has over someone else's property, eg a right of way.

A major characteristic of servitudes, implicit from the above definition, is that a servitude right and its corresponding obligation are not personal to the respective owners of the properties in question, but they run with the land; in other words, they can be exercised, or must be suffered, not only by the current owners of the properties in question, but also by any future owners who succeed them. A servitude right is therefore a real and not a personal right.[4] When a person acquires ownership of a piece of property, therefore, he thereby acquires the right to exercise any servitudes which the property enjoys and must observe any servitude rights to which it is subject. Likewise, when he disposes of the property, any such rights and obligations will pass to the new owner. A

1 Rankine *Leases* (3rd edn, 1916) chs 25 and 26; Gordon *Scottish Land Law* (1989) ch 24.
2 Bell *Principles of the Law of Scotland* (10th edn, 1899) 979.
3 See ch 1, pt 1 above.
4 See ch 1, pt 1 above.

servitude right cannot be separated from the ownership of the property in question: if an owner wants to transfer his servitude to someone else, he can only do so by transferring ownership of the property. In many ways servitudes resemble real burdens and conditions,[1] although, as we shall see later, there are important differences between the two.

We should also note from the above definition that the property whose owner enjoys a servitude right is known as the 'dominant tenement' and the property which is subject to a servitude right is known as the 'servient tenement'. The owners are generally known respectively as the 'dominant owner' and the 'servient owner'.

A notable characteristic of servitudes is that the owner of the servient tenement is not required to do anything active, but merely to suffer the restrictions in the use of his property which the servitude imposes, eg he must allow the owner of the dominant tenement access over his property, or he must refrain from erecting buildings which will interfere with the light of the dominant tenement.

A servitude must be exercised *civiliter* (courteously), ie in such a way as to interfere as little as possible with the owner of the servient tenement's property rights. It follows from this that the owner of the servient tenement is free to use his property in any way that will not affect the servitude right. In *Fraser v Secretary of State for Scotland*[2] the dominant owner objected to the servient owner planting trees on part of the servient tenement, over which she had a right of pasturage and of cutting peat. It was held that she was not entitled to prevent the servient owners from using their property in any way they wanted, provided that the needs of the servitude rights were met. They were there-fore entitled to plant trees on part of the servient tenement, provided that the servitudes could be satisfied from the part that remained.

Classification of servitudes

Servitudes have been classified in many ways, the main ones being into positive and negative, urban and rural and praedial and personal.

1 See ch 10 below.
2 1959 SLT (Notes) 36.

Positive and negative servitudes. Where there is a positive servitude, the dominant owner is entitled to perform some act affecting the servient tenement which, without the servitude, the owner of the servient tenement would be entitled to prohibit. A right of way is a good example of a positive servitude. Where there is a negative servitude, the servient owner is prohibited from performing some act which, without the servitude, he would be entitled to perform. The best (in fact the only) example of this is the servitude of light or prospect, whereby the servient owner cannot build in such a way as to interfere with the light of his neighbour.

Urban and rural servitudes. Urban servitudes relate to buildings and rural servitudes relate to land. This distinction will be illustrated when the various types of servitude are described below.

Personal and praedial servitudes. The distinction between personal and praedial servitudes is of little importance. The only personal servitude is liferent, and there is a school of thought to the effect that this should not be considered a servitude at all but a totally separate category. The only servitudes we will be considering, therefore, are praedial servitudes, ie those (in accordance with our original definition) that run with the land.

2. TYPES OF SERVITUDE

The types of servitude listed below are those traditionally recognised by Scots law. They are not necessarily the only ones, however, and there is authority for the view that new servitudes could arise provided they exhibit the necessary characteristics that distinguish the existing ones. As Lord Ardmillan said in the case of *Patrick v Napier*,[1] 'The habits and requirements of life varying and extending with advancing civilisation, improved agriculture, and multiplying necessities, may render the introduction of a new servitude possible and legitimate. But it must, in my opinion, be of a truly praedial character, similar in nature and quality to the praedial servitudes which the law has already recognised.'

Despite the great advances in civilisation since the date of that case, the traditional list of servitudes still prevails.[2] The following are some of the main categories:

1 (1867) 5 M 683 at 709, 39 Sc J 346.
2 For a recent decision on this topic, see *Mendelssohn v The Wee Pub Co* 1991 GWD 26-1518, in which it was decided that there could not be a servitude right allowing a hanging shop sign to be attached to another's property.

Urban servitudes

Support. There are two servitudes of support derived from the Roman law: *Oneris Ferrendi* ('of bearing the burden'), which is the right of the dominant owner to rest the weight of his building on the servient proprietor's wall or pillar, and *Tigni Immittendi* ('of letting in a beam') whereby the servient owner is bound to let the dominant owner insert a beam or joist in the wall of the servient tenement.

Stillicide. This servitude is also known as eavesdrop. It allows the owner of the dominant tenement to build in such a way that the rainwater falling from his house lands on his neighbour's ground; without this servitude right, he would not be entitled to do so.

Light or prospect. There are three recognised servitudes under this heading: *Non Aedificandi* ('of not building'), which prevents the owner of the servient tenement from building on his own land at all, *Altius non Tollendi* ('of not raising higher'), which prohibits him from raising his buildings above a certain height and *Non Officiendi Luminibus* ('of not harming the light'), which stops him from building in such a way as to interfere with the dominant tenement's light or view.

Rural servitudes

Way. This is a right of the owner of the dominant tenement to pass across the servient tenement. It must be distinguished from a public right of way (considered below); the latter can be enjoyed by the public at large, whereas a servitude right of way only belongs to the owner of the dominant tenement. Traditionally, a right of way could be either a footpath, a horse road or a carriage road;[1] in modern times, probably only the last of these could be used for motor vehicles.[2] Which of the three exists in a particular case will depend upon the terms of the servitude grant. If the servitude has been created by prescription,[3] the nature of the possession (ie usage) by the owner of the dominant tenement will determine the type of right. For example, if the dominant owner has habitually driven motor vehicles across the servient tenement for the required period, a right of carriage will have been created; if he has only

---

1 *Carstairs v Spence* 1924 SC 380.
2 *Smith v Saxton* 1928 SN 59.
3 See pt 3 below.

walked across it, it will be a footpath. A more burdensome servitude will include a lesser one, but not the other way about; for example, the dominant owner will be entitled to walk on a carriage road, but not drive a car on a footpath. The servient owner has no obligation to maintain or repair the road.[1]

Aquaehaustus. This gives the dominant owner the right to use a well, stream or pond in the servient tenement for the purpose of taking water or watering cattle. The dominant owner has a right of access, and also, in the case of a well, the right to clean out or repair it.

Aqueduct. This is the right to convey water through the servient tenement by means of a pipe or canal. The dominant owner has the duty of maintenance, for which he has a right of access.

Pasturage. This is the right to feed cattle or sheep on the ground of the servient tenement. The extent of the right may have been defined in the servitude grant, but otherwise will be the amount of stock the servient tenement can winter. If there is any surplus pasturage, the servient owner can use it.

Fuel, feal and divot. This is the right to cut and remove peat for fuel, and turf for fences and roofs.

3. CREATION OF SERVITUDES

A notable point about servitudes is that they need not appear in the title deeds of either the dominant or servient tenement, and a document creating a servitude need not be recorded in the Register of Sasines or registered in the Land Register. Indeed, as we will see below, it is possible to create a servitude without using writing at all. This contrasts with the case of real conditions, which not only must be created in writing but must appear or be referred to in the infeftment (the recorded title) of the owner.[2] This means that when a prospective purchaser or his solicitor is examining the title deeds of a property it is easy to see what real conditions affect it, but sometimes less easy to see what servitude rights it may enjoy, or may be subject to.

---

1 *Allan v McLachlan* (1900) 2 F 699.
2 See ch 10 below.

On the other hand, the scope of servitudes is more restricted than that of real conditions. For example, as we saw above, a servitude never involves the owner of the servient tenement in having to do anything active, but merely to suffer the restrictions in the use of his land imposed by the existence of the servitude. Real conditions, on the other hand, commonly impose active duties on the owners of property, such as maintenance of buildings, roads, fences etc.

The methods of creating servitudes are described below. Positive servitudes can be created by any of these methods, but negative servitudes, by their nature, can only be created by express grant or express reservation.[1]

It will also be helpful at this stage to distinguish between two different types of situation where a servitude can be created. The first is where the dominant and servient tenements, prior to the servitude coming into being, are already separate properties with separate owners. Only methods (1) and (5) are appropriate in such a case. The other type of situation where a servitude may be created is where an owner sells part of his property, while retaining the remaining part in his own ownership. In other words, where there was formerly only one property, there are now two. As a result of this split, it may be that one of the properties, perhaps the part sold, perhaps the part retained, now requires a servitude right (eg a right of way) over the other. It will be appropriate, therefore, for the necessary servitude right to be created at the time of the sale. By its nature, method (5) (ie prescription) is not appropriate here. In contrast, methods (2), (3) and (4) are **only** appropriate where a property is being divided.

(1) Express grant

An express grant is where the owner of the servient tenement signs a document creating the servitude. The relevant document must be probative (ie signed on the last page before two witnesses).[2] It should be recorded in the Register of Sasines (or registered in the Land Register); if it is not, it will legally bind the person signing it, but not his singular successors, ie it will not run with the land. In the case of positive servitudes, a servitude created in an unrecorded deed will eventually run with the land if the grant of the deed is followed by twenty years possession, ie it will have been created by prescription (see below). This does not apply to negative

1   *Inglis v Clark* (1901) 4 F 288.
2   See ch 1, pt 3 above.

servitudes because, as we will see shortly, they cannot be created by prescription.

A servitude can be created by express grant either in the situation where the two properties are already separate or when a property is being divided in two. In the first case, the servitude will be created in a deed of servitude signed by the servient owner, and will be delivered to the dominant owner. This may be done gratuitously; more likely, the dominant owner will pay a consideration for the right.

Where the property is being divided in two, the creation of a servitude right by express grant will be appropriate where the purchaser requires a servitude over the property being retained in the seller's ownership. For example, if the nearest road only adjoins the property being retained, the purchaser will require a right of way over the seller's remaining property. The servitude could be created by a separate deed of servitude, but most likely would be included in the disposition by which the seller transfers ownership to the purchaser.

Servitudes may also be created by Act of Parliament, which could be regarded as a form of express grant; examples of this, however, are comparatively rare.[1]

(2) Implied grant

Where part of a property is being sold and the purchaser requires a servitude over the part retained by the seller, the best way to achieve this is in the way we have just seen, ie by express grant in the disposition granted by the seller. In other words, the need for the servitude has been anticipated, and the necessary steps taken to create it. But what if the need for the servitude is overlooked, or, for some other reason, it is not expressly created at the time of the sale? This situation may be illustrated by a hypothetical example.

Mr A owns a house adjoining a main road. Behind his house is a large garden stretching back some distance, bounded by a footpath at the far end. Mr A decides to sell the bottom half of his garden to Mr B, who builds a house facing the back lane. Mr B would like vehicular access to the main road over Mr A's garden; otherwise he has to park his car some distance away and walk to it via the rear footpath. In other words, Mr B requires a servitude right of way across the land remaining in Mr A's ownership. But no such

1 See *Gordon* para 24-27.

right was expressly created at the time of the sale, and Mr A now refuses Mr B the necessary access. What is the legal position?

It is reasonably certain that Mr B would be held to have a servitude right of way by implied grant. The rule of law in such a situation is that when a person sells part of his property, he also grants the purchaser, even though this is not expressly stated, all servitude rights that are necessary for the comfortable use and enjoyment of the land purchased. In our hypothetical case, the servitude was not absolutely essential for Mr B's use of the land but, as he had no other direct vehicular access, it **was** necessary for the comfortable use and enjoyment of his property.

In *Ewart v Cochrane*,[1] the owner of a tanyard with a house and garden adjoining it built a drain leading from the tanyard to a cesspool in the garden. He later sold the tanyard, retaining the house and garden. The court held that the new owner of the tanyard could continue to use the drain: it was not absolutely necessary for the use of the property, but was required for its comfortable enjoyment.

Needless to say, it is greatly preferable to anticipate such situations and expressly create any necessary servitudes at the time of the sale.

(3) Express reservation

Here we are also dealing with a situation where a property is being divided in two for the first time. However, this time it is not the purchaser who requires a servitude over the land being retained by the seller. It is the **seller** who requires the servitude over the land that he has sold. In our hypothetical example, we should imagine that Mr A, instead of selling the back portion of his garden, has retained the back part and sold off the land at the front. To have vehicular access to the main road, he will need to reserve to himself, at the time of the sale, a servitude right of way over the front land that he sold to Mr B. To acquire this servitude right by express reservation, he will require to make it clear in the disposition to Mr B that the sale is subject to this servitude right retained by him. In such a case there will be no problem.

(4) Implied reservation

We now come to what at first sight seems an exactly parallel situation to that of implied grant. If we return to our hypothetical case, we

---

1   (1861) 23 D (HL) 3, (1861) 4 Macq 117.

see that Mr A has again sold the part of his land adjoining the road and retained the part at the back. However, this time he has neglected for some reason to expressly reserve to himself a servitude right of way over the land sold. He has inadvertently cut off his main access, rather like the man who saws off the branch of the tree he is sitting on. One would expect that, in line with example (2) above, that a servitude right would be implied. But that is not the case. The law does not regard the two cases as exactly equivalent. In an implied grant situation, the purchaser of property is impliedly entitled, **in addition** to the land he is buying, to all servitudes necessary for its comfortable use and enjoyment. Where it is the seller who requires the servitude, however, he is trying to tell the purchaser only after the event that he has in fact sold him less than he thought: on the face of it the purchaser bought land free of servitudes, and now the seller is saying that the purchaser's title should in fact be burdened with a servitude. The law is much more strict in this situation. It says that it is up to the seller to **expressly reserve** all servitudes he needs at the time of the sale.[1] A servitude **can** be created by implied reservation, but only in exceptional circumstances where it is **absolutely necessary** for the seller's use of his remaining property; it is not enough in this case that the servitude was merely necessary for his reasonable use and enjoyment of the property. Since there is a footpath adjoining the back access, the vehicular access to the front is not a necessity but only a convenience; if there were no such footpath – in other words if the back land was entirely cut off – then a servitude **might** have been created.

The strictness of the law in alleged cases of implied reservation is well illustrated by the case of *Murray v Medley*.[2] The owner of a group of buildings sold one of them together with a small area of ground. Unknown to the purchaser, a water pipe, which served both properties, ran underneath the building and land sold to him. The seller should have covered the point in his dispositon to the purchaser, by expressly reserving a servitude right of aqueduct, which would have allowed him to continue using the water pipe. But he had neglected to make such a reservation. The court refused to recognise the creation of a servitude by implied reservation. It held that a servitude of necessity was one without which the property could not be used at all, and not one merely necessary for the reasonable enjoyment of that property, and that the supply of water did not fall within this definition.

1 *Shearer v Peddie* (1899) 1 F 1201.
2 1973 SLT (Sh Ct) 75.

(5) Prescription[1]

Positive servitudes can be acquired by positive prescription. This means that the unchallenged usage of the servitude right by the dominant owner over a long period of time will by itself create the right. This does not apply to negative servitudes; as explained above, negative servitudes by their nature do not involve the dominant owner in any acts of usage which could amount to possession for the purpose of prescription, but only in having the right to stop the servient owner from doing something, such as blocking his light.

Creation of servitudes by prescription has long been recognised, and the period of possession required was formerly forty years. The relevant period is now twenty years, and the current law derives, as we saw in chapter 1, from the Prescription and Limitation (Scotland) Act 1973.[2] This states that if a positive servitude has been possessed for a continuous period of twenty years openly, peaceably and without judicial interruption, the existence of the servitude as so possessed becomes unchallengeable. Judicial interruption would occur if the dominant owner's possession were challenged by the servient owner, either in a court action or in an arbitration. Also, the nature of the possession defines the measure of the right acquired, eg the use of a footpath for twenty years would not confer a right to drive a motor car along the same route.

The dominant owner's acts of possession must be overt. In other words, it must be shown that they were known to the servient owner, or ought to have been known to him; moreover, they must be of such a character and done in such circumstances that the servient owner can be left in no doubt that a right is being asserted and what its nature is.

4. EXTINCTION OF SERVITUDES

We saw above that one of the essential characteristics of servitude rights is that they are not personal to the owners of the properties in question, but that they run with the land. In theory, therefore, a servitude right could last indefinitely. However, there are a number of ways, which we will now briefly consider, by which a servitude can be extinguished.

1 See ch 1, pt 4 above.
2 Section 3(2).

(1) Change of circumstances

If the servient tenement is acquired by compulsory purchase under statutory powers all servitudes are normally wiped out.[1] Also, if either the dominant or the servient tenement are permanently destroyed, this will also have the effect of extinguishing all servitudes.

(2) Confusione

This means 'by combination'. If the dominant and servient tenements come into the ownership of the same person, all servitudes between the two tenements are extinguished. If the ownership becomes split again at a later date, the servitudes do not automatically revive, but would normally have to be created over again.[2]

(3) Renunciation

A servitude may be expressly renounced by the owner of the dominant tenement in a probative document.

(4) Prescription

Under the Prescription and Limitation (Scotland) Act 1973,[3] a positive servitude, if not exercised by the owner of the dominant tenement for a period of twenty years, will be lost by the operation of negative prescription. This cannot apply in quite the same way with negative servitudes, since by their nature they do not require any kind of exercise by the owner. However, if the servient owner contravenes a negative servitude (eg by building higher than he should have) and the dominant owner does not challenge it over a period of twenty years, the servitude will be extinguished.

(5) Acquiescence[4]

This is an application of the principle of **personal bar,** ie a situation whereby a person by his actings (or non actings) may lose the right

---

1 See ch 18, pt 2 below.
2 However, see *Walton Bros v Magistrates of Glasgow* (1876) 3 R 1130; *Gordon* paras 24–96 to 24–98.
3 Section 8.
4 See also ch 10, pt 4 (loss of interest to enforce real conditions).

to enforce an obligation, usually because to do so in the situation that has arisen would not be in accordance with justice. Acquiescence occurs where a person sees his rights being infringed over a period of time and does nothing about it, thereby giving others the impression that he does not object to the infringement. And so, if a servient owner blocks a servitude right of way, or builds higher than he was supposed to, the dominant owner could lose his right to object by acquiescence if he does not object or take steps to enforce his right; if he changes his mind later, he may find that he is personally barred from exercising the servitude.

There is no hard and fast rule regarding the amount of contravention or degree of delay that is required for acquiescence, though it is unlikely that it would need to persist for the twenty year period required for the right to be wiped out by prescription. On the other hand, acquiescence normally only bars the person who has acquiesced and not his singular successors. For example, the owner of the dominant tenement can lose his right to enforce a servitude by acquiescence, but if he sells the property the new owner may have the right to enforce the servitude since he has not agreed to the contravention; however this probably only applies if the servitude can be easily revived, and not where the contravention has a permanent effect, eg where it consists of substantial building operations.[1] The only other exception would be if the original owner's acquiescence persisted for twenty years, because then of course the servitude would be extinguished by prescription, and this **would** be binding on the singular successors of the dominant owner.

(6) Lands Tribunal for Scotland

As we have already seen,[2] under the Conveyancing and Feudal Reform (Scotland) Act 1970,[3] the owner of property subject to a land obligation may apply to the Lands Tribunal for Scotland to have the obligation varied or discharged. This is normally considered in the context of superior and vassal when the vassal wants rid of a real condition which the superior, or an adjoining proprietor, wants to enforce.[4] However, servitudes are also classed as land obligations for the purpose of the Act.[5] The servient owner may

1 *Gordon* para 24–89.
2 See ch 2, pt 2 above.
3 Section 1.
4 See ch 10 below.
5 See eg *Spafford v Bryden* 1991 SLT (Lands Tr) 49.

therefore apply to the Lands Tribunal who may vary or extinguish the servitude if they consider that one or more of the three statutory criteria have been met.[1]

5. PUBLIC RIGHTS OF WAY

A public right of way superficially resembles a servitude right of way, but in fact it is not a servitude at all. The only person who can enforce a servitude right of way is the owner for the time being of the dominant tenement; a public right of way, on the other hand, can be enforced (or vindicated) in an application to the court by any member of the public, or by a local authority.

The method by which a public right of way is invariably created is by prescription, ie by the assertion of the right by members of the public, openly, peaceably and without judicial interruption, for a continuous period of twenty years.[2] Likewise, it may be extinguished by the long negative prescription, if it falls into disuse for the twenty year period.[3]

In establishing a public right of way, the nature of the possession is important: the members of the public must be traversing the land in question by a purposeful route, entering from one public place and exiting at another.[4]

In the recent case of *Cumbernauld and Kilsyth District Council v Dollar Land (Cumbernauld)*[5] it was held that a public right of way can comprise in whole or in part the line of an artificial structure, such as an elevated walkway in a town centre.

1 See ch 10 below.
2 Prescription and Limitation (Scotland) Act 1973, s3(3).
3 Ibid, s8.
4 *Strathclyde (Hyndland) Housing Association Ltd v Cowie* 1983 SLT (Sh Ct) 61.
5 1991 SLT 806.

10. Real burdens and conditions

1. INTRODUCTION

(1) Distinction between real burdens and real conditions

Although it is common to speak of real burdens and real conditions as if they were essentially the same thing, there are important differences between them, most notably in terms of enforcement.

Real burdens are a form of security over heritable property, usually for money, but possibly also for the performance of some other obligation. They are generally enforceable between the original contracting parties both by personal action, in the form of an action for payment, interdict or implement, and real action in the form of adjudication or poinding of the ground; and in other cases only by real action.[1] It has been suggested that real burdens are now obsolete, although they continue to exist in the form of feuduties.

Real conditions, on the other hand, are obligations affecting the use and enjoyment of land. Examples of such conditions are those imposed by superiors as to buildings to be erected on the feu, their use and maintenance. Such conditions can be enforced both by real actions in appropriate cases and by personal action, for example, interdict or specific implement. Real conditions are now very common and the rest of this chapter will be primarily concerned with them, although the rules relating to constitution are similar for real burdens and real conditions.[2]

(2) Real and personal conditions

Personal conditions are conditions which are only enforceable between the original parties to the contract creating them. Real conditions in contrast are enforceable against the owner of the land

---

1 See below, pt 7.
2 For a fuller discussion of the differences see K Reid 'What is a Real Burden?' (1984) 29 JLSS 9. See the land certificate in the Appendix for typical real conditions affecting residential property.

for the time being whether or not he was a party to the original contract. The rationale for creating conditions affecting property as real conditions is therefore clear. If the conditions are left as personal conditions they can be evaded simply by transferring the property to a third party. This third party would then not be bound by the conditions as he was not a party to the original agreement imposing the conditions. He would, however, still be bound by a real condition. Because real conditions affect individuals by virtue of their ownership of land they are said to run with the land. In this respect they resemble servitudes.[1]

2. CREATION OF REAL CONDITIONS[2]

Real conditions can be created both in feudal grants and in dispositions of property. The principal differences between the two relate to enforcement and will be considered in that context. Before a condition will be regarded as a real condition certain requirements must be fulfilled.[3]

(1) Condition must appear or be referred to in dispositive clause

The condition must appear or be referred to in the dispositive clause[4] of the deed giving the current proprietor title to the land. Although historically there was a requirement to repeat all conditions affecting a piece of land at length in every deed transferring that land, all that is now necessary is a reference to a recorded deed which contains the conditions in full. The reference must appear in the dispositive clause as this is the clause which determines the extent of the rights obtained by the proprietor in his land. The deed referred to need not be a document transferring an interest in the property. It could, for example, be a deed of conditions, the function of which is to set out common conditions affecting a number of properties. Such deeds of conditions are common in tenemental properties and in new housing developments. They have the advantage that reference

---

1 See ch 9, pt 1.
2 Halliday *Conveyancing Law and Practice* (1985) paras 19–18 to 19–40; McDonald *Conveyancing Manual* (4th edn, 1989) paras 10–8 to 10–20; Gordon *Scottish Land Law* (1989) paras 22–30 to 22–54.
3 *Tailors of Aberdeen v Coutts* (1840) 1 Rob App 296; *Wells v New House Purchasers* 1964 SLT 2.
4 See ch 17, pt 1.

to them avoids the necessity of inserting conditions at length into the individual conveyances of each flat or house as it is sold off.[1]

(2) Clear intention to create continuing obligation

There must be a clear intention in the deed creating the condition to create a continuing real condition affecting land rather than merely imposing an obligation on one of the original contracting parties.[2] No special form of words is needed to create a real condition: all that is needed is that the words clearly and unequivocally express the intention to do so. The condition must be one of a continuing nature, eg a restriction on the use of the property, rather than one involving the performance of a single act; in this latter case performance of the act will discharge the condition.

(3) Condition must affect land

The condition must be one which affects land or the use of land and the land affected must be clearly specified. There is a suggestion that real conditions must be related to protecting the amenity of the land affected, the amenity of neighbouring property or the comfortable enjoyment of such property.[3]

(4) Condition must be clearly specified

The condition must be clearly specified and the extent of any obligation it imposes must be definite and must leave the proprietor in no doubt as to what is required of him. The main reason for the requirement for clarity is that there is a common law presumption in favour of freedom of use of land and any restriction on this must be clear and will be interpreted strictly *contra proferentem* ie against the interests of the person having the right to enforce the condition. A subsidiary reason is that a proprietor's only guide to the restrictions affecting his property is the terms of conditions appearing in recorded deeds. The proprietor will therefore be bound only by what the deeds contain rather than what might be presumed to be the

1 See also ch 7, pt 5; ch 17, pt 3.
2 *Peter Walker & Son (Edinburgh) v Church of Scotland General Trustees* 1967 SLT 297.
3 See *Aberdeen Varieties Ltd v James F Donald (Aberdeen Cinemas) Ltd* 1940 SLT 58 at 61, 63 and 65; *Wells v New House Purchasers* 1964 SLT 2 at 4.

intentions of the original contracting parties,[1] and the whole terms of any condition must be discoverable simply by looking at the deed creating it; for example, a restriction which referred to an Act of Parliament to define a term was held to be invalid.[2]

As illustrations, a condition restricting a proprietor from doing anything which 'may injure the amenity of the place and neighbourhood' was considered precise enough,[3] while a condition requiring the maintenance of a flow of water through a mill lade to cleanse and drain the remainder of the lade to the reasonable satisfaction of the disponer was held to be too vague.[4]

(5) Condition must not be contrary to law or public policy or useless or vexatious or inconsistent with the nature of property

Examples of this would be cases where the restrictions virtually prevented the proprietor from making any 'useful' use of the property at all, or cases where the sole purpose of the restriction was the restraint of trade, which is contrary to public policy.[5]

(6) Condition need not be accompanied by an irritant or resolutive clause

Although strictly unnecessary, such a clause is common in practice. Its effect is to allow the superior to irritate the feu if the vassal breaches any of the conditions.[6]

3. ENFORCEMENT RIGHTS[7]

An individual seeking to enforce a real condition must establish that he has both title and interest to do so. Title involves the

1 *Anderson v Dickie* (1915) 1 SLT 393.
2 *Aberdeen Varieties Ltd v James F Donald (Aberdeen Cinemas) Ltd* 1940 SLT 58.
3 *Mannofield Residents Property Co Ltd v Thomson* 1983 SLT (Sh Ct) 71.
4 *Lothian Regional Council v D V Rennie & Co* 1991 SLT 465 (this citation may be incorrect when the bound volume of SLT appears as the pages in the issue containing the report were arranged in random order), but see the dissenting judgement of Lord McCluskey.
5 *Aberdeen Varieties Ltd v James F Donald (Aberdeen Cinemas) Ltd* 1940 SLT 58; *Phillips v Lavery* 1962 SLT (Sh Ct) 57.
6 See below, pt 5.
7 *Halliday* paras 19–41 to 19–60; *McDonald* paras 17–1 to 17–12; *Gordon* paras 22–55 to 22–66.

possession of a legally recognised right to enforce, interest is dependent on the breach of conditions adversely affecting the interests of the person wishing to enforce. There are four possible situations where the question of title and interest to enforce are likely to arise; as between superior and vassal, as between disponer and disponee, as between co-feuars and as between co-disponees. Each of these will be considered in turn, followed by a discussion of the circumstances in which interest to enforce can be lost.

(1) Superior and vassal

In cases where the superior is seeking to enforce conditions against a vassal, title and interest are readily established. The superior's legal right to enforce is clear, deriving from the continuing contract between superior and vassal which is at the root of the feudal system of tenure. Interest is readily assumed by the courts and the onus falls on the vassal to establish that the superior has in fact lost the necessary interest to enforce the condition.

(2) Disponer and disponee

As noted above real conditions can be effectively created in dispositions of property. In these circumstances the disponer is in a similar position to the superior as far as rights to enforce the condition are concerned. It is now clear that conditions imposed in a disposition can be enforced both by subsequent owners of the disponer's interest and against subsequent owners of the disponee's interest.[1]

(3) Co-feuars

The normal situation in the law of contract is that the only people entitled to enforce the terms of a contract are the parties to that agreement. In certain circumstances, however, a *ius quaesitum tertio* is created, giving a third party a right to enforce the terms of the contract against one of the contracting parties. In the context of feudal tenure such a right can give co-feuars the right to enforce real conditions against each other.

---

1 *Aberdeen Varieties Ltd v James F Donald (Aberdeen Cinemas) Ltd* 1940 SLT 58 at 65; *Wells v New House Purchasers* 1964 SLT 2 at 6.

In order for such a right to exist it must be conferred either by express provision in the titles of the co-feuars[1] or by implication from the terms of these titles. Creation by implication can only arise where the terms of the title deeds indicate a clear intention to create a *ius quaesitum*. Indications of such an intention are reference to a common plan of development, appearance of the same or similar conditions in the titles of the co-feuars or an undertaking by the superior to insert such similar conditions in each of the feu grants in a neighbourhood. Such indications are not in themselves conclusive, and the courts will look at all the circumstances of the case before reaching a conclusion as to intention. A reservation by the superior of the right to vary conditions will be fatal to an attempt to establish a *ius quaesitum* by implication, though not where the *ius quaesitum* is expressly conferred.[2]

A *ius quaesitum* may also arise on the subdivision of a property. In such cases each of the proprietors of a subdivision will be entitled to enforce the conditions applying to the original property against each other.[3]

Finally, as well as establishing title to enforce, the co-feuar must establish an interest to enforce. In the case of a co-feuar this must take the form of a patrimonial interest, ie that the co-feuar is suffering some form of financial loss as a result of the breach of conditions. The onus is therefore the reverse of the previous two cases where the party seeking to enforce was presumed, in the absence of evidence to the contrary, to have an interest to enforce.

(4) Co-disponees

The same considerations relating to title and interest apply to co-disponees as apply to co-feuars.

4. LOSS OF INTEREST TO ENFORCE

The person seeking to enforce may have lost his interest to do so; and the onus is on the person claiming loss of interest to prove his claim, at least against a superior or disponer.

1 *Lawrence v Scott* 1965 SLT 390.
2 *Gray v MacLeod* 1979 SLT (Sh Ct) 17; *Lawrence v Scott* 1965, *supra* at 396.
3 *Lees v North East Fife District Council* 1987 SLT 769.

Loss of interest can occur in three ways.

(1) Bad faith

Bad faith on the part of the superior can lead to his losing interest. Bad faith might take the form of refusing to waive or alter a condition for no good reason or, more probably, of demanding an excessive amount in return for alteration or discharge.[1]

(2) Acquiescence

Acquiescence is a form of personal bar which prevents enforcement action being taken where the person entitled to enforce an obligation has failed to take action against a breach of the obligation over a period of time.[2] In the present context the obligation involved would be a real condition.

Before a failure to take action can amount to acquiescence a number of conditions must be fulfilled:

(a) *Knowledge of breach.*   The party entitled to enforce the condition must know of the breach of the condition.

(b) *Passage of time.*   The breach must be allowed to continue without action for a reasonable period of time. What is reasonable will depend on the circumstances of each individual case.

(c) *Must not be minor.*   The breach must be one which is substantial and not merely minor or trivial.

(d) *Expense to person bound.*   The person bound by the condition must have incurred some expense which is not trivial before acquiescence can be successfully pleaded.[3]

Once acquiescence has occurred it can operate as a bar to enforcement action, not only in respect of the original breach, but also in respect of breaches of the same condition by others bound by it. For example if a superior failed to take action against one person on an estate who built an extension in contravention of a real condition, that acquiescence could also prevent the superior taking action against any other feuars who do the same. In this

---

1   *Howard de Walden Estates Ltd v Bowmaker Ltd* 1965 SLT 254, where it was decided that a demand for £1,250 was not excessive.
2   See also ch 9, pt 4.
3   *Ben Challum Ltd v Buchanan* 1955 SLT 294. This case also contains a general discussion of acquiescence.

situation the superior's acquiescence would not prevent enforcement by a co-feuar having a *ius quaesitum tertio*.[1]

The bar on enforcement, however, only extends to the condition breached. Other conditions affecting the property can still be enforced.

Where there have been departures from the terms of real conditions affecting an area, but these have been specifically authorised by the person entitled to enforce the conditions, these changes will not be evidence of acquiescence barring action against someone who breaches a condition without consent.[2]

(3) Change of circumstances

This refers to the situation where there has been such a substantial change in circumstances that there would be no benefit to those entitled to enforce the condition in allowing them to do so. This point was argued in *Howard de Walden Estates Ltd v Bowmaker Ltd*,[3] where it was suggested that a residential area had become so penetrated by commercial uses that the superiors had lost interest to enforce a condition requiring residential use of a property. Rejecting this the court considered that the appropriate test was as follows:

'To exclude any interest on the part of the superior the defenders must show not merely that the area has become partly commercial, but that it has wholly lost its residential character.'[4]

In this case only two of thirteen houses in the immediate vicinity had come to be used for commercial purposes; this was not enough to establish a change of circumstances.

5. ENFORCEMENT REMEDIES[5]

There are two main means of enforcement of real conditions; personal action and irritancy.

---

1 *Lawrence v Scott* 1965 SLT 390.
2 *Howard de Walden Estates Ltd v Bowmaker Ltd* 1965 SLT 254; *North British Railway Co v Clark* (1913) 1 SLT 207 at 210.
3 1965 SLT 254.
4 At 266; compare this with s1(3)(a) of the Conveyancing and Feudal Reform (Scotland) Act 1970.
5 *Gordon* paras 22–67 to 22–71.

(1) Personal action

In some cases the appropriate means of enforcement will be by way of personal action; for example, an action for debt where the condition requires a contribution to the costs of maintenance of common property[1] or an action for interdict where the condition is designed to be restrictive, eg to prevent additional building.[2] This is the only form of action open to co-feuars and co-disponees.

(2) Irritancy[3]

The second remedy which is usually available to the superior, and may, depending on the terms of the disposition, be available to the disponer,[4] is conventional irritancy. For the purposes of simplicity the remainder of this section refers only to superiors; this should be read to include disponers. This is only available to enforce real conditions if it is specifically provided for in the vassal's title by means of an irritant and resolutive clause. Irritancy allows the superior to recover the *dominium utile* from the vassal without compensation.[5]

Irritancy is not an automatic process; in other words, the *dominium utile* does not automatically revert to the superior on the mere happening of a breach of condition. Before that can happen the superior must raise an action for declarator of irritancy in the Court of Session or sheriff court. Decree in the action will operate to transfer the *dominium utile* to the superior. Once the action for declarator has been started the vassal has no automatic right to comply with the condition and purge the irritancy; that is a matter for the discretion of the court. The court has considerable discretion as to whether to allow the vassal a further period to comply with a condition requiring some action,[6] and whether or not to grant declarator.

Irritancy also has the further, dramatic, effect of setting aside any rights to land which may have been obtained by a third party from the vassal. An illustration of this would be the situation where A grants a feu to B Ltd, a firm of builders, who build houses on the land and sell them off to individual purchasers. If B Ltd then

---

1 *Wells v New House Purchasers* 1964 SLT 2.
2 *Mannofield Residents Property Co Ltd v Thomson* 1983 SLT (Sh Ct) 71.
3 *Halliday* paras 17–122 to 17–126.
4 *Gordon* para 23–16.
5 *Ardgowan Estates Ltd v Lawson* 1948 SLT 186.
6 *Precision Relays v Beaton* 1980 SLT 206 (requirement to construct factory buildings).

breaches one of the real conditions affecting the property, A is entitled to raise an action for declarator of irritancy against them. If successful not only will B Ltd lose any rights in the land, but so also will all the purchasers from B Ltd. In order to protect the interests of such third parties they must be notified of any action which could result in irritancy.[1]

6. VARIATION AND DISCHARGE OF REAL CONDITIONS

(1) Voluntary

Voluntary discharge describes the situation where the superior agrees, often in exchange for some consideration, to alter or discharge a real condition. This can be done either by minute of waiver or by Charter of Novodamus.

(a) Minute of waiver.[2]   This is a brief document executed by the superior, waiving or discharging the condition for the future, with the result that the condition no longer affects the property. The minute of waiver does not need to be recorded or registered to be effective, but unless this is done the minute is binding only on the superior granting it and not on anyone acquiring the superiority from him.[3]

(b) Charter of novodamus.[4]   Where real conditions are to be altered, or where some conditions are being discharged and others substituted, a charter of novodamus will be appropriate. The procedure involves the superior making a new feudal grant to the vassal incorporating the new or altered conditions. Strictly speaking this should be preceded by a reconveyance of the *dominium utile* by the vassal to the superior. This, however, is unnecessary as a result of a statutory provision that absence of such a reconveyance will not affect the force or validity of the charter of novodamus.[5]

The advantage to the superior of this means of altering or discharging conditions is that it enables him to continue to exercise control over the use of the land. Thus, for example, the superior

1 *See Halliday* para 17–123 for a full discussion of the notification requirements.
2 *McDonald* para 17–17.
3 Land Registration (Scotland) Act 1979, s18.
4 *Halliday* paras 17–96 to 17–98; *McDonald* para 17–16.
5 Conveyancing (Scotland) Acts Amendment Act 1887, s3.

may discharge a prohibition on building and insert in the Charter conditions relating to the buildings to be erected. In contrast, if the prohibition had simply been discharged by a minute of waiver the superior would have no means of regulating any building on the land.

(2) Variation or discharge by the Lands Tribunal for Scotland[1]

The voluntary procedure for securing the variation of real conditions had disadvantages as far as the vassal was concerned. The superior might refuse consent or might charge a substantial consideration, and unless the vassal could establish loss of interest he would remain bound by the condition and any development, however apparently reasonable, would be prevented. In order to remedy this situation the Conveyancing and Feudal Reform (Scotland) Act 1970 introduced a procedure by which the Lands Tribunal for Scotland could vary or discharge what the Act described as 'land obligations'.[2]

On the other hand there are advantages in the voluntary procedures and someone seeking discharge or variation of a condition affecting land will normally try to achieve this by agreement. This is worthwhile for a number of reasons. In the first place if an agreement can be reached right away with the person entitled to enforce a condition (usually the superior), the vassal's plans will not be delayed by having to wait for a Lands Tribunal hearing. Secondly, knowing that the vassal can now go to the Lands Tribunal, the superior will be motivated to be much more modest in his financial demands, or may not even charge at all; so getting a waiver from the superior may well prove cheaper to the vassal than incurring legal costs, not to mention the cost of a delay to his plans. Finally, the outcome of the Lands Tribunal hearing is by no means certain; if they are not satisfied that one of the criteria are met, they will refuse an application,[3] and even if they are satisfied they have the discretion to refuse an application.[4] Doing a deal with the superior therefore avoids this uncertainty.

1   *Halliday* paras 19-64 to 19-94; *McDonald* paras 17-18 to 17-34; *Gordon* ch 25; Halliday *The Conveyancing and Feudal Reform (Scotland) Act 1970* (2nd edn, 1977) ch 2.
2   See W M Gordon 'Variation and Discharge of Land Obligations' in D J Cusine (ed) *A Scots Conveyancing Miscellany* (1987), 67 for a discussion of this development and the relationship between the 1970 Act and the equivalent English legislation.
3   See *Pickford v Young* 1975 SLT (Lands Tr) 17.
4   Conveyancing and Feudal Reform (Scotland) Act 1970, s1(3).

If agreement is impossible then resort will be had to the Lands Tribunal; though an early article on the Lands Tribunal indicated that the majority of applications were settled, perhaps suggesting that an application to the Tribunal can focus the minds of the parties on agreement.[1]

(a) *Definitions and jurisdiction.* The Lands Tribunal is given power to vary or discharge land obligations. A land obligation is defined as an obligation relating to land enforceable by the proprietor of an interest in land by virtue of being such a proprietor and binding on the proprietor of another interest in that land or other land by virtue of their being such a proprietor.[2] An interest in land is any interest which is capable of being owned or held as a separate interest and to which title can be recorded in the Register of Sasines or registered in the Land Register.[3] The party entitled to enforce a land obligation is referred to as the benefited proprietor, the party bound by it as the burdened proprietor.[4]

These definitions are wide enough to cover not only real conditions but also other restrictions and burdens affecting land. Examples are servitudes,[5] which of course do not have to be created by a formal deed, rights of pre-emption,[6] and conditions in registrable leases (ie leases for more than twenty years) whether or not the lease has actually been recorded or registered.[7] However an irritancy clause is not a land obligation which the Tribunal can alter.[8]

Certain conditions affecting land are excluded from the jurisdiction of the Tribunal, preventing them from varying such conditions. The main exclusions are obligations to pay feuduty or ground annual, obligations relating to the right to work minerals, and obligations imposed in connection with the lease of an agricultural holding.[9] In addition the Tribunal has no power to vary an obligation imposed within two years of the date of application.[10] In the case of obligations

---

1 N Gow 'The Lands Tribunal for Scotland' (1973) 18 JLSS 109.
2 Conveyancing and Feudal Reform (Scotland) Act 1970, s1(2).
3 Ibid, s2(6).
4 Ibid.
5 See ch 9.
6 *Banff & Buchan District Council v Earl of Seafield's Estate* 1988 SLT (Lands Tr) 21.
7 *McQuiban v Eagle Star Insurance Company* 1972 SLT (Lands Tr) 39; *British Steel plc v Kaye* 1991 SLT (Lands Tr) 7; see also ch 8.
8 *Highland Regional Council v Macdonald-Buchanan* 1977 SLT (Lands Tr) 37.
9 Conveyancing and Feudal Reform (Scotland) Act 1970, Sch 1.
10 Ibid, s2(5).

created in feu deeds or in dispositions, the two year period starts
to run on the date of delivery of the deed to the burdened proprietor.[1]

Where a dispute arises as to the validity of a land obligation the
Tribunal has taken the view that this question should be decided
by application to court and that they have no jurisdiction to deal
with such questions.[2] They do however have power to decide whether
or not a benefited proprietor has title to enforce a land obligation.[3]

(b) Making the application.   The application for variation or discharge is made by the burdened proprietor. Once the application is
made the Tribunal will notify any burdened or benefited proprietors.
The definition of benefited proprietors includes not only the superior
or landlord, but also any co-feuars having a *ius quaesitum tertio.*

The Tribunal will also notify adjoining or neighbouring proprietors
who are likely to be affected by the change proposed in the application
even though they have no enforcement rights and, therefore, are not
benefited proprietors.[4] Such people are referred to as affected persons.

Benefited proprietors have a right of audience at the Tribunal
hearing if they object; affected persons have no such right, but may
be heard at the discretion of the Tribunal.[5]

Even if the parties agree that the application should be granted
at the hearing the Tribunal must still be satisfied that grounds exist
for the change sought[6] and may require to hear evidence to
substantiate the application.[7]

Finally, the land obligation in respect of which the application
is made must impede the proposed new use of the land. If it does
not the Tribunal has suggested that they would simply refuse the
application on its merits,[8] although in the case of *Banff & Buchan
District Council v Earl of Seafield's Estate*[9] they appeared to take
the view that, while the condition in respect of which the application
was made did not affect the changes in status of the property
proposed, they would, nevertheless, vary the condition to take
account of problems which **might** arise.

1   *Watters v Motherwell District Council* 1991 SLT (Lands Tr) 2.
2   *Smith v Taylor* 1972 SLT (Lands Tr) 34; *CWS v Ushers Brewery* 1975 SLT
    (Lands Tr) 9.
3   *Smith v Taylor, supra.*
4   Conveyancing and Feudal Reform (Scotland) Act 1970, s2(2); see also *Gorrie
    & Banks Ltd v Musselburgh Town Council* 1974 SLT (Lands Tr) 5 at 7.
5   Ibid, s2(2).
6   *British Steel plc v Kaye* 1991 SLT (Lands Tr) 7.
7   *Robertson v Church of Scotland General Trs* 1976 SLT (Lands Tr) 11.
8   *Solway Cedar Ltd v Hendry* 1972 SLT (Lands Tr) 42.
9   1988 SLT (Lands Tr) 21.

(c) Grounds for application. The grounds for application and on which the Tribunal may vary or discharge land obligations are:

i. That by reason of changes in the character of the land affected by the obligation or of the neighbourhood thereof or other circumstances which the Tribunal may deem material, the obligation is or has become unreasonable or inappropriate.[1]

ii. That the obligation is unduly burdensome compared with any benefit resulting or which would result from its performance.[2]

iii. That the existence of the obligation impedes some reasonable use of the land.[3]

Each of the grounds is independent of the others and the Tribunal only have to be satisfied that one of the grounds exists in order for them to grant the order sought. For this reason it is common for applications to be based on more than one of the grounds, and frequently on all three. It should also be noted that the Tribunal retains a discretion and is not bound to grant an application even if one or more of these conditions is satisfied.

i. Change of circumstances. There are really four elements to this ground:

(a) **Change in the nature of the land.** Applications based on this are not particularly common, though some examples of reported and unreported cases are cited by Halliday.[4] It is clear that increased competition leading to a decline in a business carried on by the applicant is not a change in the character of the land,[5] nor can the applicant rely on changes in the land which he has brought about,[6] possibly in breach of the land obligation.[7]

(b) **Change in the neighbourhood.** The extent of the neighbourhood considered depends on the circumstances of the individual

---

1 Conveyancing and Feudal Reform (Scotland) Act 1970, s1(3)(a).
2 Ibid, s1(3)(b).
3 Ibid, s1(3)(c).
4 *The Conveyancing and Feudal Reform (Scotland) Act 1970* (2nd edn) paras 2-19 to 2-22; *Halliday* para 19-75.
5 *Bolton v Aberdeen Corporation* 1972 SLT (Lands Tr) 26.
6 *Solway Cedar Ltd v Hendry* 1972 SLT (Lands Tr) 42, where the applicants had contrived to make enough room in a development for an extra house which was beyond the number permitted in the relevant obligation.
7 *North East Fife District Council v Lees* 1989 SLT (Lands Tr) 30.

case. In past cases it has extended from a small number of neighbouring properties, eg an enclave of six villas,[1] through part[2] or all[3] of a housing estate to the whole of Pitlochry.[4]

The applicant must be able to establish that there has been some change since the obligation was imposed, and any changes in contemplation when the obligation was imposed will be irrelevant to this task.[5]

Changes taken account of by the Tribunal have included housing developments,[6] a decline in the number of schoolchildren in the area,[7] loss of the area's residential character and the growth of tourism in the area.[8] (Although in one case this last development was discounted on the basis that the town concerned was the reverse of an attraction for tourists.)[9] Subdivision of houses to provide more residential accommodation is not sufficient to change the character of an area.[10]

(c) **Changes in other circumstances**. Under this heading the Tribunal has considered changes in social habits regarding the consumption of alcohol,[11] the disappearance of domestic staff, where a house had additional rooms to accommodate them,[12] the decline in demand for industrial premises on an industrial estate,[13] and the change of location of a swimming pool building.[14] Other points argued unsuccessfully in applications have been the increase in demand for home ownership and the contents of a Scottish Development Department (SDD) circular[15] and the fact that fulfilment of an obligation to build a number of houses was more difficult and expensive than originally contemplated.[16]

1   *Mercer v MacLeod* 1977 SLT (Lands Tr) 14.
2   *Bolton v Aberdeen Corporation* 1972 SLT (Lands Tr) 26.
3   *CWS v Ushers Brewery, supra.*
4   *Manz v Butter's Trs* 1973 SLT (Lands Tr) 2.
5   *CWS v Ushers Brewery, supra.*
6   *Leney v Craig* 1982 SLT (Lands Tr) 9.
7   *Highland Regional Council v Macdonald-Buchanan* 1977 SLT (Lands Tr) 37.
8   *Manz v Butters Trs, supra; Owen v Mackenzie* 1974 SLT (Lands Tr) 11.
9   *CWS v Ushers Brewery, supra.*
10   *Main v Lord Doune* 1972 SLT (Lands Tr) 14.
11   *Manz v Butters Trs, supra; Pickford v Young* 1975 SLT (Lands Tr) 17.
12   *Morris v Feuars of Waverley Park* 1973 SLT (Lands Tr) 6.
13   *British Bakeries v Edinburgh District Council* 1990 SLT (Lands Tr) 33.
14   *North East Fife District Council v Lees* 1989 SLT (Lands Tr) 30.
15   *Grampian Regional Council v Viscount Cowdray* 1985 SLT (Lands Tr) 6.
16   *James Miller & Partners v Hunt* 1974 SLT (Lands Tr) 9.

(d) **Changes must render obligation unreasonable or inappropriate.** In addition to establishing that there has been a change in circumstances the applicant must also satisfy the Tribunal that these changes make the obligation unreasonable or inappropriate. The consequence of this requirement is that success in establishing a change in circumstances does not always or automatically lead to discharge or variation of the obligation.[1]

ii. *Obligation unduly burdensome.* The decision on whether the obligation is unduly burdensome depends on weighing the benefits to the benefited proprietor against the burden on the burdened proprietor. Any benefits accruing to third parties as a result of the obligation are irrelevant to this process.[2] The subsection covers not only positive obligations imposed on the burdened proprietor, but also restrictive or negative conditions.[3]

To be considered, the benefit must be one which arises from the performance of the obligation. The benefit of being able to charge a consideration in exchange for the grant of a minute of waiver or charter of novodamus discharging the obligation is irrelevant,[4] so also is a benefited proprietor's loss of the ability to control a development involving both his and the applicant's land.[5]

Where there is no direct benefit to the benefited proprietor from the performance of the obligation, a very light burden on the burdened proprietor will be sufficient to bring this subsection into operation.[6] More generally, in the case of *Lothian Regional Council v George Wimpey*[7] the Tribunal expressed the view that to succeed, the relevant land obligation 'must, in practice, have become a relatively pointless one giving no real benefit'.[8] In that case they appeared to suggest that restrictions of the type normally found in housing developments (in this instance restricting occupation to one family) would not be unduly burdensome as the owner could relieve himself of it by selling and buying in a more suitable location. On the other hand the Tribunal has taken the view that an

---

1 For example *Leney v Craig* 1982 SLT (Lands Tr) 9; *Tully v Armstrong* 1990 SLT (Lands Tr) 42.
2 *Manz v Butters Trs* 1973 SLT (Lands Tr) 2.
3 *McQuiban v Eagle Star Insurance Company* 1972 SLT (Lands Tr) 39.
4 *West Lothian Co-operative Society Ltd v Ashdale Land and Property Company* 1972 SLT (Lands Tr) 30.
5 *United Auctions (Scotland) Ltd v British Railways Board* 1991 SLT (Lands Tr) 71.
6 *Manz v Butters Trs, supra*, where the burden was that a hotelier was losing out on bar profits as a result of the obligation.
7 1985 SLT (Lands Tr) 2.
8 At 3.

obligation will not be unduly burdensome if it allows some profitable use of the property, though not the **most** profitable use,[1] that there is no undue burden in maintaining a dwellinghouse as such when this is done by neighbouring proprietors,[2] and that a right of preemption is not unduly burdensome, rather it is an inconvenience.[3]

iii. *Obligation impedes some reasonable use.* Of all the grounds this is the one on which applicants are most likely to succeed, even if they have failed on the other grounds.

This ground looks to the future, unlike the first which looks to the past, and is concerned with the reasonableness of the use proposed by the applicant. The question as to whether the use is reasonable depends on the whole surrounding circumstances of the case,[4] and the task of the applicant is only to establish that the obligation involved impedes **some** reasonable use of the land and not **the** reasonable use of the land.[5] This means, then, that the applicant does not have to establish that the obligation prevents the land from being put to **any** reasonable use at all, only **a** reasonable use as proposed by him.

One of the indicators of reasonableness of use that the Tribunal will take into account is the grant of planning permission for the proposed use and overall planning policy for the area.[6] Grant of planning permission for the proposed use is however not conclusive as to the reasonableness of that use, and the Tribunal will take its own decision.[7] In a number of cases applications have been refused despite the grant of planning permission.[8] The reason for this is that the Tribunal has taken the view that:

'The considerations to which a planning authority give weight may be very different to those which the tribunal must have in mind, and while there may be no justification on planning grounds for prohibiting a particular

1 *Smith v Taylor* 1972 SLT (Lands Tr) 34.
2 *Main v Lord Doune* 1972 SLT (Lands Tr) 14; *Leney v Craig* 1982 SLT (Lands Tr) 9.
3 *Banff & Buchan District Council v Earl of Seafield's Estate* 1988 SLT (Lands Tr) 21.
4 *Murrayfield Ice Rink Ltd v Scottish Rugby Union* 1973 SLT 99 at 106.
5 *Main v Lord Doune, supra.*
6 For an outline of the law relating to development control and the need for planning permission, see ch 12, pt 2.
7 *Gorrie & Banks Ltd v Musselburgh Town Council* 1974 SLT (Lands Tr) 5 at 7.
8 *Solway Cedar Ltd v Hendry* 1972 SLT (Lands Tr) 42; *Cameron v Stirling* 1988 SLT (Lands Tr) 18; *Tully v Armstrong* 1990 SLT (Lands Tr) 42; see also *Mercer v MacLeod* 1977 SLT (Lands Tr) 14, though in this case the situation was complicated by a change of planning policy in relation to the area after the grant of permission.

use of land, the person in right of a feudal obligation may have a strong, continuing interest to enforce it, so that it may be entirely reasonable and appropriate that it should stay unchanged.'[1]

The Tribunal views planning decisions as being concerned with questions of public right whereas it is concerned with questions of safeguarding private rights.[2] In addition it has been pointed out that planning procedures do not necessarily provide for the canvassing of the opinions of all of those likely to be affected by a proposed development before permission is granted.[3] The grant of planning permission will be especially significant where the obligation has been imposed on what are effectively planning grounds.[4] Refusal of planning permission will also be significant.[5]

Another factor considered by the Tribunal to be important is the effect of the proposed change on the amenity of the area. Lack of effect on amenity will be persuasive in favour of granting the change sought,[6] though the fact that the benefited proprietor will suffer some harm to amenity is not in itself a ground for refusal as it can be dealt with by way of compensation.[7] In the context of amenity the Tribunal will consider whether or not granting the change would be the 'thin end of the wedge' opening the way to other changes in the area.[8]

Other factors considered in deciding whether or not the proposed use is reasonable have included a social need for the proposed use,[9] the encouragement of tourism, the lack of a suitable alternative site,[10] grant of a licence,[11] very small size of plot/garden for proposed

---

1 *British Bakeries (Scotland) Ltd v City of Edinburgh District Council* 1990 SLT (Lands Tr) 33 at 34.
2 *Main v Lord Doune* 1972 SLT (Lands Tr) 14 at 17.
3 *Ross & Cromarty District Council v Ullapool Property Co Ltd* 1983 SLT (Lands Tr) 9 at 13. See also Halliday *The Conveyancing and Feudal Reform (Scotland) Act 1970* (2nd edn) para 2-42.
4 *British Bakeries (Scotland) Ltd v City of Edinburgh District Council, supra.*
5 *Murrayfield Ice Rink Ltd v Scottish Rugby Union* 1973 SLT 99.
6 *Morris v Feuars of Waverley Park* 1973 SLT (Lands Tr) 6; *British Bakeries (Scotland) Ltd v City of Edinburgh District Council, supra.*
7 *Smith v Taylor* 1972 SLT (Lands Tr) 34.
8 *Mercer v MacLeod* 1977 SLT (Lands Tr) 14.
9 *Main v Lord Doune, supra* (nursery).
10 *Ross & Cromarty District Council v Ullapool Property Co Ltd, supra.*
11 *CWS v Ushers Brewery* 1975 SLT (Lands Tr) 9 (change granted); contrast *Bolton v Aberdeen Corporation* 1972 SLT (Lands Tr) 26 (change refused).

house,[1] the views of local residents regarding the proposed use,[2] the unwillingness of women to enter public bars to purchase carry-outs[3], and the objectives of the person seeking to uphold the obligation. In *Bolton* the Tribunal expressed the view that where a benefited proprietor 'in maintaining a private obligation is genuinely endeavouring to control a particular environment the tribunal will be slow to interfere with that control'.[4]

The Tribunal is also concerned that the proposed new use is the true reason for the application being made and that there is not some ulterior motive. For example, in an application for discharge of a servitude right of way allegedly based on its impeding a reasonable use of the land, the Tribunal took the view that the true motive of the applicants was the closing of an allegedly dangerous footpath and refused the application.[5]

Finally, the Lands Tribunal may not grant a variation under this subsection where due to exceptional circumstances money could not compensate the benefited proprietor for any loss or disadvantage he would suffer as a result of the granting of the discharge or variation.[6]

(d) Imposition of conditions by Lands Tribunal. In granting an application the Tribunal can impose any conditions they consider reasonable,[7] usually for the protection of the amenity of the area, eg restrictions on the height of buildings[8] and requirements for sound insulation.[9]

(e) Compensation. Compensation can be awarded by the Tribunal, following the grant of a variation or discharge, in two circumstances.

The first is where the benefited proprietor suffers substantial loss or disadvantage as a result of the variation or discharge being granted.[10] The loss must be substantial and will usually take the form of a reduction in the market value of the benefited proprietor's property as a result of the change. Compensation will be assessed

---

1 *Solway Cedar Ltd v Hendry* 1972 SLT (Lands Tr) 42; *Cameron v Stirling* 1988 SLT (Lands Tr) 18.
2 *Bolton v Aberdeen Corporation* 1972 SLT (Lands Tr) 26.
3 *Owen v Mackenzie* 1974 SLT (Lands Tr) 11; *CWS v Ushers Brewery* 1975 SLT (Lands Tr) 9.
4 At 30.
5 *Spafford v Brydon* 1991 SLT (Lands Tr) 49.
6 Conveyancing and Feudal Reform (Scotland) Act 1970, s1(4).
7 Ibid, s1(5).
8 *Gorrie & Banks Ltd v Musselburgh Town Council* 1974 SLT (Lands Tr) 5.
9 *Leney v Craig* 1982 SLT (Lands Tr) 9.
10 Conveyancing and Feudal Reform (Scotland) Act 1970, s1(4)(i).

as the difference between the 'before' and 'after' values of the property.[1]

In the *CWS* case, however, the Tribunal also stated that, 'following English authority, we leave for consideration in a future case whether compensation can ever be claimed under s 1(4)(i) in respect of personal loss or disturbance unrelated to heritage.'[2]

Claims for compensation must relate to harm to the benefited proprietor's proprietary interest in his property,[3] so that claims based on the superior being deprived of the right to irritate the feu,[4] for compensation for removal of the superior's right to extract money in exchange for a minute of waiver or charter of novodamus, and for a share in the development value of the property released by the change[5] have all been refused.

The second situation in which compensation may be ordered is where, because of the existence of the obligation, a reduced consideration was paid for the interest in land at the time of the grant containing the obligation.[6] The only reported cases on this have concerned claims for compensation because a reduced feuduty was charged in consequence of the existence of the restrictive condition. In the only case where an award of compensation was made the method of calculation adopted was to take the difference between the actual feuduty and what it would have been in the absence of the condition and apply to that figure an appropriate multiplier, in that case, fifteen.[7]

Where the Tribunal orders payment of compensation, the variation or discharge only takes effect once payment of compensation has been made and that fact is endorsed on the order making the variation or discharge.[8] The Tribunal also has power to impose a time limit for the payment of compensation.[9]

(f) Relationship of applications to irritancy proceedings. Breach of a land obligation by an applicant is no bar to his making an application for its variation or discharge, even if an action for irritancy has

---

1 *CWS v Ushers Brewery* 1975 SLT (Lands Tr) 9.
2 *Supra* at 14.
3 *United Auctions (Scotland) Ltd v British Railways Board* 1991 SLT (Lands Tr) 71.
4 *Highland Regional Council v Macdonald-Buchanan* 1977 SLT (Lands Tr) 37.
5 *Robertson v Church of Scotland General Trs* 1976 SLT (Lands Tr) 11.
6 Conveyancing and Feudal Reform (Scotland) Act 1970, s1(4)(ii).
7 *Gorrie & Banks Ltd v Musselburgh Town Council* 1974 SLT (Lands Tr) 5.
8 Lands Tribunal for Scotland Rules 1971, Rule 5(2).
9 Ibid, Rule 5(3).

already been raised.[1] Where such an action has been raised the effect
on that action of the grant by the Tribunal of an order varying
or discharging the obligation is one for the court hearing the action
to decide.[2] Where no action has been raised the effect of a variation
or discharge on the anterior breach of the obligation by the burdened
proprietor is again a question for the courts to decide. In the words
of the Tribunal in *Highland Regional Council v Macdonald-Buchanan*
'[T]he question of whether a variation order will prevent the superior
from now irritating the feu, on the ground of past failure to [comply
with the obligation], remains open and is for the courts to determine
– should the superior decide to raise an action for irritancy.'[3]

Any irritancy clause in the deed containing the varied obligation
attaches to the obligation as varied. More precisely it will only be
effective 'in so far as it would have been effective if the obligation
had to that extent been varied or discharged by the person entitled
to enforce the obligation.'[4] This wording has led the Tribunal to
suggest that 'It may thus still be open to a defaulting burdened
proprietor confronted by an action of decree of declarator of irritancy
and removing to persuade the court that a Tribunal order is equivalent
to a waiver by the benefited proprietor; or the equivalent of purgation;
or that it would be oppressive in the face of such an order to grant
decree.'[5]

(g) Grounds for refusal of application.   As well as cases which are
excluded from the Tribunal's jurisdiction, in cases where the
obligation does not impede the proposed use, cases where money
would not be adequate compensation, and cases where the grounds
for discharge are not made out, the Tribunal will refuse an
application, even if the grounds are made out, if the making of
the order sought would impose a greater burden on the benefited
proprietor or on someone else. In *Murrayfield Ice Rink Ltd v Scottish
Rugby Union*, where the additional burden would have been increased
demand for car parking on the benefited proprietor's land, the Court
of Session stated 'there is no provision in the [1970] Act ... which
empowers the Tribunal, even when they are relieving the burdened
proprietor of some obligation, to impose an extended obligation on

1   *Ross & Cromarty District Council v Ullapool Property Co Ltd* 1983 SLT (Lands
    Tr) 9; *British Steel plc v Kaye* 1991 SLT (Lands Tr) 7.
2   *British Steel plc v Kaye, supra* at 8 H–J.
3   1977 SLT (Lands Tr) 37 at 40.
4   Conveyancing and Feudal Reform (Scotland) Act 1970, s1(6).
5   *Highland Regional Council v Macdonald-Buchanan* 1977 SLT (Lands Tr) 37 at
    39.

some other land in which the burdened proprietor (or, indeed, anyone else) has an interest.'[1]

7. FEUDUTIES[2]

The obligation to pay feuduty is a particular form of real burden affecting property. It takes the form of an obligation on the vassal to make an annual monetary payment to the superior for the use of the *dominium utile*. The background to feuduties and the provisions prohibiting the creation of new feuduties have been considered in chapter 2.

Allocation of feuduty[3]

Allocation of feuduty is the process by which a proprietor of heritable property which contributes to a *cumulo* feuduty can have a portion of that *cumulo* feuduty allocated to his property. A *cumulo* feuduty exists where a number of separate properties contribute towards the payment of a single feuduty which is fixed as the feuduty applying to the larger area. For example, a piece of land for which a feuduty of £20 pa was payable might be divided into four and sold to four separate proprietors without anything being done to divide up the feuduty. The four proprietors would then be liable to contribute towards the *cumulo* feuduty of £20. By contrast, an allocated feuduty exists where a particular feuduty is fixed for each particular property; thus, in the above example, if a feuduty of £5 had been fixed on each of the properties sold, each proprietor would have had an allocated feuduty. A common example of *cumulo* feuduty occurs in flatted property, where each proprietor of a flat contributes towards the feuduty which is fixed on the piece of ground on which the building is erected.

Contribution to a *cumulo* feuduty has two disadvantages as far as the individual proprietor is concerned. First, the superior can look to each individual proprietor for payment of the whole of the *cumulo* feuduty, leaving the proprietor to recover from the others contributing to the *cumulo*.[4] Second, each individual proprietor can be held liable by the superior for a breach of any of the other real

---

1   1973 SLT 99 at 107.
2   *McDonald* ch 16; *Gordon* paras 22–03 to 22–28.
3   *Halliday* paras 17–34 to 17–40; Halliday *The Conveyancing and Feudal Reform (Scotland) Act 1970* (2nd edn) ch 3.
4   *Nelson's Trs v Tod* (1904) 6 F 457.

conditions applying to the property by any of their co-contributors to the *cumulo* feuduty.

Clearly, it is desirable to try to avoid these liabilities and this can be done by having the *cumulo* feuduty allocated. Once a feuduty is allocated each proprietor is only liable for the payment of the allocated feuduty and performance of his own obligations to the superior.

Allocation could formerly only be achieved by reaching agreement with the superior. This might be difficult since the superior's security for payment of the feuduty and ease of recovery would be reduced if the feuduty was divided up amongst individual proprietors. Superiors might, therefore, be unwilling to agree to allocation, or might demand an increase in the feuduty in exchange.

Under the Conveyancing and Feudal Reform (Scotland) Act 1970 it is now possible to have a portion of a *cumulo* feuduty allocated without the superior's consent. This is done by the vassal serving a notice of allocation on the superior at least three months before the next date on which payment of the feuduty is due. This notice will indicate the proportion of the *cumulo* feuduty which is to be allocated to the vassal's property. If there is no objection to the notice or the proposed allocation it will take effect as at the next date for payment of feuduty.[1]

The superior may object to the notice by way of representation to the Lands Tribunal for Scotland[2] which will then adjudicate on the dispute. In doing so the Tribunal must, unless it is impracticable, allocate a portion of the feuduty for all the proprietors liable to contribute towards the *cumulo*.[3] The order made by the Tribunal will become effective at the next date for payment of feuduty which is three months or more after the making of the order.[4]

Allocation of feuduty should be clearly distinguished from apportionment of feuduty, which is simply an informal agreement between the vassals contributing to a *cumulo* feuduty as to the proportion each will pay. An apportionment is not binding upon the superior.

Procedure for redemption of feuduty[5]

As noted in chapter 2, part 2 above it is now possible for a vassal to redeem his feuduty without the superior's consent, and an allocated

1   Conveyancing and Feudal Reform (Scotland) Act 1970, s3.
2   Ibid, s4.
3   Ibid, s4(1).
4   Ibid, s5.
5   *Halliday* paras 17–41 to 17–63.

feuduty must be redeemed if the property to which it attaches is sold.

(a) Voluntary redemption.   The vassal serves a notice of redemption on the superior at or before any term of Whitsunday (28 May) or Martinmas (28 November)[1] and by payment of the redemption price and any arrears of feuduty up to the date of payment, redeems the feuduty. The redemption price is the sum of money required to purchase sufficient 2.5 per cent consolidated stock to produce an annual income equivalent to the feuduty being redeemed.[2]

(b) Compulsory redemption.   Whenever a property to which an allocated feuduty attaches is sold, the feuduty attaching to that property is deemed to be redeemed as at the date of entry (or date of completion of the contract or date of execution of the disposition if either of those are later than the date of entry).[3] The responsibility for paying the redemption price rests with the seller, with the exception noted below. The superior, however, has a right of security over the property for a period of two months from the redemption date, and, within that period, can obtain payment of that sum from the purchaser if it is not reasonably practicable to get it from the seller.[4]

In cases where entry is taken by an authority possessing compulsory purchase powers it is the acquiring authority which is liable to make payment of the redemption price.[5]

The amount due to the superior in cases of compulsory redemption will be the redemption price and any amount of feuduty due for the current year up to the date of redemption.

(c) Effect of redemption.   The effect of redemption of feuduty is simply to remove the obligation to pay feuduty, and all other real burdens and conditions affecting the property remain in place and enforceable. More generally the effect of compulsory redemption is the gradual extinction of feuduties, except in those cases where there is a *cumulo* feuduty. The latter situation exists in relation to most flatted properties and these will continue to be burdened by feuduties. In such cases it is, of course, possible for all of the proprietors contributing to the feuduty to voluntarily redeem it.

1   Term and Quarter Days (Scotland) Act 1990.
2   Land Tenure Reform (Scotland) Act 1974, s4.
3   Ibid, s5(2).
4   Ibid, s5(6), (7).
5   Ibid, s6; see also ch 18, pt 2.

This does not seem to have happened to any great extent in practice, largely because the amount of the feuduty is insignificant.

Enforcement of feuduties[1]

Feuduties can be enforced by way of the same remedies noted above in relation to real conditions, ie personal action and irritancy. There are significant differences, however, in the provisions relating to irritancy. In the first place the superior's right to irritate has a statutory basis (and is, therefore, referred to as legal irritancy) which allows it where five years feuduty is unpaid.[2] The second significant difference is that the vassal has a right to purge the irritancy by payment of the arrears until the decree of declarator of irritancy is recorded in the Register of Sasines or registered in the Land Register.[3]

In addition to these remedies the superior also has a hypothec (ie a right in security) over the vassal's moveable property for the last and current feuduty, and can proceed by way of adjudication and poinding of the ground.[4]

All of this last group of remedies, together with personal action and irritancy, are available to the superior to enforce other real burdens.

8. OCCUPANCY RIGHTS

These are not strictly speaking real conditions affecting property, but since they confer rights over property which can limit the proprietor's dealings with that property they are dealt with here.

Prior to the coming into effect of the Matrimonial Homes (Family Protection) (Scotland) Act 1981 the position of a spouse who was not the owner or tenant of the family home was a precarious one. It was well established that she had no legal right to occupy the home and could be removed at the will of the other spouse.[5] The situation where one spouse alone, usually the husband, owned or

---

1 *Halliday* paras 17-19 to 17-32; *McDonald* paras 16-1 to 16-6.
2 Feuduty Act 1597 (amended by Land Tenure Reform (Scotland) Act 1974, s 15). The five year period supersedes any shorter period stated in a deed.
3 Conveyancing (Scotland) Acts Amendment Act 1887, s4; Conveyancing Amendment (Scotland) Act 1938, s6(4); Land Registration (Scotland) Act 1979, s29(2).
4 See ch 11, pt 3.
5 *MacLure v MacLure* (1911) 1 SLT 6; *Millar v Millar* 1940 SLT 72.

was the tenant of the family home was common. One of the purposes of the 1981 Act was to provide some protection for the other spouse, usually the wife.

The legislation is designed to provide this protection in relation to what it describes as 'matrimonial homes'. A matrimonial home means any home[1] provided or made available by one or both of the spouses as, or which has become, a family residence.[2] The definition also includes gardens attached to the home but specifically does not include a home provided by one spouse for the other spouse to live separately in.

Spouses are divided into entitled and non-entitled spouses, the entitled spouse being the one who is owner or tenant of the matrimonial home. Occupancy rights in the matrimonial home are then conferred upon the non-entitled spouse. The nature of the rights depends on whether or not the non-entitled spouse is in occupation of the matrimonial home. If so, the right is to continue in occupation, if not, the right is to be allowed to enter and occupy the home.[3] Application must be made to court for the exercise of the right in the latter case, and the courts also have the power to make orders regulating, declaring and restricting occupancy rights.[4] In certain circumstances the court may also make an order excluding the entitled, or indeed the non-entitled, spouse from the matrimonial home.[5]

The significance of occupancy rights for property law is that the occupancy rights of a non-entitled spouse are, subject to the exceptions noted below, preferable to those obtained by a third party (eg a purchaser of the property) in a voluntary dealing with the entitled spouse. The consequence of this is that any such third party will not be entitled to occupy the matrimonial home or any part of it if there is a non-entitled spouse with occupancy rights.[6] 'Dealing' is not very clearly defined in the legislation, but it certainly includes sale and the granting of a security over the property.

The occupancy rights of the non-entitled spouse are not protected against a third party acquiring rights in a dealing with the entitled spouse where the non-entitled spouse has consented to the dealing, where the non-entitled spouse has renounced her occupancy rights, where a court order has been made dispensing with the consent

1   Including houses, caravans, houseboats and 'other structures'.
2   Matrimonial Homes (Family Protection) (Scotland) Act 1981, s22.
3   Ibid, s1(1).
4   Ibid, s3.
5   Ibid, s4.
6   Ibid, s6(1).

of the non-entitled spouse,[1] and where the special provisions, considered in the relevant chapters concerning sale and granting of securities apply.[2] In each of these cases therefore the rights of the third party dealing with the entitled spouse will be protected from claims to exercise occupancy rights by a non-entitled spouse.

Occupancy rights may be terminated in the following ways: the ending of the marriage; passing of the long negative prescription period of twenty years without exercise of the rights; cessation of the entitled spouse's entitlement to occupy the matrimonial home; non-exercise of the rights for a period of five years following a disposal by the entitled spouse; destruction of the matrimonial home; and, renunciation of the rights by the non-entitled spouse.

1   This can be done if she is unable to consent or is withholding consent unreasonably.
    Matrimonial Homes (Family Protection) (Scotland) Act 1981, s7.
2   Ibid, s6(3).

11. Heritable securities

1. INTRODUCTION

Heritable securities are grants of security over heritable property which, in case of default by the debtor, will generally allow the creditor to recover the amount owed by sale of the property. Because the security relates to an interest in land it must take the form of a formal deed,[1] and for the creditor to have a real right it must be recorded in the Register of Sasines or registered in the Land Register. The most common situation in which a heritable security will be granted is where property is purchased with the assistance of a loan and the lender takes a security over the property purchased.

The precise form of the security will depend on when it was granted. The only means of creating a heritable security since 1970 has been by way of a standard security.[2] However, as will be discussed in chapter 17 relating to examination of title, it is important when property is being bought to ensure that any previous securities have been discharged properly. For this reason we will consider first the main forms of pre-1970 security.[3] In addition, companies may create floating charges, which are general securities over all of their property, heritable and moveable. These will be considered at the end of the chapter.[4]

2. PRE-1970 SECURITIES

(a) Bond and disposition in security[5]

The bond and disposition in security was a deed containing two

---

1   See ch 1, pt 3 on contractual requirements, and Appendix for specimen deed within the charge certificate.
2   Conveyancing and Feudal Reform (Scotland) Act 1970, s1.
3   For a brief discussion of other forms see Halliday *Conveyancing Law and Practice* (1985) ch 32.
4   See also ch 3, pt 4.
5   *Halliday* ch 33; McDonald *Conveyancing Manual* (4th edn, 1989) paras 21-1 to 21-21; Gordon *Scottish Land Law* (1989) paras 20-03 to 20-83.

parts.[1] First was a personal undertaking by the debtor to repay the loan or perform any other obligation for which the security was granted. Second was a conveyance of heritable property belonging to the debtor in security of performance of his obligations. This was expressed to be 'redeemably as aftermentioned yet irredeemably in the event of sale by virtue hereof.' In other words it was a conveyance which only became effective as a transfer of the property to the creditor if the debtor defaulted and the creditor exercised his right of sale, and which expressly recognised the debtor's right to redeem the security.

On default by the debtor there are a number of remedies open to the creditor. He can proceed by way of summary diligence, relying on the clause of consent to registration for execution in the bond.[2] He can raise an action of maills and duties which would allow him to enter into possession of the security subjects and collect rents and other sums due from the subjects. Poinding of the ground and adjudication are also available to the creditor as remedies. The principal remedy, as with contemporary securities, is the right of sale.

The right of sale has to be exercised according to a comparatively detailed statutory code.[3] In brief, this involves service of a calling-up notice giving the debtor three months notice to repay the loan.[4] If this is not complied with the creditor can proceed to sale. Prior to 1970 this could only be done by public roup; since then it has also been possible to sell by private bargain.[5] There are detailed rules relating to the number and location of advertisements required[6] and the selling creditor must obtain the best price that can reasonably be obtained.[7] Purchasers from a selling creditor are given certain statutory protection.[8] This protection is in similar terms to that given to a purchaser from a selling creditor under a standard security and will be considered more fully in that context.

Where the property has been exposed for sale by public roup and has failed to raise an offer sufficient to pay off the selling creditor's security and any prior and *pari passu* (ie of equal standing to the

---

1 A statutory form is provided in the Titles to Land Consolidation (Scotland) Act 1868, Sch FF.
2 See ch 3, pt 4.
3 Explained in detail in *Halliday* paras 33-21 to 33-38.
4 Conveyancing (Scotland) Act 1924, s33; Conveyancing and Feudal Reform (Scotland) Act 1970, s33.
5 Conveyancing and Feudal Reform (Scotland) Act 1970, s35.
6 Conveyancing (Scotland) Act 1924, s38.
7 Conveyancing and Feudal Reform (Scotland) Act 1970, s35(1).
8 Conveyancing (Scotland) Act 1924, s41(2); Conveyancing and Feudal Reform (Scotland) Act 1970, ss32, 38.

security held by the selling creditor)[1] securities, the creditor can apply for a decree of foreclosure; that is a judgement transferring the security subjects to him.[2] If such a decree is granted it operates from the date of recording or registration of an extract to transfer the property to the creditor.

As indicated above, the debtor in the bond and disposition in security retains a right of redemption which can be exercised on giving three months notice to the creditor.[3]

A bond and disposition in security can be validly discharged in a number of ways. First, by recording an express discharge of the bond in the appropriate statutory form.[4] Second, as with any other debt, by simple repayment, although it is clearly desirable that there is some evidence obtained of this for exhibition to prospective purchasers etc. Third, the security could be extinguished by the operation of prescription if there were no payments of principal or interest for twenty years;[5] here again any third party would require clear evidence of this, and would not necessarily be satisfied with a simple assurance that the debt had prescribed. Fourth, the debt will be discharged if the same person acting in the same capacity becomes both debtor and creditor in the bond. Finally, there is provision for the debtor to obtain a discharge by consigning the amount due under the bond where a discharge cannot be obtained from the creditor.[6]

It is also possible to restrict the extent of the property covered by the heritable security; this is done by the creditor granting a deed of restriction,[7] which may or may not be accompanied by a partial discharge of the bond.

(b) Cash credit bond[8]

The major limitation of the bond and disposition in security was that it could only secure advances made prior to the infeftment of the creditor. This meant that it could not be used to cover fluctuating sums or advances made after this, and could therefore not be used to secure overdrafts or further advances. Any further

1 See below, pt 3(e).
2 Heritable Securities (Scotland) Act 1894, s8; see below, pt 3(f)(vii).
3 Conveyancing (Scotland) Act 1924, s32.
4 Ibid, Sch K, Form 3.
5 Prescription and Limitation (Scotland) Act 1973, ss7–10.
6 Conveyancing (Scotland) Act 1924, s32.
7 Ibid, s30.
8 *Halliday* paras 33–72 to 33–76; *Gordon* paras 20–84 to 20–85.

advances would have to be secured by a separate bond and disposition in security. In order to overcome this the Debts Securities (Scotland) Act 1856 allowed securities to be created which covered sums advanced after infeftment, provided that the sum secured did not exceed a definite sum stated in the security and consisting of principal and three years interest at 5 per cent. This security was the bond of cash credit. Aside from this allowance for future advances it was similar in form, enforcement and discharge to the bond and disposition in security.

McDonald notes[1] that the bond of cash credit was not commonly used; the reason for this was that the same objectives could be achieved with more flexibility by the *ex facie* absolute disposition.

(c) *Ex facie* absolute disposition[2]

The *ex facie* absolute disposition took the form of an unqualified and absolute conveyance of the security subjects granted by the debtor to the creditor and recorded in the Register of Sasines. There was no indication in the deed that the transfer of the property was a grant in security. In other words, the deed, apart from the specification of the consideration which was usually expressed to be for 'certain good and onerous causes', was identical to a disposition on sale. Because of this there were no problems about securing future advances or fluctuating amounts, nor was it necessary, as with the bond of cash credit, to fix a maximum sum in advance.

In addition to the disposition there was a collateral agreement between the debtor and creditor which was not normally recorded and which disclosed the true nature of the transaction and contained a considerable number of provisions regarding the loan and the security subjects. This agreement normally dealt with the following matters:

(i) An acknowledgement of the true nature of the transaction, ie that the conveyance was truly in security for a loan and not absolute or irrevocable.

(ii) A personal undertaking by the debtor to repay the loan according to the terms of the agreement.

---

1 Para 21-36.
2 *Halliday* ch 34; *McDonald* paras 21-37 to 21-52; *Gordon* paras 20-86 to 20-102.

(iii) Details regarding the size of the loan, instalments and interest rates.

(iv) Provision for the debtor to redeem the loan and a procedure for doing this.

(v) Obligations would be imposed on the debtor in connection with the upkeep and maintenance of the security subjects. In practice these provisions are similar to the standard conditions 1–7 applying to standard securities and considered below.[1]

(vi) The powers of the creditor on default either in respect of repayment or other terms or conditions would be specified. Again, in practice, those were similar to those now existing in relation to standard securities.

The main remedies available to the creditor are a right of entry into possession, if that was provided for in the agreement, and the right of sale. There is no statutory regulation of the exercise of the right of sale as exists in relation to the bond and disposition in security. The selling creditor is, however, bound to exercise his power of sale *bona fide* considering the interests of the debtor and to take reasonable steps to obtain a full and fair market price.[2]

Prior to 1970 the *ex facie* absolute disposition could only be properly discharged by a reconveyance of the property to the debtor or by a conveyance by the creditor with consent of the debtor if the debtor sold the property before the debt was fully paid off, as would be quite common in mortgage transactions. Since then, recording of a short statutory form is sufficient to discharge the security and vest the land 'in the person entitled thereto'.[3] This form of words led Professor Halliday to suggest that where the debtor was not infeft, and therefore did not appear clearly on the record as the person entitled to the land, a reconveyance should be used rather than the statutory discharge.[4] His later view, however, is that 'In the normal case where the loan is repaid by the original debtor to the original creditor the statutory form of discharge may be used: there is then no doubt that the debtor is the person in whose favour the deemed reconveyance is granted.'[5]

The advantage of the *ex facie* absolute disposition as a security was that it was possible for further advances to be made, for the

---

1 Conveyancing and Feudal Reform (Scotland) Act 1970, Sch 3.
2 *Rimmer v Thomas Usher & Son Ltd* 1967 SLT 7.
3 Conveyancing and Feudal Reform (Scotland) Act 1970, s40 and Sch 9.
4 'Ex Facie Absolute Dispositions and their Discharge' (1980) 25 JLSS 54; see also *McDonald* para 21–52.
5 *Halliday* para 34–17.

amount of the loan to fluctuate, and for changes to be made in the rate of interest. There were, however, certain disadvantages; there was a possibility (admittedly remote) of fraud by the creditor, the collateral agreement was often a lengthy and unwieldy document, and, as the apparent owner of the property, the creditor could be required by the superior to fulfil the feudal obligations attaching thereto.[1]

3. STANDARD SECURITIES[2]

(a) Introduction

As a result of the defects and difficulties affecting the existing forms of security, and following the publication of the report on *Conveyancing Legislation and Practice*,[3] these earlier forms of security were effectively abolished from 29 November 1970.[4] This was achieved by a provision in section 9 of the Conveyancing and Feudal Reform (Scotland) Act 1970 to the effect that after that date any attempt to create a heritable security in a form other than a standard security would be void.

A standard security can be granted over any interest in land capable of being owned or held as a separate interest and to which title can be recorded in the Register of Sasines or registered in the Land Register.[5] This definition is wide enough to include not only ownership interests in land but also registrable leases[6] and even other heritable securities since these are also interests in land capable of separate infeftment.

The debt secured by the standard security can be any obligation to pay money, except feuduty or any other periodical sum payable in respect of land, or an obligation *ad factum praestandum*.[7] Thus as well as being used to secure a loan or an overdraft a standard security might also secure the performance of some other

---

1 See *Halliday* para 32–06; *Conveyancing Legislation and Practice* (1966) Cmnd 3118 para 105.
2 *Halliday* chs 36–40; Cusine *Standard Securities, passim*; *McDonald* ch 22; *Gordon* paras 20–128 to 20–213; Halliday *The Conveyancing and Feudal Reform (Scotland) Act 1970* (2nd edn, 1977) chs 6–10.
3 (1966) Cmnd 3118, paras 102–106.
4 Conveyancing and Feudal Reform (Scotland) Act 1970, ss9(4), 54(2).
5 Ibid, s9(8)(b); Land Registration (Scotland) Act 1979, s29(1).
6 See ch 8, pt 1.
7 Conveyancing and Feudal Reform (Scotland) Act 1970, s9(8)(c).

non-monetary obligation (eg completion of a building) by the debtor.

A standard security may be granted by someone other than the debtor and the person granting need not be infeft in the interest and may deduce title in the security deed.[1] Deduction of title involves the uninfeft proprietor linking his ownership of the interest in land, via a series of deeds and documents, back to the last recording or registration of the interest.[2]

(b) Forms

Two forms of standard security are provided for, imaginatively entitled Form A and Form B,[3] and actual security deeds must conform to these 'as closely as may be'.[4]

In Form A the security is achieved in one deed which contains a brief personal obligation which is given statutory meaning[5] and a grant of security over the interest in land.[6] Form B consists of two separate deeds, the grant of security, and a separate agreement which will be referred to in the security and which will contain details of the personal obligation secured. This separate agreement will not usually be recorded in the Register of Sasines or registered in the Land Register.

Regardless of the form used the security deed will contain certain common clauses. First of these is a description of the interest in land. In Sasine transactions and transactions inducing first registration, this should take the form of a particular description; a description by reference to a general name or a statutory description by reference.[7] In securities over an interest already registered in the Land Register all that is necessary is reference to the title number of the property.[8] The Keeper will, however, apparently accept descriptions simply by reference to the postal address of the property.[9] In any

---

1   Ibid, s12.
2   See also ch 17, pt 1.
3   Ibid, Sch 2.
4   Ibid, s53(1); for styles see *Halliday* paras 37-12 to 37-46; Cusine *Standard Securities* paras 4.37–4.42.
5   Conveyancing and Feudal Reform (Scotland) Act 1970, s10(1).
6   The charge certificate in the Appendix contains an example of a Form A security.
7   Ibid, Sch 2, Note 1; see also ch 17, pt 1.
8   Land Registration (Scotland) Act 1979, s15(1).
9   *Cusine* para 4.19; see also his article on 'Descriptions in Standard Securities' (1990) 35 JLSS 98.

event it is unnecessary to refer to burdens affecting the property in the description.[1]

Secondly there will be an importation of the standard conditions (see below) and any variation thereof, and finally there will be a grant of warrandice.[2]

Because Form A contains a personal obligation it also contains a clause of consent to registration for execution; this will normally be found in the separate agreement in Form B.

(c) Standard conditions[3]

The standard conditions set out in Schedule 3 of the Conveyancing and Feudal Reform (Scotland) Act 1970 apply to all standard securities, either in the form in which they appear in the Schedule or as varied. Variation is very common in practice and will be considered in the next section. The effect of the unvaried conditions is as follows:

Standard condition 1. This obliges the debtor to maintain the security subjects in a good state of repair to the reasonable satisfaction of the creditor, permits the creditor, on giving notice, to inspect the premises, and requires the debtor to remedy any defects or disrepair within a reasonable time fixed by the creditor.

Standard condition 2. The debtor must complete any unfinished building or works forming part of or affecting the security subjects to the reasonable satisfaction of the creditor. Demolition or alteration of, or addition to, any part of the security subjects requires the consent of the creditor and must also comply with the terms of any consent or approval required by law.

Standard condition 3. The debtor must:

(a) observe all of the title and other conditions affecting the property;
(b) make prompt payment of all monetary burdens payable in respect of the property (eg feuduty, rates, council tax);
(c) comply with any statutory requirements affecting the property.

---

1 Conveyancing (Scotland) Act 1924, s9(1).
2 See ch 15.
3 *Halliday* ch 38; *Cusine* ch 5.

Standard condition 4.   Within fourteen days of receipt by the debtor the creditor must be given notice of any planning or other notice or order affecting or likely to affect the security subjects. The debtor must comply with the terms of any such notice or order and if required by the creditor object, or join with the creditor in objecting to or making representations regarding the notice or order.

Standard condition 5.   The debtor must insure, or permit the creditor to insure, the security subjects to the extent of their market value and pay the premiums on such a policy as they fall due. Any possible claims under the policy must be notified to the creditor within fourteen days.

Standard condition 6.   The debtor must not let or sub-let the security subjects without the prior written consent of the creditor.[1]

Standard condition 7.   The creditor may perform any obligation imposed on the debtor by the standard conditions where the debtor fails to and may recover any reasonable expenses so incurred from the debtor. Where the creditor has to enter on to the security subjects to implement this condition he may do so on giving seven days notice.

Standard condition 8.   The creditor is entitled, subject to any provision in the security, to call up the standard security in the manner prescribed by s 19 of the Conveyancing and Feudal Reform (Scotland) Act 1970 (see below, pt (f)(i)).

Standard condition 9.   The debtor shall be held to be in default:

(a)   where a calling-up notice in respect of the security has been served and has not been complied with;
(b)   where there has been a failure to comply with any other requirement arising out of the security;
(c)   where the proprietor of the security subjects has become insolvent.

Paragraph 2 of the condition details what is to be considered as insolvency and includes someone who is notour bankrupt and a company in respect of which a receiver has been appointed.

---

1   As to the consequences for the lessee of a letting without the creditor's consent, see *Trade Development Bank v Warriner & Mason* 1980 SLT 223; *Trade Development Bank v David W Haig (Bellshill) Ltd* 1983 SLT 510.

Standard condition 10.   Where the debtor is in default the creditor has the following remedies, which must be exercised in accordance with the provisions of Part II of the Conveyancing and Feudal Reform (Scotland) Act 1970, in addition to any others arising from the contract to which the standard security relates:

(a)   sale of the security subjects;
(b)   entering into possession of the security subjects and receiving any monetary payment due from them;
(c)   where the creditor enters into possession he may let them;
(d)   where the creditor enters into possession all rights relating to the granting of leases and management and maintenance of the property pass to him;
(e)   effecting repairs to the property and carrying out such reconstruction, alteration and improvement of the subjects as would be expected of a prudent proprietor to maintain the market value of the subjects. In exercise of this power the creditor may enter the subjects at any reasonable time;
(f)   application may be made for a decree of foreclosure.

Standard condition 11.   This condition details the procedure for the exercise of the debtor's right of redemption.

Standard condition 12.   The debtor is personally liable for all of the creditor's legal and other expenses arising out of the constitution and enforcement of the standard security.

Where the standard security is granted by someone other than the debtor the obligations imposed in standard conditions 1–7 are imposed on the proprietor of the security subjects. In such cases both the proprietor and the debtor may exercise the right of redemption.

(d) Variation of standard conditions

As noted above, there is provision for variation of the standard conditions by agreement between the parties.[1] There are three exceptions to this ability to vary. The provisions relating to the power of sale and to foreclosure cannot be varied, for example by substituting another procedure for that set out in the 1970 Act, and although the right of redemption can be denied to the debtor,

1   Conveyancing and Feudal Reform (Scotland) Act 1970, s11(3).

if it exists the procedure for its exercise set out in standard condition 11 cannot be varied.[1]

Variation of standard conditions is very common in practice and can be effected either in a separate deed (which need not be recorded in the Register of Sasines or registered in the Land Register) or by provision in the standard security itself.[2] Building societies and some other institutional lenders favour a deed of variation registered in the Books of Council and Session.

Common variations include an obligation to insure for reinstatement rather than market value, a prohibition against parting with possession of the security subjects rather than letting or sub-letting, and a provision permitting the creditor to deal with the debtor's moveable property in the event of him taking possession of the security subjects.[3]

(e) Ranking[4]

Where there are two or more standard securities over the same property the question of ranking may arise. Ranking is concerned with the relative position of the securities and is a particular concern when the security subjects are sold and do not raise enough to pay off all of the securities in full. In such a situation the ranking of the securities will determine the order in which they are paid off.

As between two securities the ranking may be prior and postponed, in which case the prior security would be paid first, with the postponed taking whatever was left, or the two may rank *pari passu*, ie equally, with the proceeds going equally to the creditors in both securities.

As illustration, take the position where the Priory Local building society and the Bank of Paisley each hold standard securities for £25,000 over Greene's house, the securities being registered respectively on 21 January 1990 and 2 February 1991. The house is sold for £40,000. In this case the building society's security ranks prior to the bank's and so they would be paid off in full leaving the bank with £15,000. If both securities had been registered on the first date the two would have ranked *pari passu* and bank and building society would each receive £20,000.

In general the ranking of securities is determined by the date

1 Ibid.
2 Ibid, Sch 2, Note 4.
3 See *Cusine* paras 5.16–5.30 for a fuller discussion of common variations.
4 *Cusine* ch 7.

of recording or registration, so that a security recorded or registered earlier will rank prior to one recorded or registered later. Where securities are recorded or registered on the same day they will rank *pari passu*.

This order of ranking can be changed by express agreement in the form of a ranking clause in the securities, a separate ranking agreement, or by the holder of an earlier security consenting to a change in the normal order in the body of the later security. There are two situations where such changes will need to be made. The first is where two securities will be recorded on the same day and one is to be postponed to the other, and the second is where a later security is to rank prior to or *pari passu* with an earlier security.

Where the creditor in a recorded or registered standard security receives notice of the creation of a subsequent security the preference in ranking of that creditor is restricted as regards the creditor in the new security. The preference is restricted to the amount advanced at the time of the notice, any future advances the creditor is bound by contract to make, interest, and any expenses of the creditor in connection with the security.[1] There has been some dispute about the effect of this provision. One view was that the earlier creditor had no security for any sums advanced after the date of notice of the second security.[2] On the other view all that was restricted was the first creditor's preference in ranking, so that the effect of the provision was that security still existed for future advances, but this was postponed to the security of the second creditor.[3] The latter view appears preferable, although Cusine points out that further advances are rarely, if ever, made in these circumstances.[4]

(f) Creditor's remedies 1: Remedies provided for in the standard conditions[5]

As noted above, standard condition 10 confers a variety of rights on the creditor in the event of default by the debtor. The remedies specified in that standard condition and the statutory provisions

---

1 Conveyancing and Feudal Reform (Scotland) Act 1970, s13(1).
2 G Gretton 'Ranking of Heritable Creditors' (1980) 25 JLSS 275, (1981) 26 JLSS 280.
3 J Halliday 'Ranking of Heritable Creditors' (1981) 26 JLSS 26; *Halliday* para 36–20.
4 *Standard Securities* para 7.12; see also *Gordon* para 20–141 where this view is stated without comment.
5 *Halliday* ch 39; Cusine *Standard Securities* ch 8.

regarding their exercise are the subject of this section. The following section will consider other remedies available to the creditor.

The principal remedies provided for by standard condition 10 are the power of sale, entry into possession and letting, repair reconstruction and improvement, and foreclosure.

The creditor acquires the right to exercise these remedies in one of three ways: service of a calling-up notice, service of a notice of default, or application to the sheriff court under section 24 of the Conveyancing and Feudal Reform (Scotland) Act 1970.

(i) Calling-up notice.   In terms of standard condition 8 the creditor has the right to serve a calling-up notice, subject to the terms of the security and any rule of law. Thus, for example, the security may provide for payment by instalments and preclude the creditor from requiring full repayment so long as these are being paid.

The calling-up notice requires repayment of the loan in full within two months of the date of service of the notice.[1] The sum stated in the notice should be correct at the date of service. If the sum is stated in the notice as being subject to adjustment the person on whom the notice is served may require the creditor to supply the debtor with a statement of the final amount within one month of the date of service of the notice. If this is not done the notice is deemed to be of no effect.[2]

The notice is served on the proprietor of the security subjects rather than on the debtor; these, as we have noted, may not be the same.[3] However, if the creditor wishes to preserve a right of action against the debtor under the latter's personal obligation a copy of the calling-up notice must be served on him.[4]

The statutory requirements as to service must be strictly adhered to. In *Hill Samuel & Co v Haas*[5] a notice addressed to Mr and Mrs Haas was held to be invalid when Mrs Haas alone was the proprietor.[6]

The period of notice may be shortened or dispensed with by the person(s) on whom the notice is served, though the agreement of any creditors holding securities postponed to or *pari passu* with that of the serving creditor and of any non-entitled spouse must be obtained to do this.[7]

---

1   Conveyancing and Feudal Reform (Scotland) Act 1970, Sch 6, Form A.
2   Ibid, s19(9).
3   Ibid, s19(2).
4   Ibid, s 19(5).
5   1989 SLT (Sh Ct) 69.
6   *Supra* at 70, G-I.
7   Conveyancing and Feudal Reform (Scotland) Act 1970, s19(10).

Failure to comply with a calling-up notice entitles the creditor to exercise any of the rights in standard condition 10.

(ii) Notice of default. A notice of default can be served where there has been a failure to comply with any requirement arising out of the security (other than failure to comply with a calling-up notice) and the failure is remediable.[1] Halliday suggests that '[d]efault in payment of interest or of a periodic instalment of capital and interest, or breach of an obligation under standard condition 1, 2, 3 or 5, or failure to implement an obligation undertaken in the personal obligation or in a variation of the standard conditions, are obvious examples.'[2]

The other requirement, apart from default, is that it should be remediable. Thus a failure to comply with standard condition 4 which meant that, for example, the time for appealing against a closing order had passed, might not be remediable, and therefore a notice of default would not be appropriate.

The notice of default is served on the debtor 'and, as the case may be, on the proprietor' and must be in conformity with the statutory form.[3] It gives one month's notice to remedy the default, subject to the same provisions as to shortening of notice as apply to calling-up notices.[4]

Anyone served with a notice of default can object to it by application to the sheriff court within fourteen days,[5] but if this is done the creditor may make a counter-application seeking leave to exercise any of the remedies available to him.[6]

If the notice of default is not complied with, the creditor can immediately exercise the powers of sale, repair reconstruction and improvement and foreclosure.[7] Should the creditor wish to make use of any of the other remedies provided for in standard condition 10 (ie those involving entering into possession of the security subjects) application must be made to the sheriff court.[8] The exercise of these remedies is subject to the proviso that, after the expiry of the period of notice in the notice of default, the debtor or proprietor may redeem

---

1 Conveyancing and Feudal Reform (Scotland) Act 1970, s21 (1); standard condition 9(1)(b); see also *United Dominions Trust Ltd v Site Preparations Ltd (No 2)* 1978 SLT (Sh Ct) 21 at 23.
2 *Halliday* para 39–19.
3 Conveyancing and Feudal Reform (Scotland) Act 1970, s21(2) and Sch 6, Form B.
4 Ibid, s21(3).
5 Ibid, s22(1).
6 Ibid, s22(3).
7 Ibid, s23(2).
8 Ibid, s24.

the security without notice, provided that this is done before conclusion of an enforceable contract to sell the security subjects.[1]

(iii) Application under section 24.   An application under section 24 may be made where the debtor is in default in the sense explained above in relation to the notice of default, and is also the appropriate means of proceeding where the proprietor is insolvent. Where the debtor is in default there is no need to precede the application by service of a notice of default.[2] The application is for warrant to exercise any of the standard condition 10 remedies and any other remedies which may be provided for in the security.

(iv) Sale.   Once the creditor has obtained the right to exercise the power of sale this may be done either by public roup or by private bargain.[3] The only statutory requirements imposed on the creditor are that there must be advertisement of the property and that reasonable steps should be taken to ensure that the price is the best that can reasonably be obtained.[4] There is no further specification of the nature of the advertising needed, such as that which exists in the case of sale under a bond and disposition in security, but clearly the advertising would have to be extensive enough to ensure that the best possible price was obtained.[5] The onus of establishing that the best possible price was not obtained rests on the debtor.

In addition to the statutory provision there is also a common law requirement that the seller 'must pay due regard to the interests of the debtor when he comes to sell the security subjects.'[6]

The selling creditor does not require consent from any other creditor to proceed with the sale.

Once the security subjects are sold the proceeds are applied firstly in payment of the selling creditor's expenses, secondly in payment of any prior security where the property is not being sold subject to it, thirdly in payment of the selling creditor's security and any others ranking *pari passu* with it, fourthly in payment of any postponed securities, and finally any surplus is payable to the debtor.[7]

---

1 Ibid, s23(3).
2 Although *Halliday* (para 39-35) suggests that this is the preferable course.
3 Conveyancing and Feudal Reform (Scotland) Act 1970, s25.
4 Ibid.
5 *Dick v Clydesdale Bank plc* 1991 SLT 678; see also *Cusine* paras 8.27-8.29.
6 *Dick v Clydesdale Bank plc, supra* at 681A per Lord President Hope, who also approved Halliday's statement (para 33-27) that the creditor is in a position of quasi-trustee for the debtor.
7 Conveyancing and Feudal Reform (Scotland) Act 1970, s27(1).

If the proceeds of sale are insufficient to repay all of the debtor's securities he will remain liable for the outstanding amount under the personal obligation.

The disposition by the selling creditor disburdens the property of his security and any securities ranking *pari passu* with or postponed to it. (Including inhibitions lodged against the debtor after the date of infeftment of the creditor under the standard security.)[1] Separate discharges of prior securities must be obtained if the property is to be sold free of all securities.

If the debt has ceased to exist prior to the sale or if there is any irregularity in the sale procedure or its preliminaries the title of a purchaser who receives a disposition bearing to be granted by a selling creditor will be protected from challenge provided that he has purchased in good faith and for value and on the face of it the seller's exercise of his power of sale was regular.[2]

(v) Entering into possession. On entering into possession of the security subjects the creditor is entitled to receive any rents, feuduties or ground annuals payable to the proprietor and may also let the subjects for up to seven years, or longer with the consent of the sheriff court.[3] The creditor also has assigned to him all the rights and obligations of the proprietor relating to the management and maintenance of the subjects.[4]

A creditor in possession is not liable for arrears of common charges arising before his entry into possession, but would be liable for those arising after this.[5] He is also not liable for the standard community charge,[6] but would be liable to be entered on the valuation roll and so liable for rates if he was receiving the rents and profits of the security subjects.[7]

(vi) Repair reconstruction and improvement. Under standard condition 1 the creditor has power to require the debtor or proprietor to carry out repairs in the absence of default. The additional powers obtained on default are that the creditor may enter the property

1 *Newcastle Building Society v White* 1987 SLT (Sh Ct) 81.
2 Conveyancing (Scotland) Act 1924, s41(2); Conveyancing and Feudal Reform (Scotland) Act 1970, s32.
3 Conveyancing and Feudal Reform (Scotland) Act 1970, s20(3).
4 Ibid, s20(5).
5 *David Watson Property Management v Woolwich Equitable Building Society* 1990 SLT 764.
6 *Northern Rock Building Society v Wood* 1990 SLT (Sh Ct) 109.
7 *Armour on Valuation for Rating* (5th edn) para 12–05. The same liability will presumably arise in relation to the proposed council tax.

to carry out work at all reasonable times and may effect such reconstruction, alteration and improvement as would be expected of a prudent proprietor to maintain the market value of the subjects.

(vii) Foreclosure. Where the security subjects have been exposed for sale by public roup[1] at a price not exceeding the amount due under the selling creditor's security and any securities ranking prior to or *pari passu* with it, and no purchaser has been found, the creditor may, after two months, apply to the court for decree of foreclosure.[2] The court may grant the debtor or proprietor three months to pay the amount due under the security, order re-exposure, or grant a decree of foreclosure. The effect of a decree of foreclosure, once an extract has been recorded or registered, is to transfer the subjects irredeemably to the creditor with effect from the date of recording or registration and to disburden the property of any securities postponed to that held by the foreclosing creditor.[3] The title obtained by the creditor is not open to challenge on the ground of any irregularity of the foreclosure proceedings or any prior notices.[4]

The value of the property to the creditor will be the price at which it was last exposed for sale, which must not exceed the amount due under the foreclosing creditor's security and any prior or *pari passu* security. The debtor will remain personally liable for any amount by which this price is less than the sum required to repay the outstanding debt to the foreclosing creditor.[5]

(viii) Conclusion. Of these remedies sale is the one which will be used most often in practice. The advantage of this from the creditor's point of view is that, in normal market conditions, it enables him to recover the debt which he is owed. The remedies involving entry onto the property and carrying out of repairs are unlikely to be commonly used because of administrative inconvenience. Foreclosure will generally only be used where the security is worth less than the debt owed.

(g) Creditor's remedies 2: other remedies

The remedies provided in standard condition 10 are stated to be without prejudice to any other remedy arising out of the contract

1 See ch 15, pt 5.
2 Conveyancing and Feudal Reform (Scotland) Act 1970, s28(1).
3 Ibid, s28(6).
4 Ibid, s28(8).
5 Ibid, s28(5),(7).

to which the standard security relates. The contract, then, may provide additional remedies for the creditor. As well as these there are three other remedies generally available to the creditor. These are enforcement of the personal obligation, poinding of the ground, and adjudication.

(*i*) *Personal obligation.* The personal obligation may be enforced by court action; either an action for debt or, where the security has been granted to secure an obligation *ad factum praestandum*, an action for implement. In addition, where there is a clause of consent to registration for execution (as there will be in a Form A security and will usually occur in the agreement ancillary to a Form B security) the creditor may proceed by way of summary diligence.

(*ii*) *Poinding of the ground.* The creditor may attach the debtor's moveable property situated on the security subjects and proceed to sale.

(*iii*) *Adjudication.* Adjudication involves a judicial transfer of the security subjects to the creditor in satisfaction of the loan. Application is made to the Court of Session for decree of adjudication. The drawback of the remedy is that the transfer does not become final until the passing of a ten year period (known as the 'legal') after the recording or registration of the extract decree.

(*iv*) *Conclusion.* These remedies are rarely used. In the case of the first two the reason is that any amount raised would probably be quite inadequate to repay the debt outstanding.

(h) Restrictions on creditor's remedies

As we have noted above if the creditor sells the security subjects he must obtain the best price that can reasonably be obtained. However it appears that this does not give the debtor any right to prevent a sale at what he considers to be an inadequate price; instead his remedy is to raise an action for damages after the event.[1]

There is, however, an unreported case referred to in *Armstrong, Petitioner*[2] of a judicial factor on the estate of a bankrupt partnership

1 *Associated Displays Ltd v Turnbeam Ltd* 1988 SCLR 220; *Dick v Clydesdale Bank plc* 1991 SLT 678.
2 1988 SLT 255.

being granted interdict against a creditor to prevent him exercising any of his standard condition 10 remedies. There is also, in *Armstrong, Petitioner* an *obiter dictum* to the effect that 'A heritable creditor cannot use his powers for the primary purpose of advancing his own interests at the expense of the debtor when he has the alternative of proceeding in a more equitable manner.'[1]

(i) Variation, assignation and restriction.[2]

It is possible to vary the provisions of a recorded or registered standard security by means of a variation endorsed on the security or by a separate deed of variation. In either case, the variation must be duly recorded or registered.[3] Variation would be appropriate, for example, when the amount of the loan was being increased. The only restriction on variation is that it cannot be used when the same end could be achieved by an assignation, discharge or restriction of the security.

Standard securities can be assigned by the creditor, and a statutory form is provided.[4]

It is also possible to restrict the scope of a standard security, in other words to disburden part of the security subjects. This can be done either in the form of a deed of restriction[5] or by a partial discharge and deed of restriction when some of the outstanding loan is also repaid.[6]

(j) Discharge[7]

In most cases the standard security will be discharged by the execution of a discharge in the statutory form,[8] followed by recording in the Register of Sasines or forwarding to the Land Register to be given effect to.[9]

---

1   1988 SLT 255 at 258c. See also the criticism of this case in *Cusine* para 8.25.
2   *Halliday* paras 40-01 to 40-34, 40-44 to 40-49; Cusine *Standard Securities* paras 6.01–6.12.
3   Conveyancing and Feudal Reform (Scotland) Act 1970, s16 and Sch 4, Form E.
4   Ibid, s14 and Sch 4, Forms A and B.
5   Ibid, s15(1) and Sch 4, Form C.
6   Ibid, s15(2) and Sch 4, Form D.
7   *Halliday* paras 40-63 to 40-72; Cusine *Standard Securities* paras 10.02–10.10.
8   Conveyancing and Feudal Reform (Scotland) Act 1970, s17, Sch 4, Form F.
9   See *Registration of Title Practice Book* G2.40 and G3.30.

The standard security will also be extinguished by payment of the debt in full or performance of the other obligation secured; it is, however, desirable to get a formal discharge as evidence of payment or performance.

Finally, the security may be discharged by confusion, where the same person acting in the same capacity becomes both debtor and creditor in the security.

(k) Redemption[1]

The debtor's right of redemption can, as we noticed earlier, be dispensed with by variation of the standard conditions. However, even when that has happened a security over a private dwelling house can still be redeemed after twenty years.[2]

The procedure for redemption is set out in standard condition 11. Where, despite repayment of the debt in full or performance of the other obligation, the debtor is unable to obtain a discharge there is provision for him to be released from the security.[3]

(l) Matrimonial Homes (Family Protection) (Scotland) Act 1981[4]

In order to protect the creditor in a standard security from the occupancy rights of any non-entitled spouse an affidavit to the effect that the security subjects are not a matrimonial home, a renunciation of occupancy rights by the non-entitled spouse, or a consent to the dealing by the non-entitled spouse will have to be produced by the debtor. Previously the requirement was for this evidence to be produced prior to the granting of the security, but this is no longer the case.[5]

(m) Standard securities granted by companies

As noted in the introduction, the creditor's right in a standard security only becomes real on recording of the security in the Register of

---

1 *Halliday* paras 40-50 to 40-62; Cusine *Standard Securities* paras 10.11–10.15.
2 Land Tenure Reform (Scotland) Act 1974, s11.
3 Conveyancing and Feudal Reform (Scotland) Act 1970, s18(2).
4 See also ch 10, pt 8.
5 Matrimonial Homes (Family Protection) (Scotland) Act 1981, s8(2A) (inserted by the Law Reform (Miscellaneous Provisions) (Scotland) Act 1985, s13(8) and amended by the Law Reform (Miscellaneous Provisions) (Scotland) Act 1990, s74 and Sch 8).

Sasines or registration in the Land Register. In addition to this, securities granted by companies must also be registered in the Companies Register of Charges within twenty-one days of being granted. Failure to register means that although the charge is valid against the company it is void against any liquidator or administrator in insolvency proceedings and against any other creditor having a security interest in the subject matter of the unregistered security.[1]

Late registration may be allowed following application to court.[2] Once the relevant provisions of the Companies Act 1989 come into force[3] late registration will be allowed without application to court, but will impose certain penalties on the creditor. These are that the date of priority of the charge in a question of ranking is the date of registration rather than the date of creation of the charge, and that the charge is void against the liquidator or administrator in insolvency proceedings started within six months if the company was unable to pay its debts at the time of registration of the charge or became so as a result of registration.

4. FLOATING CHARGES[4]

(a) Introduction

Fixed charges, such as the standard security, attach to a specific piece of property which cannot be disposed of without either the charge continuing to affect it or, alternatively, being discharged on repayment of the loan or debt. A floating charge in contrast is a charge over part or all of a company's assets which allows the company to continue to deal with these assets and does not attach specifically to them until the charge crystallises. On crystallisation the charge fixes on the assets and becomes a fixed charge over them.

The distinction has also been expressed as follows 'A specific [fixed] charge . . . is one that without more fastens on ascertained and definite property or property capable of being ascertained or defined; a floating charge, on the other hand, is ambulatory and shifting in its nature, hovering over and so to speak floating with the property which it is intended to affect, until some event occurs or some act is done which causes it to settle and fasten on the subject of the charge within its reach and grasp.'[5]

---

1 Companies Act 1985, ss410, 415.
2 Ibid, s420.
3 Section 95 inserting new ss 399 and 400 into the 1985 Act.
4 *Halliday* ch 41; *McDonald* ch 23.
5 *Illingworth v Houldsworth* [1904] AC 355 at 358 per Lord Macnaghten.

The significance of the floating charge is that it allows the company to grant a security over its assets and at the same time deal with them without the consent of the creditor being necessary for each transaction as it would be with a fixed security. It would clearly be impracticable to grant a fixed security over the stock in trade of a company, however a floating charge would not affect the companies ability to deal.

(b) Constitution and registration

Floating charges can be created over any assets of a company including heritable property. Although this is the case they need not be recorded in the Register of Sasines or registered in the Land Register. The same requirements as to registration in the Register of Charges apply to them as apply to standard securities.

There is no specific form of floating charge. A style is given in *Halliday*.[1]

(c) Crystallisation

Crystallisation occurs on the happening of one of three events: if an event specified in the instrument of charge occurs (eg if the assets of the company fall below a certain level); on the appointment of a receiver; on the commencement of winding up.

(d) Ranking[2]

Floating charges commonly contain ranking clauses which specifically prohibit the subsequent creation of fixed or floating charges ranking prior to or *pari passu* with them. Where such a clause exists any subsequent charge, fixed or floating, will be postponed to the earlier floating charge. In the absence of express provision, fixed charges granted before the crystallisation of a floating charge will rank before that charge, even if granted subsequently. As between floating charges the order of ranking is determined by the order of registration.

---

1 Para 41–05.
2 See also G Gretton 'Searches' (1989) 34 JLSS 50 at 51.

12. Statutory restrictions on property rights

1. INTRODUCTION

In this section of the book, we have been systematically exploring the second half of Erskine's definition of property, ie the extent to which a property owner's rights are qualified by law or paction.[1] So far the emphasis has been on the second of these qualifications, namely the restrictions on his rights which a property owner accepts voluntarily upon himself, though in some cases – in the case of real conditions, for example – it is true that the agreement may have been imposed upon him by a previous owner, or by the superior. In modern times, however, the most comprehensive restrictions on an owner's rights are imposed by the state (by means of legislation) and implemented (usually) by local authorities.

There are good reasons, of course, for this official intervention. While the law is prepared to allow a property owner the maximum freedom to use his property as he wants, it is desirable in the public interest that he should conform to some systematic policy for land use so that (say) a factory emitting noxious fumes is not placed in the middle of a residential area. It is also desirable that any buildings he erects conform to acceptable standards of construction, and that its inhabitants are not endangered by inadequate fire precautions.

Our main concerns in this chapter will be the legislation on town and country planning, the regulations regarding building control, and local authority housing controls. However, we will finish with a brief indication of various other statutory intrusions which property owners and would-be developers should be aware of and, if necessary, investigate further.

---

1 See ch 1, pt 1 above.

2. PLANNING LAW

Administrative structure

Town and country planning is a function in which all levels of government are involved. Central government, in conjunction with Parliament, is responsible for the legislation to provide the overall framework for the system, as well as a number of important statutory instruments which fill in the details. Also, the Secretary of State (in the present context the Secretary of State for Scotland), in addition to providing a constant stream of advice to local authorities (on planning legislation, policy procedures and best practice), hears appeals against the decisions of local planning authorities (usually the district council) in individual cases. He also has the power to 'call in' (ie take over the decision on) planning applications of significant national interest, and is responsible for compiling a list of buildings of special architectural or historical interest to which special planning controls apply.

The regional councils (representing the nine local authority regions) form the upper of the two tiers of local government in Scotland. As regards planning, they are responsible for compiling a structure plan, a document setting out the strategic planning policy for their area; they can also 'call in' planning applications from a district council in respect of developments that are of regional importance.

Each region comprises a number of districts, thirty-six of which have planning powers. These are run by district councils, who are on the front line in the planning process. Prominent among their many planning functions is the responsibility for compiling a local plan for their area, a map-based plan giving land use policies and allocating preferred land uses (eg residential, industrial, or even specific uses such as sites for schools or hospitals); their most extensive function, however, is to act as local planning authority, making decisions on individual planning applications.

The structure and local plan for any particular area are known collectively as the development plan.

In some of the less heavily populated areas of Scotland, the regional and district council planning functions are combined in one body, eg in the region alone, or in the islands councils, in which all the regional and district functions are combined. For planning purposes, these councils are known as general planning authorities.

Scottish planning law is consolidated in the Town and Country Planning (Scotland) Act 1972. Since then there have been a number of amendments, most recently in the Planning and Compensation Act 1991. As in other areas of law, England has parallel legislation, which corresponds in many (though not all) respects with its Scottish equivalent.

Development control

Any property owner who wants to carry out development on his land must first (subject to some of the exceptions mentioned below) apply to the local planning authority (usually the district council) for planning permission. Before looking further at the relevant procedure, however, we must first see what is legally meant by development.

Meaning of development.   This is defined as (a) the carrying out of building, engineering, mining or other operations in, on, over or under land or (b) the making of any material change in the use of any buildings or other land.[1] The definition of building operations includes demolition.[2]

It will be seen that development includes (as we would expect) activities that result in land or buildings being physically altered in some way; however it also extends beyond this to changes of use (even without any physical alteration) that are considered sufficiently radical to amount to a material change of use, eg a change from a residential to a commercial use. What amounts to a material change of use is a matter of fact depending on the circumstances of a particular case. However, the situation is greatly clarified by the Use Classes Order,[3] a statutory instrument that classifies property uses into sixteen different classes of use; these include shops (Class 1), financial, professional and other services (Class 2), food and drink (Class 3), business (Class 4), and six classes of industrial use. There are also a number of excluded uses (eg petrol filling stations or public houses). And so, if a change of use falls within the same class (eg from a newsagent to a chemist) there is no development; but where the existing use and the proposed use fall within different classes, or one of them is an excluded use, it will be a material change of use and so amount to development.

For the avoidance of doubt, certain other kinds of activity are specifically excluded from or included within the definition of

1   Town and Country Planning (Scotland) Act 1972, s19(1).
2   Planning and Compensation Act 1991, s44.
3   Town and Country Planning (Use Classes) (Scotland) Order 1989.

development. Those excluded include internal alterations to a building that do not materially affect the exterior (provided that they do not extend below ground level),[1] and (perhaps surprisingly) agriculture and forestry. Specifically included within the definition of development is the use of what was previously a single dwellinghouse as two or more dwellinghouses.

Permitted development. If an activity does not fall within the definition of development, then no planning consent is required before it can be carried out. If, however, it does qualify as development this does not automatically mean that permission will be required. For example, development by the Crown (which includes the government) does not require permission. Nor does certain development by local authorities. The most extensive exception relates to those classes of activity detailed in a statutory instrument known as the General Development Order.[2] This contains twenty-two classes of permitted development which comprise either relatively minor activities, or else, for some other reason, deserve to be included within a special category. The effect of the General Development Order is to grant planning consent in advance to all development falling within one of these classes, so that individual applications are not required.

The classes of permitted development include extensions to dwellinghouses, garages and other outhouses (all Class 1), and walls and fences (Class 2), subject in all cases to their conformity within certain size and locational limitations. (The permitted development rights applying to dwellinghouses, however, do not apply to flats). Also included are satellite dishes (Class 1) and temporary buildings and works (Class 4). Under Class 3, certain changes of use which, in strict terms of the Use Classes Order qualify as development, are given permitted development status, because they involve moving away from rather than towards a use which is thought to require control. For example, changing from a newsagents shop (Class 1) to a fish and chip takeaway (Class 3) would still require permission; however, a change from a hot food takeaway to a newsagent (which immediate neighbours might consider an improvement) is permitted development for which no consent is required.

Under Article 4 of the General Development Order, the Secretary of State may give a direction that a certain class or classes of permitted

---

1 Town and Country Planning (Scotland) Act 1972, s19(2)(a).
2 Town and Country Planning (General Development)(Scotland) Order 1981, Sch 1 (as amended).

development, or all of them, may have their permitted development status withdrawn in a particular area, or even with regard to a particular site. If an owner is thereafter refused consent for a development that would normally have been permitted, he may be entitled to compensation. Probably the most common use of Article 4 directions is in relation to conservation areas (see below), and usually the Secretary of State's action will be at the request of the planning authority

Planning applications

Planning applications are made on a form supplied by the planning authority, and should be accompanied by detailed specifications of any building or other operations that are proposed. If he wants, the applicant can obtain permission in two stages, by first applying for *outline permission*, ie by submitting a completed form and site plan alone. This allows him to test whether the development is acceptable in principle before he has gone to the expense of hiring architects and other professionals to design his development in detail. If successful in obtaining outline permission, he may then convert this to a full permission (which would enable the development to proceed) by obtaining his detailed specifications (known in this context as *reserved matters*) and submitting them in turn to the planning authority for approval.

Alternatively, he may submit a full application right away. This (because of its nature) would be the method used for a material change of use, and would also be appropriate for small developments. In certain other circumstances (eg in a conservation area) local planning authorities will not accept outline planning applications, but only full ones.

Notification and publicity. Certain interested parties must be notified of a proposed development in order to give them the opportunity to make representations to the planning authority should they feel this to be necessary. These include immediate neighbours and also any agricultural tenant who may lose his security of tenure if his landlord obtains permission for a non-agricultural use.[1] Also, there is no legal requirement that the person making a planning application must be the owner of the property on which the development is to take place; he may, for example, be a tenant, or an intending owner who wants to be sure of planning consent

1 See ch 8, pt 4 above.

before proceeding with his purchase. However, if the applicant is not the owner, the owner must be notified of the application in case he wants to make representations to the planning authority regarding the application.

In certain circumstances a press advert is also required, eg where the planning authority agrees that there are too many neighbours to notify individually or where someone with a notifiable interest cannot be traced. It is also required in cases where the public interest is involved, eg where the proposal is contrary to the development plan, where it involves alteration to or demolition of a listed building, or where it is one of the activities listed in the General Development Order and known as a *bad neighbour development*; this last category includes things that might affect the amenity of a residential area, eg slaughterhouses, scrap yards, wildlife parks, public houses, theatres, cinemas and many others.

Planning authority's decision.   Planning authorities have a wide discretion in deciding planning applications. However, they must have regard to any representations from members of the public and people with a notifiable interest. Above all, they have a duty to make their determination in accordance with the development plan unless material considerations indicate otherwise. This last provision was added by the Planning and Compensation Act 1991[1] and marks a change in emphasis from the previous law, under which the planning authority's obligation was to have equal regard to the development plan and other material considerations. This means that, while planning authorities are still not bound by the provisions of local and structure plans, there is now a presumption in favour of comforming with them.

'Material considerations' have not been given statutory definition, either in the old or the new law; in the past they have been held by the courts to include a wide variety of things such as amenity, the desirability of retaining the existing use, the safety of the public and users of the development, the need for the development, the availability of alternative sites, and the current policy advice from central government.[2]

Conditional consents.   Planning authorities may grant unconditional permission, refuse an application, or grant consent 'subject to such

---

1   Section 58.
2   Eric Young & Jeremy Rowan-Robinson *Scottish Planning Law and Procedure* (1985) ch 9.

conditions as they think fit.'[1] The function of planning conditions includes regulating the development or use of, or carrying out works on, land under the control of the applicant, eg by the provision of access roads or amenity land. They can also be used to protect trees on the site (see below).

Although the above provisions appear to give planning authorities unfettered discretion in the imposition of conditions, the courts have the power to declare planning conditions *ultra vires* if they believe that they have been made for an ulterior motive and not a planning purpose, that they do not fairly and reasonably relate to the development or that they are so unreasonable that no reasonable planning authority could have imposed them (eg by requiring works on land outwith the applicant's control).[2] Planning conditions may also be held to be unnecessary,[3] or void from uncertainty.[4]

Appeals.   Where planning permission has been refused, or granted subject to conditions, the applicant may within six months appeal to the Secretary of State, who has the power to reverse or amend the planning authority's decision. The applicant is entitled to a public hearing, though is encouraged to make a written submission instead. Appeals are heard by a reporter, ie an official appointed by the Secretary of State; although the reporter's duty is theoretically to 'report' his findings back to the Secretary of State, reporters now have the delegated power themselves to make the decision on most kinds of application.

The Secretary of State's decision is final on the merits of an application; there is a further right of appeal to the Court of Session on legal grounds, eg if the decision is *ultra vires*, or the statutory procedures have not been conformed to.

If an applicant who has been refused consent, or granted one subject to conditions, believes that this renders the land of no reasonably beneficial use to him, he may serve a purchase notice on the planning authority; this may result in the planning authority being compelled to purchase the property on the same terms as if it had been a compulsory purchase.

Planning agreements.   In many cases it makes sense for the developer

---

1 Town and Country Planning (Scotland) Act 1972, s26(1).
2 *Newbury District Council v Secretary of State for the Environment* [1981] AC 578; *BAA v Secretary of State for Scotland* 1979 SLT 179; *Birnie v Banff County Council* 1954 SLT (Sh Ct) 90.
3 *BAA v Secretary of State for Scotland, supra.*
4 *David Lowe & Sons v Musselburgh Town Council* 1974 SLT 5.

to consult the planning authority in advance of submitting his application in order to sound out their opinion and negotiate the terms of any conditions that are likely to be imposed. These may be embodied in a contract between the developer and the planning authority,[1] which the planning authority can then follow up with an unconditional consent, thereby speeding matters up and precluding the possibility of an appeal. If recorded in the Register of Sasines, the planning agreement will bind future owners and occupiers of the development as well as the party who signed it.

Planning agreements are becoming increasingly common nowadays. They obviously suit developers because they expedite matters and eliminate uncertainty; and planning authorities can use this to negotiate *planning gain,* ie the inclusion in the development of some extra amenities in the public interest, which the developer, if left to his own devices, might have omitted on strictly economic grounds. The use of planning agreements, however, is somewhat controversial, and the government has been reviewing their status for some time.

Revocation of planning consent. It is open to a planning authority to decide that an existing lawful development or land use (old or new) is no longer desirable (eg if it creates a nuisance in a residential area) and require it to be removed.[2] They are even entitled to change their mind and revoke consent for a development which has not been completed, or even started.[3]

Obviously this withdrawal of consent is not the fault of the owner, who may claim compensation for any loss he has sustained as a result. Alternatively, if he can establish that the revocation of consent renders his property of no reasonably beneficial use, he may serve a purchase notice on the planning authority, requesting them to take it off his hands (see above).

Planning consent is automatically revoked for a development not begun within five years or (where outline consent has been obtained first) within two years of the approval of reserved matters. If a development is begun within the relevant time limit, but then apparently abandoned, the planning authority may serve a *completion notice* upon the developer; this gives the latter a specific period (not less than twelve months) within which to complete the development,

---

1 Town and Country Planning (Scotland) Act 1972, s50.
2 Ibid, s49.
3 Ibid, s42.

otherwise planning consent will be withdrawn and the developer open to enforcement proceedings (see below).

Enforcement of planning control

Obviously there would be little point in having a system of development control if there was no way of enforcing it against those who carry out unauthorised developments, or contravene any conditions attached to a consent. Accordingly, where there is a breach of planning control in the form of an unauthorised operation, or material change of use, the planning authority may serve an **enforcement notice** on the owner, occupier or other person having an interest in the land.[1] Where there has been breach of a planning condition, they may send a **breach of condition notice** which, unlike an enforcement notice, is not subject to appeal.[2] Where a breach of planning control is only suspected, they may send a **planning contravention notice**, requiring further information.[3]

An enforcement notice will state a date when it becomes effective, and at any time before that date the recipient may appeal against the notice to the Secretary of State. The enforcement notice is rendered ineffective pending the outcome of the appeal; however, if emergency measures are required to stop the breach, the planning authority may achieve this by following up the enforcement notice with a *stop notice*.[4]

Immunity from enforcement. Where the breach consists of an unauthorised building, mining, engineering or other operation, it becomes immune from enforcement after four years if no enforcement proceedings have been taken within that period. The same applies to an unauthorised material change of use where the new use is as a single dwelling. All other breaches (ie other material changes of use and breaches of planning conditions) become immune after ten years.

Failure to obey enforcement, etc, notices. Failure to obey any of the types of notice mentioned above is an offence, which could result in the party in breach incurring a substantial fine. The planning

---

1   Town and Country Planning (Scotland) Act 1972, s84 (substituted by the Planning and Compensation Act 1991, s37).
2   Planning and Compensation Act 1991, s34.
3   Ibid, s33.
4   Town and Country Planning (Scotland) Act 1972, s87 (as amended by the Planning and Compensation Act 1991, s41).

authority also have power to remove any unauthorised development at the expense of the person responsible for it.

Certificate of lawful use or development.[1] A person who wants confirmation that an existing use or development is lawful (eg if it was originally unauthorised, but may now be immune, or if there is some doubt as to whether permission was legally required) may apply to the planning authority for a certificate of lawful use or development. The issue of such a certificate creates an irrefutable presumption as to the lawfulness of any activity which it covers. A developer may also apply for such a certificate in respect of an intended development in order to ascertain, in doubtful cases, whether or not planning consent is required.

Special controls

There are certain special matters with regard to which it is felt that restrictions beyond the normal development control system should be imposed. These include controls relating to listed buildings, conservation areas, tree preservation and reclamation of waste land among others.[2] Here we will give a brief account of the first three of them.

Listed Buildings. The Secretary of State maintains a list of buildings which are considered to be of special architectural or historical interest. In such cases a special consent (known as *listed building consent*) is required; the application is made to the planning authority, but the Secretary of State must be notified and may call in the application. Listed building consent is required for changes which in relation to other buildings would be permitted development (eg small extensions or dormer windows) or not even development at all (eg internal alterations).

An owner has no right to contest the fact that his building has been listed in the first place; however if he is refused listed building consent, or granted a conditional consent, he is entitled to appeal to the Secretary of State in the normal way, and one of his possible grounds of appeal is to challenge the merits of the listing.

Planning authorities have the discretion to award grants to owners of listed buildings in order to help with their maintenance. An owner who allows a listed building to fall into disrepair may be served

---

1 Planning and Compensation Act 1991, s42.
2 For a full treatment of all of these see *Young & Rowan Robinson* ch 19.

by the planning authority with a repairs notice, and this may be followed up by a compulsory acquisition if necessary.

Conservation areas. A local planning authority (not the Secretary of State in this case) can declare a whole area to be of special architectural or historical interest. All buildings in the area are given special protection, and trees are also protected. The Secretary of State may declare certain conservation areas to be of outstanding merit, which makes them eligible for grants towards their enhancement.

Tree protection. We saw earlier that agriculture and forestry were notable exclusions from our general definition of development, which means that planning consent is not normally required to fell or otherwise damage trees. However, there are three exceptions to this general rule:

(1) The planning authority may impose a *tree preservation order* upon any tree or group of trees, which makes it an offence to fell or otherwise harm them without the planning authority's consent.

(2) When granting planning consent for a development, a planning authority has power to impose a planning condition protecting trees within the area concerned.

(3) If trees are located within a conservation area, they may not be felled or otherwise harmed unless the planning authority have first been given notice. If the authority do not impose a tree preservation order within six weeks of such notice, the applicant may proceed.

3. BUILDING CONTROL[1]

There are two aspects to building control. The first of these is a set of regulations governing buildings. These regulations, known as the building standards regulations, are designed to ensure the health, safety, welfare and convenience of people making use of buildings. The second aspect is the control of new building works by local authorities.[2] Each aspect will be considered in turn.

---

1 See F McManus *Environmental Health Law in Scotland* (1989) ch 9.
2 In this context the local authority is the district or islands council, except in Highland, Dumfries and Galloway, and Borders regions where building control is a regional function.

Building standards regulations

The current building standards regulations are the Building Standards (Scotland) Regulations 1990.[1] These take the form of a series of very general statements of requirements to be met by new buildings and are supplemented by more detailed Technical Standards which are published as a separate volume.

Certain classes of buildings are exempted from the building regulations. The principal exceptions include: agricultural buildings, caravans, most garages and garden huts, greenhouses and nuclear shelters.[2] The exceptions for garages, huts and greenhouses do not apply if they are very large (exceeding thirty square metres), or, in the case of garages or huts, if they are close to a dwellinghouse or a property boundary.

It is also possible to apply to the Secretary of State, and in some cases the local authority, for relaxation of or dispensation with the building regulations. This may be done in respect of a particular building, or, more unusually, in respect of a class of buildings. The effect of a relaxation is that the application of particular building standards requirements is relaxed for the building or buildings, but there are still some requirements to be met. A dispensation simply dispenses with particular requirements for the building or buildings.[3]

Building control

Subject to the exceptions below, application must be made to the local authority for a building warrant before the commencement of any building operations. The term 'building operations' includes works of construction, demolition or change of use. In this context change of use means either a change in use of a building bringing it within the scope of the building regulations for the first time, or a change which will result in more onerous requirements of the regulations applying to the building. Certain types of work do not need a building warrant; these include: replacement of a fixture by another of the same general type (fixtures include windows, roof coverings and sanitary appliances), replacement of a window by another not of the same general type (eg replacement of single by double glazing), installation of gas or solid fuel central heating, and

1 SI 1990/2179.
2 Building Standards (Scotland) Regulations 1990, Sch 1.
3 Building (Scotland) Act 1959 ss4, 4A.

insulation, including cavity wall insulation.[1] It should be noted that although these works do not require a building warrant they must, when completed, meet any relevant requirements of the building regulations. One common type of situation is not covered by these exceptions, namely the conversion of attic space from storage space to accommodation; such work requires a building warrant.

If the authority is satisfied that the proposed works will comply with the building standards regulations they must grant the warrant. The works must then be completed in accordance with that warrant.[2]

Once the works are complete it is an offence to occupy the property unless a completion certificate or certificate of temporary occupation has been granted. A completion certificate will be granted if the works have been carried out in accordance with the building warrant.[3]

The local authority has enforcement powers in respect of buildings constructed without a building warrant or in breach of the terms of a warrant. Ultimately they can require the owner to undertake works to remedy the situation and if he does not do so they are empowered to do the work themselves and charge him.[4] Authorities also have power to require works to existing buildings to make them comply with the building standards regulations.[5]

In some cases where work has been undertaken in breach of the building control legislation the local authority will be prepared to issue what is sometimes described as a letter of comfort. This indicates that they will not take enforcement action in respect of the breach.

Finally, local authorities have the power to take action against dangerous buildings and to require the owners to take steps to remove the danger caused by the state of a building.[6]

4. LOCAL AUTHORITY HOUSING CONTROLS[7]

The Housing (Scotland) Act 1987 consolidated local authority powers and responsibilities in relation to housing. Most of it is therefore concerned with the public sector, but it also brings together most

1 Building Standards (Scotland) Regulations 1990, Sch 2.
2 Building (Scotland) Act 1959, s6.
3 Ibid, s9.
4 Ibid, s10.
5 Ibid, s11.
6 Building (Scotland) Act (1959), s13.
7 *McDonald* paras 19–44 to 19–60; F McManus *Environmental Health Law in Scotland* ch 11; C Himsworth *Public Sector Housing Law in Scotland* (3rd edn (1989)) chs 11, 12.

of the powers that local authorities have to take action against houses in the private sector.

The nature of the action that can be taken depends on whether or not the house falls below the tolerable standard. For this to be the case the house must fail to meet one or more of a series of criteria. These include the house being substantially free from damp, having a water closet for the exclusive use of the occupants of the house and having an adequate supply of hot and cold water.[1]

If a house is below the tolerable standard the authority has a number of options. If the house is part of a larger building (eg in a tenement) they can serve a closing order. The effect of this is that the property can no longer be used for human habitation.[2] Alternatively they can serve a demolition order where the whole building is below the standard. This requires demolition of the property.[3] In both cases the owners have a right of appeal and may also seek suspension orders, suspending the operation of the closing or demolition order for a period. The normal reason for granting a suspension order is to allow the owner to bring the property up to the tolerable standard.[4] More positively an improvement order can be served on a sub-tolerable house which requires its improvement. There is a right of appeal to the sheriff against this, and if the owner does not comply with the order the authority may, in order to carry out the works themselves, acquire the house by agreement or compulsorily.[5]

Where an authority is faced with an area of housing which falls below the tolerable standard they may decide to declare a housing action area. This may require the improvement and/or demolition of housing in the area. Declaration of a housing action area gives an authority considerable compulsory purchase powers.[6]

In the case of a house not falling below the tolerable standard a repairs notice can be served if it is in a state of serious disrepair. This notice requires specified repairs to be made to the property.[7] Where the disrepair is not serious the authority has power under the Civic Government (Scotland) Act 1982 to require repairs to be carried out.[8] In the event of failure to act by the owners the

1 Housing (Scotland) Act 1987, s86.
2 Ibid, s114.
3 Ibid, s115.
4 Ibid, s117.
5 Ibid, s88.
6 Ibid, ss89–104; see also ch 18 on compulsory purchase generally.
7 Ibid, s108.
8 Civic Government (Scotland) Act 1982, s87.

authority is empowered, in both cases, to carry out the necessary work and charge the owner.

There are two further points which should be noted in relation to repairs notices and notices under the Civic Government (Scotland) Act 1982. Firstly, there is a right of appeal to the sheriff. Secondly, in cases where the authority carry out the work and charge the owners, the owners who are charged and responsible for payment are those at the time the demand is made, not those at the time the notice was served or the work carried out.[1]

The counterpoint of the enforcement powers of local authorities is the grant system which they administer and which makes grants available for repairs to and improvement of properties.[2]

5. OTHER STATUTORY CONTROLS

There is a wide variety of other statutory provisions which affect, directly or indirectly, heritable property or the uses which are made of it. Examples include the Control of Pollution Act 1974 relating to noise; Sewerage (Scotland) Act 1968 dealing with the maintenance of drains and sewers and the control of discharges into them; Fire Precautions Act 1971 requiring certain premises to have specified means of fire escape, fire certificates etc; Health and Safety at Work Act 1974; Offices, Shops and Railway Premises Act 1963; Factories Act 1961; and the Weeds Act 1959.

In addition there are a number of statutes which require the licensing of properties for certain uses. Examples are the sale of alcohol,[3] residential and nursing homes,[4] amusement arcades,[5] and the provisions of the Civic Government (Scotland) Act 1982 which allow local authorities to introduce schemes for the licensing of, for example, sex shops[6] and places of public entertainment.[7]

---

1 *Howard v Hamilton District Council* 1985 SLT (Sh Ct) 42; *Purves v City of Edinburgh District Council* 1987 SLT 366.
2 Housing (Scotland) Act 1987, Pt XIII; see C Himsworth *Public Sector Housing Law in Scotland* (3rd edn) ch 12 for details.
3 Licensing (Scotland) Act 1976.
4 Social Work (Scotland) Act 1968 (as amended by the Registered Establishments (Scotland) Act 1987); Nursing Homes Registration (Scotland) Act 1938.
5 Lotteries and Amusements Act 1976.
6 Section 45 and Sch 2.
7 Section 41.

13. Pre-contract procedures

1. INTRODUCTION

The main theme of this part of the book will be the legal procedures involved in the transfer of ownership of heritable property. Such procedures will normally be the concern of the solicitors acting respectively for the purchaser and seller, and they begin when a formal offer is made with a view to concluding missives. However, this is the culmination of an earlier process during which the property has been put on the market, negotiations have taken place with prospective purchasers, surveys of the property may have been instructed, and (in some cases) competing offers have been received by the seller. These preliminary procedures may be dealt with by a solicitor or surveyor or (particularly in the case of residential property) by a professional estate agent, who need in fact have no professional qualification at all. There is much recent law on these matters, in particular the legislation relating to estate agency and misdescription of property, and a number of cases relating to the legal liability of surveyors. It will therefore be useful to include a brief coverage of these subjects.

2. ESTATE AGENTS ACT 1979

The need for legislation in the area of estate agency was felt for a very long time before anything actually materialised on the statute book. One of the main perceived difficulties was the bureaucratic implications of introducing a comprehensive system for registration of estate agents. The Estate Agents Act 1979 got round this by introducing a system of negative licensing; this meant that there was no need for estate agents, in order to practise, to be registered or professionally qualified in any way. However, bad estate agents could be weeded out by a system of blacklisting which could be triggered off by a number of specified offences.

The 1979 Act itself barely made the statute book, having been passed on the very last day before Parliament was dissolved prior to the general election in that year. This haste in pushing it through had at least two fairly profound effects.

The first of these related to the fact that the proposals (and this was agreed by both parties in the House of Commons) were originally thought of as a consumer measure, which meant that they were intended only to apply to residential estate agency. However, a late House of Lords amendment slipped through unnoticed, making the Act apply to **all** estate agency, ie to those (mainly surveyors) acting in the acquisition or disposal of commercial and industrial property also.

The other (possible) consequence of haste was that the Act consisted mainly of a framework, with many of the offences that could lead to the blacklisting of an estate agent being left to be spelled out by the government in future delegated legislation. With one major exception (the accounts regulations) little of that delegated legislation materialised for more than a decade, leaving the Act substantially toothless; only in 1991 was much of the necessary dentistry completed by a series of regulations empowered by the Act;[1] These followed upon a report by the Director General of Fair Trading (the official entrusted with enforcement of the Act) based on his experience of the Act's operation and wide consultation of various interested bodies.

Scope of the Act

Work that could be described as estate agency is regularly undertaken by persons in a variety of professional categories, and so the Act does not attempt a definition of an estate agent; instead it defines estate agency itself, and applies to all persons (subject to certain stated exceptions) involved in that type of work. The definition of estate agency is a wide and complex one, but in essence it comprises all work involving the disposal or acquisition of an interest in land, provided that the transaction is carried on in the course of a business.[2] In Scotland, an interest in land means one in respect of which a title can be recorded in the Register of Sasines or registered in the Land Register;[3] the main transactions included, therefore, are sales of heritable property and leases of more than twenty years.

---

1 The Estate Agents (Specified Offences) (No 2) Order 1991, SI 1991/1091; The Estate Agents (Undesirable Practices) Order 1991, SI 1991/1032; The Estate Agents (Provision of Information) Regulations 1991, SI 1991/859.
2 Estate Agents Act 1979, s1(1).
3 Ibid, s2(1)(c).

As noted above, the Act applies to transactions involving all types of heritable property, ie commercial and industrial as well as residential property.

Excluded categories.   Four of these relate to specific functions, often carried out by people who engage in estate agency work, which are specifically excluded from the application of the Act; these are planning applications, surveys and valuations (unless incidental to other estate agency work), credit brokerage and insurance brokerage. The second of these means (for example) that a surveyor carrying out a survey on behalf of a building society would not thereby be affected by the Act.[1]

The remaining four exclusions refer to specific categories of person whose activities might otherwise be caught up (perhaps only technically) within the definition of estate agency work; these are solicitors, publishers of advertisements (eg newspapers advertising properties for sale), receivers of mortgage interest (eg the creditor under a standard security exercising his power of sale) and employees of estate agents.

Perhaps the most controversial of these is the exclusion of solicitors from the Act's application. This is partly an acknowledgement that solicitors, unlike unqualified estate agents, have their own professional body in the form of the Law Society to regulate their activities; more probably it reflects the fact that English solicitors do not generally become involved in estate agency work (ignoring the fact, of course, that their Scottish counterparts frequently **do** become involved in such work.) In any case, surveyors (to whom the Act **does** apply) are also regulated by a professional body in the form of the Royal Institution of Chartered Surveyors.

Operation of the Act

As stated above, the Estate Agents Act imposes no requirement for estate agents to be registered or licensed in any way. A negative approach is adopted instead, whereby anyone can operate as an estate agent unless he has been declared by the Director General of Fair Trading to be unfit to practise. The Act, together with the regulations made under it, imposes a number of duties upon estate agents, as well as stating a number of business practices to be undesirable. Breach of any of these duties, or involvement in a prohibited practice, will consititute a 'trigger offence', entitling the Director General

---

1 But see pt 4 below with regard to their common law liability.

to act against the agent concerned. Such action could consist of a complete prohibition against practising estate agency at all, or could take the form of a partial ban prohibiting certain types of activity only, eg handling clients' money. The Director General also has power to issue a warning order, which may be followed up later, if necessary, by a ban or partial ban.

Appeals against an order by the Director General of Fair Trading may be made to the Secretary of State and thereafter (on points of law only) to the courts. An estate agent who is the subject of an order may, at a later date, apply to the Director General to have it revoked. The Director General must keep a register of orders under the Act, which is open to the public.

The Director General has wide powers of investigation allowing him to enter business premises and seize books and documents if he has reasonable cause to suspect that an offence has been committed under the Act. He may also require any other person to furnish information or produce documents.

Trigger offences

A trigger offence by an estate agent is one which gives the Director General of Fair Trading the right to make a warning order, or impose a complete ban on an estate agent from practising. Broadly speaking, trigger offences fall into two categories, the first being the commission of one of a number of criminal offences (including a number of statutory offences listed in regulations), or the engaging in an activity which is prescribed by regulations as an undesirable practice. A person who has been declared bankrupt is also prohibited from practising. Secondly, a number of definite duties are imposed upon estate agents in connection with the carrying out of their work, and breach of any of these duties is also a ground for a warning or a bar.

Prohibited offences: criminal convictions.   An estate agent may be the subject of a warning or a bar if he has been convicted of an offence involving fraud or other dishonesty, or violence.[1] The same applies to offences under a number of specified statutes including the Company Directors Disqualification Act 1986, the Consumer Credit Act 1974, the Consumer Protection Act 1987, the Data Protection Act 1984, the Financial Services Act 1986 and the Trade

---

1   Estate Agents Act 1979, s3(1)(a)(i).

Descriptions Act 1968.[1] The offences include specified unlawful acts by company directors and many types of misrepresentation and other forms of misleading conduct.

Undesirable practices.   An estate agent may also be barred for engaging in any one of a number of undesirable practices.[2] These fall into three categories:

(1)   Failure to disclose a personal interest in writing. This is dealt with below in relation to duties of estate agents.

(2)   Practices relating to the arrangement and performance of services by the estate agent. These relate to situations where the estate agent provides certain financial or other services for a prospective purchaser (eg the obtaining of mortgage facilities). This is a common situation, but of course it could create a potential conflict of interest between the prospective purchaser and the seller to whom the estate agent's main duty lies. In such cases, the estate agent is prohibited from discriminating against a prospective purchaser on the ground that he will not be making use of their services. Also, when an offer has been received, the seller must be sent in writing before missives have been concluded an accurate list of any services by the estate agent which the person making the offer may be paying for.

(3)   Other matters. These include misrepresentation by the estate agent about the existence or details of any offer, or as to the existence or status of any prospective purchaser. The estate agent also has a duty to forward to his client promptly and in writing details of any offers received from potential purchasers; this may be partially contracted out of if the seller agrees in writing (eg in the contract with the estate agent) that he does not want to receive details of certain categories of offer (eg offers under a certain amount).

Duties of estate agents[3]

Failure by an estate agent in any of these statutory duties may result in a warning order or a bar by the Director General of Fair Trading.

---

1   See the Estate Agents (Specified Offences) (No 2) Order 1991, SI 1991/ 1091 for a full list of the statutes and offences involved.
2   The Estate Agents (Undesirable Practices) (No 2) Order 1991, SI 1991/1032.
3   Estate Agents Act 1979, s18; the Estate Agents (Provision of Information) Regulations 1991 SI 1991/859.

Information to Clients.   As soon as practicable after the estate agent and client enter into communication, and before they are legally committed, the estate agent must provide certain information in writing to the client. This includes full details of the circumstances, particulars and amount of any payment to be made by the client; if this is not complied with and the agent sues for payment, the court has power to reduce the amount payable or dismiss the agent's claim altogether. He must also disclose details of any services offered to prospective purchasers (whether provided by him or another person) from which he would receive financial benefit. Finally, if the estate agent uses certain standard terms in relation to the transaction, the contract between agent and client must include, in a prominent position, an explanation of these terms using the wording prescribed in the regulations. The terms referred to are 'sole selling rights', 'sole agency' and 'ready, willing and able purchaser', or any other terms that have the same meaning; broadly speaking, the meaning assigned by the regulations to these expressions entitles the estate agent to payment when the property is sold, even if the purchaser was found by the seller himself or another agent. He is also entitled to payment for a sale taking place after the contract between him and the seller has ended, if the purchaser was originally found by him. And if he introduces a purchaser, the estate agent must be paid even if the sale does not go ahead.

Disclosure of personal interest[1].   An estate agent is required to declare in writing a personal interest in respect of any property of which he is attempting to secure the disposal or acquisition. 'Personal interest' is defined to include the interest of an associate (who could be either a business associate or a relative) and also the interest of an employer or employee. In addition, an estate agent may not take a deposit in connection with any property in which he or an associate has an interest.

Pre-contract deposits[2].   This refers to the English practice whereby a pre-contract deposit or 'earnest money' is paid to an estate agent during the negotiations for a sale of land. The Act regulates this practice in England, but totally prohibits it in Scotland, where it has never operated in the past.

---

1 Estate Agents Act 1979, s21; the Estate Agents (Undesirable Practices)(No 2) Order 1991, SI 1991/1032 Article 2(a) and Sch 1.
2 Estate Agents Act 1979 ss19, 20.

Clients' Money[1].   As defined in the Act, this only includes deposits paid by a client to an estate agent in connection with the acquisition of an interest in land. An estate agent is prohibited from accepting clients' money at all unless he is insured by way of an authorised indemnity bond to cover fraud and dishonesty.[2] As well as possibly incurring a warning order or a ban, breach of this provision may lead to a criminal prosecution. The clients' money must be paid into a clients' account maintained by the estate agent for that purpose; also, the estate agent must account for interest on clients' money where the deposit exceeds £500 and the interest on it exceeds £10.[3]

3. PROPERTY MISDESCRIPTIONS ACT 1991

It was felt for a long time that the failure of the Trade Descriptions Act 1968 to apply to property was a serious omission; the purchase of a house, after all, is probably the single largest financial transaction regarding which a consumer would benefit from legal protection. This problem has now been addressed by the Property Misdescriptions Act 1991.

The Act makes it an offence to make a false or misleading statement about a prescribed matter in the course of an estate agency business or a property development business.[4] A 'prescribed matter' is defined as any matter relating to land which is specified in an order made by the Secretary of State.[5]

The Act only gives rise to criminal and not to civil liability; in particular it is stated that no contract shall be void or unenforcable only because an offence has been committed under the Act. Presumably, however, this does not affect the normal civil liability (including the effect on contractual validity) resulting under the common law from misrepresentation, whether innocent, fraudulent or negligent.

Estate agency business is given the same definition as in the Estate Agents Act (see above) with the important exception that the relevant activities of solicitors and employees of estate agents (which were specifically excluded from the former Act) **are** included within the scope of the present one.[6] Furthermore, it is specifically provided

---

1   Estate Agents Act 1979, ss12–17.
2   Ibid, s16.
3   Estate Agents (Accounts) Regulations 1981, SI 1981/1520.
4   Property Misdescriptions Act 1991 s1(1).
5   Ibid, s1(5)(d).
6   Ibid, s1(5)(e)

that an employee may be prosecuted under the Act even where his employer is not.[1]

However, there is a specific exclusion in respect of false or misleading statements made in the course of conveyancing work.[2] Also, it would appear that a statement made by the owner of the property in question, since he would not be acting as an estate agent, would normally incur no liability under the Act; however, if the owner was also a professional property developer, he could be caught up in the definition of property development business.

A statement is defined as being made in the course of a property development business only if it is made (a) in the course of a business concerned wholly or substantially with the development of land and (b) relates to the sale or lease of a building (or part of a building) constructed or renovated in the course of the business.

The Act also defines what is meant by a false or misleading statement.[3] 'False' means false to a material degree. A statement is misleading (even though the statement itself is not false) if a reasonable person could be expected to infer a false state of affairs from it; this may result either from something in the misleading statement, or an omission from it. A false or misleading statement may be made orally or in writing, or not even in words at all (eg by pictures or any other method of signifying meaning).[4]

A person prosecuted under the Act may be liable (on summary conviction) to a fine of up to the statutory maximum or (on conviction on indictment) to an unlimited fine.[5] It is a defence for him to show that he took all reasonable steps and exercised all due diligence to avoid committing the offence.[6]

An officer of a corporate body (eg a company director), or the partner of a firm may be liable under the Act.[7]

Anyone incurring liability under the Act becomes immune from prosecution either three years after the offence or a year after it is discovered by the prosecutor, whichever is the earlier.[8]

The enforcement authorities are the local weights and measures authorities.[9]

1   Ibid, s1(2)
2   Ibid, s1(1)
3   Ibid, s1(5)
4   Ibid, s1(5)(c)
5   Ibid, s1(3)
6   Ibid, s2
7   Ibid, s4
8   Ibid, s5
9   Ibid, s3 and Schedule.

4. SURVEYS

In virtually all cases a prospective purchaser will have had some form of survey carried out on the property before making an offer for it. This section considers the various types of survey available and the question of surveyor's liability for negligence.

(i) Types of survey

(a) Mortgage valuations. The most basic type of survey is the mortgage valuation, and this is the type which is most commonly encountered in relation to the purchase of houses. It is estimated that 90 per cent of purchasers rely on this type of survey.

The legal basis for this type of survey is the Building Societies Act 1986 which requires building societies, before they lend money on security of a property, to obtain a report on any factor likely to materially affect the value of the property[1]. This practice is also followed by other lenders.

The mortgage valuation involves a reasonably careful visual inspection of the property lasting about thirty minutes, which should draw attention to any obvious features likely to affect the value of the property. It will not usually involve lifting carpets, moving furniture or the inspection of roof and sub-floor spaces. However, where the valuer sees some signs of possible trouble he is required to 'follow the trail of suspicion' behind furniture and under carpets[2].

Some consternation was caused when it was suggested in *Martin v Bell-Ingram*[3] that the valuer carrying out this sort of survey had two duties. The first was to the lender to draw attention to any matter which might affect the value of the property; the second was to the prospective purchaser to draw to his attention any matter which might influence his decision as to whether or not to buy the property. Clearly this second responsibility is potentially far more extensive than the first. This potential, however, is limited by the fact that the court could not actually instance any matter which fell under the second responsibility which would not already be covered by the first.

---

1   Building Societies Act 1986, s13(1)(c).
2   *Roberts v J Hampson & Co* [1989] 2 All ER 504 at 510, quoted with approval in *Smith v Eric S Bush* [1989] 2 All ER 514 at 525.
3   1986 SLT 575.

(b) RICS housebuyers report and valuation.   This is a more extensive survey and the report is presented on a pre-printed form. The areas covered are clearly explained before the survey is undertaken, and the survey excludes certain things, eg sub-floor inspection and the testing of services. Most building societies and other lenders offer the option of this type of survey, but it is seldom taken up.

(c) Full structural survey.   This is the most extensive and expensive type of survey. The precise form of the survey will depend on the precise terms of engagement of the surveyor but could involve a full survey of all areas of the building and the testing of all services.

(d) Specialist reports.   It is not uncommon to find in a mortgage valuation a requirement that a specialist report on some matter be obtained, particularly in relation to older properties. A common example is a report by timber specialists on the state of the wood-work. These reports are generally obtained from specialist contractors.

(ii) Liability of surveyors

(a) To client.   Surveyors are liable to their client, with whom they have a contract, for any loss which he suffers as a result of the surveyor's negligence. This liability arises from an implied term in the contract that the surveyor will display the level of ability expected of a reasonably competent member of the profession.

(b) To third parties.   As noted above the commonest type of survey encountered in practice is the mortgage valuation. In these cases the report is instructed by the lending institution, and their client (the purchaser), who will be relying on the report and may suffer loss if it is inaccurate, therefore has no contractual relationship with the surveyor. However, it is now clear, following the general principles of the law of delict, that such clients have a claim against the surveyor for any loss suffered as a result of relying on a negligent report.[1]

The basic claim in such cases is for the difference between the lesser of the price paid or negligent valuation on the one hand, and the true value of the property on the other. In addition, claims

1   *Martin v Bell-Ingram* 1986 SLT 575; *Smith v Eric S Bush* [1989] 2 All ER 514.

may be made for distress and disturbance, additional legal and other expenses, and even physical injury.

(iii) Exclusion of liability

(a) *In contract.*   Any attempt to exclude liability for negligence is subject to the requirement imposed by the Unfair Contract Terms Act 1977 that it is fair and reasonable in the circumstances.[1]

(b) *Non-contractual.*   Where there is no contract between the surveyor and the person ultimately relying on his report, as in the case of mortgage valuations, liability can be excluded by a non-contractual disclaimer. Disclaimers of this sort were commonly found on mortgage application forms. Until 1 April 1991 they were completely effective in Scotland as there was no requirement, as exists in England and Wales, for such disclaimers to be fair and reasonable.[2]

Section 68 of the Law Reform (Miscellaneous Provisions) (Scotland) Act 1990 brought Scots law in line with that in England and Wales. On the basis of English decision, non-contractual disclaimers will not be fair and reasonable where the survey is of a house in the medium price range. However, where the property is particularly expensive, or where the transaction is a commercial one, the courts have indicated that they would take the opposite view.[3]

1   Section 16.
2   *Robbie v Graham & Sibbald* 1989 SLT 870.
3   *Smith v Eric S Bush* [1989] 2 All ER 514, at 532 c-e.

14. Registration of title[1]

In previous chapters we have made frequent mention of registration of title and the new Land Register for Scotland which is gradually replacing the Register of Sasines. In the chapters that follow, as we discuss in some detail the procedures for transfer of ownership, it will crop up even more frequently. It will probably help comprehension and place the subsequent detail in a proper context if we first give a brief overview of the new system.

THE LAND REGISTER FOR SCOTLAND

The system of recording deeds in the General Register of Sasines, as it has evolved over the centuries, is an efficient and practical one. Nevertheless, in the context of the sale of heritable property, the system has its limitations. As we saw in chapter 1,[2] in order to demonstrate his legal right to sell, a seller of heritable property has to exhibit a prescriptive progress of title deeds, as well as any other deeds which affect his ownership, such as deeds containing real conditions. It is therefore necessary for the purchaser's solicitor, in order to protect his client's interest, to examine and check the validity of each of these deeds. If the property changes hands again, the new purchaser's solicitor will have to repeat the same work.

Another difficulty arose from the fact that the descriptions in dispositions and feu charters of the property being sold were often vague or imprecise, in some cases referring in general terms to the name of a landowner's estate. In other cases exact boundaries might be specified, and/or a plan supplied, but, with the passage of years, identifying features, such as boundary walls or fences, roads, other buildings, or the names of adjoining proprietors might have changed

---

1 Land Registration (Scotland) Act 1979; see also McDonald *Conveyancing Manual* (4th edn, 1989) ch 36 and *The Registers of Scotland* (booklet by the Keeper, 1989).
2 See also ch 16 below.

sufficiently to make precise identification of the boundaries uncertain. Even modern titles could create problems, eg if a title was recorded in conformity with a builder's plan and it subsequently transpired that the building had not been erected on the exact site shown there.

It should be emphasised that none of this is a criticism of the registration of deeds as such. It merely shows the desirability of developing the system even further, so that not only individual deeds, but the succession of deeds that establish the title to a particular property can be registered as a unity.

This is the function of the Land Register for Scotland. It was created under the Land Registration (Scotland) Act 1979, in order to establish a system, not just of registration of title deeds, but of **registration of title**. As we will see in a moment, this system is designed to deal with the criticisms discussed above.

The process of registering the title to a particular piece of property involves a significant amount of work for the Keeper's staff. First of all, they have to do the same job as a purchaser's solicitor under the old system, ie examine a prescriptive progress of deeds to make sure that the owner has a good title. If they are satisfied that he has, the Keeper will grant an indemnity, ie he will give a state guarantee that the title is valid. This makes it unnecessary for the solicitors of future purchasers to undertake the time-consuming process of examining the title again, thereby shortening and simplifying the conveyancing procedure. After the Keeper has granted indemnity, it is possible that a third party may establish the grounds for a successful challenge of the title; in such a case the party may be entitled to compensation, but only in limited circumstances will the Keeper be required to prejudice the title of the current possessor by rectifying his title sheet (see below).

The process of simplification is further achieved during the registration process by the gathering together of all essential information from the title deeds into a single document. This is kept by the Keeper in the form of a computer record, called the title sheet, and a printout of the title sheet is issued to the owner in the form of a land certificate.[1] The land certificate comprises four main sections:

(1) **Property section.** This states briefly the property interest being registered, eg that of proprietor, or perhaps tenant. It also identifies the property very briefly by its address and a reference to the title plan (more of which below).

(2) **Proprietorship section.** This will give the name of the person

---

1 For a specimen land certificate see the Appendix.

whose interest is being recorded, the date of registration, the price and the date of entry.

(3) **Charges section.** This will specify any standard securities over the property, eg in favour of the building society that granted a loan over it. The creditor will be issued with a separate certificate, known as a charge certificate,[1] that will include a copy of the standard security and provide the necessary title document for his interest.

(4) **Burdens section.** This is the only section that normally extends to any length. In it is gathered together the conditions from all the deeds that were referred to for burdens.

Whenever the property is resold, the title sheet is updated and a fresh land certificate issued to the new owner. This prevents the land certificate from becoming cluttered up with out of date information, such as a list of past owners, or details of standard securities that have been paid off and discharged. Only the current information is shown, which means that all the necessary details relating to the title can continue to be contained in a single document.

The final great advantage of registration of title is that the description of the property is very much simplified. The Keeper maintains a series of Ordnance Survey master plans, and when a title is registered, the property is outlined on the appropriate plan and a copy included in the land certificate. The process of registration involves matching the description in the existing titles with the Ordnance Survey plan, but, once that has been done, the property can be identified in the deeds relating to future transactions simply by a plan reference number.

It will be seen that the process of first registration for even a single property involves much work by the keeper's staff, although in subsequent transactions the procedure is much simplified and the work greatly reduced. Nevertheless, before registration of title can be complete throughout Scotland, this process of first registration will have to be undertaken in respect of each separate property in the country. Obviously this will take some time. It is therefore being undertaken in a piecemeal fashion, one county at a time. (It will be remembered that the divisions of the General Register of Sasines correspond to the old Scottish counties). After a county becomes operational for registration, the title of each property there has to be registered on the first occasion the property is sold. So far only four counties have become operational for registration, namely Renfrew (which became operational on 6 April 1981), Dunbarton

---

1   For a specimen charge certificate see the Appendix.

(4 October, 1982), Lanark (3 January 1984) and Glasgow (30 September 1985).

As we saw, registration normally only happens when a property is being sold. At other times, the Keeper has the discretion to allow a voluntary registration at the request of the owner, although he is entitled to refuse. The Keeper also has the power to compel registration, whether or not the property is being sold. This would be appropriate, for example, if a majority of the titles in a particular county had been registered and it was desirable to register the remainder so that the division of the Register of Sasines for that county could be shut down and the transfer to the Land Register complete. So far, however, no counties have reached that stage and that particular power of the Keeper has not yet been exercised.

15. Voluntary transfer[1]

Ownership rights in heritable property can be transferred in three ways:

1. By voluntary transfer.
2. By compulsory transfer, eg following compulsory purchase[2] or bankruptcy.
3. By transmission to heirs on the death of the proprietor.

Here we will be concerned only with the first situation, that of voluntary transfer, and, in particular, the transfer of the *dominium utile* in a piece of land. Similar, though not identical, principles apply to the sale of superiorities and the *dominium plenum*.

Transfers of land can be effected by two main methods:

1. **Sale by private bargain.** Here sealed offers are submitted to the seller, or more usually his solicitor, who then accepts one of them. This form of sale involves three main stages:

(a) Conclusion of a contract for the sale and purchase of the property. Since this contract is made by the exchange of letters between purchaser and seller, or their solicitors, it is referred to as the missives stage. Once this contract is concluded the purchaser has a personal right to require a transfer of the property to him.[3]

(b) Delivery by the seller of a conveyance of the interest in the property in favour of the purchaser in exchange for payment of the price or other consideration. At this stage, as noted below, the purchaser still only has a personal right to the property.

(c) Completion of the purchaser's title to the property via the

---

1 Halliday *Conveyancing Law and Practice* (1986) ch 15; McDonald *Conveyancing Manual* (4th edn, 1989) ch 28; Sinclair *Handbook of Conveyancing Practice in Scotland* (2nd edn, 1990) chs 3, 18–20.
2 See ch 18.
3 See ch 1, pt 1.

process of infeftment. Once this is done the purchaser obtains a real right to the property.

2. **Sale by public auction.** Usually in Scotland this takes the specific form of a sale by public roup, though sales of this nature are comparatively rare. They are considered more fully in part 5 below.

1. THE MISSIVES STAGE

The initial stage of the purchase/sale of heritable property usually involves the making of an offer to purchase the property by the prospective purchaser, followed by an acceptance of that offer by the seller. There is nothing to prevent this being done the other way round, and having an offer to sell accepted by the purchaser. As well as containing an agreement to sell/purchase the property at an agreed price, the missives will also contain a number of terms and conditions relating to the agreement which are designed by the respective solicitors to safeguard their clients' interests. Once missives have been concluded (ie an offer has been accepted) a legally binding contract exists between seller and purchaser and either can be compelled to perform his part of the bargain by legal action.

Before discussing the specific contents of missives, it should first be noted that since missives are simply a form of contract three basic contractual requirements must be fulfilled:

1.   The parties must have contractual capacity. This means generally that they must be under no legal disability arising from insanity or age,[1] but also, more particularly, in relation to companies and trustees that they are acting within the scope of the powers conferred on them. For a fuller discussion of contractual capacity see chapter 1, part 3.

2.   The offer and acceptance must be in writing. This requirement arises from the general rule that all contracts relating to heritage must be in writing, which is fully discussed in chapter 1, part 3.

3.   There must be *consensus in idem*, ie the offer and acceptance must meet each other's terms. In most cases the offer takes the form of a lengthy document containing a large number of conditions. Unless prior negotiations have taken place it is unusual for the offer to meet with a simple acceptance; more

1   Age of Legal Capacity (Scotland) Act 1991.

usually the acceptance will seek to modify, qualify or remove some of these conditions and possibly add conditions in the interests of the seller. Such a qualified acceptance is legally regarded as a counter-offer which displaces the original offer and must be accepted by the prospective purchaser to conclude a contract. This process of counter-offer is often repeated several times before a final offer is accepted and a contract concluded.

As a result of this view that a qualified acceptance is a counter-offer it is not open to either party to withdraw qualifications they have imposed in a qualified acceptance and accept an earlier offer; the earlier offer simply no longer exists for acceptance.[1] There are, however, some unusual cases where there are effectively two offers open for acceptance and one of the parties can withdraw his offer and accept the other.[2] It is possible to withdraw an offer verbally as long as this is done before it is accepted.[3]

In addition to these general contractual requirements there are some more specific requirements to be fulfilled:

1. The parties and the subject matter (ie the property) must be sufficiently well described to allow them to be clearly identified.[4] This is usually done simply by reference to the postal address of the property, or in new houses by reference to the plot number. Where areas of land are involved in the transaction it is advisable to have a plan of the property attached and referred to in the missives. Where a flat is involved floor and position must be clearly stated.

2. The price or other consideration, or a procedure for arriving at the price or consideration, must be specified in the missives.[5] In most cases the consideration will be the payment of money, or, occasionally, the transfer of another piece of land, but, in accordance with the general law of contract in Scotland, it is possible to enter into a binding gratuitous contract for the transfer of heritage.

3. It used to be considered that it was essential to include in the missives a date of entry; that is, a date on which the price would be paid and entry to the property given. It now seems

---

1   *Rutterford Ltd v Allied Breweries Ltd* 1990 SLT 249.
2   *Findlater v Maan* 1990 SLT 465.
3   *McMillan v Caldwell* 1991 SLT 325 at 329 J–L.
4   *Grant v Peter G Gauld & Co* 1985 SLT 545.
5   *MacLeod's Executor v Barr's Trs* 1989 SLT 392.

clear that this is not required.[1] Prudence, of course, suggests
that a date of entry is included in missives to give certainty
as to when the transaction is likely to be concluded.

Standard conditions in missives[2]

A simple agreement containing details of the parties, property and
price is, of course, sufficient to constitute a binding contract for
the sale of heritage. Most missives, however, contain in addition
a large[3] (and seemingly growing) number of standard conditions
which vary according to the type of property concerned. These extra
conditions are added to make explicit or alter the common law
obligations of the parties, to provide protection for one or other
of the parties or to deal with a particular aspect of the transaction.
What follows is a review of the common standard conditions and
other conditions applicable to particular types of property.[4]

1. Vacant possession. Missives will normally require vacant
possession to be given on the date of entry. If this provision is
not included the seller's obligation is simply to give possession within
a reasonable time. If a property is being bought subject to a lease
or leases this would be mentioned here. In such cases there will
be no vacant possession of the property let, but the right to collect
rent will be transferred on the date of entry. In addition conditions
will be included dealing with the terms of the leases.

2. Payment of price and interest. At common law the position is
that in 'a contract for the sale of heritage, where it is stipulated
that the price is to be paid on a particular date, payment of the
price on the appointed date is not, in general, an essential condition
of the contract and failure to pay on that date does not entitle the
seller to rescind'.[5] All that is required is payment within a reasonable
time of the date of entry. The exception to this general rule is where

---

1 *Sloan's Dairies v Glasgow Corporation* 1976 SLT 147; *Gordon District Council
v Wimpey Homes Holdings Ltd* 1988 SLT 481.
2 *Halliday* paras 15-22 to 15-118 and style at 15-136; *McDonald* paras 28-31 to
28-65; *Sinclair* paras 3.15-3.33 and pp 193-197.
3 In comparison, see the style of missive at p 173 in the 3rd edn of Burns *Conveyancing
Practice* published in 1926.
4 More exhaustive treatment can be found in *Halliday* paras 15-22 to 15-148 and
McDonald ch 28.
5 *Rodger (Builders) Ltd v Fawdry* 1950 SLT 345 at 350 per Lord Sorn.

punctual payment is expressly provided for in the missives, and this is now done as a matter of course.

It is now also common practice to include a condition requiring the payment of interest if payment of the price is not made on the date of entry. This alters the common law rule that interest is only payable if the purchaser takes entry without paying the price.[1] The rate of interest is usually fixed by reference to the prevailing mortgage or bank base rate, and the condition will normally not apply where the failure to pay arises as a result of the fault of the seller; for example if the seller cannot provide a marketable title on the date of entry.[2]

3. Marketable title and clear searches. This condition elucidates the seller's common law obligation to produce a marketable title to the property and will be considered more fully when that obligation is considered in chapter 16. The condition may add to the common law obligation, and the precise terms will depend on whether the transaction will result in recording of the title in the Register of Sasines or registration of the title in the Land Register and, in the latter case, on whether it is a first registration or registration of a property already registered there.

4. Feuduty. In the case of an allocated feuduty this condition provides either that the feuduty has been redeemed or that it will be redeemed on sale and suitable evidence exhibited. Where the property is affected by a *cumulo* feuduty the amount will be mentioned and provision made for apportionment at the date of entry. A material difference between the feuduty stated in the missives and the actual feuduty is grounds for rescission by the purchaser.[3]

5. Rates and local taxes. This condition will specify the rateable value of the property and provide for apportionment of rates around the date of entry. Such a condition is, of course, now only applicable to non-domestic properties, but similar provision may be necessary for domestic properties with the introduction of the Council Tax.

6. Minerals. It is normal to make some mention of minerals, if only to confirm that there are no mineral rights attaching to the property. This is because, as explained in chapter 4, it is assumed

1 *Tiffney v Bachurzewski* 1985 SLT 165.
2 *Bowie v Semple's Exrs* 1978 SLT 9; see also ch 14.
3 *Bremner v Dick* 1911 SLT 59.

that a purchaser buying a piece of land purchases it *a coelo usque ad centrum*.[1] Therefore, if minerals are found to be excluded and this is not made known to the purchaser prior to the agreement to purchase he will be entitled to withdraw from the contract of purchase on the grounds that he will not get all that he agreed to buy. This condition may also contain provisions as to rights of entry to the surface, support, and compensation, to guard against the rare situations where the owner of minerals is entitled to enter the surface to work them or where compensation for damage to the surface is excluded. These provisions will be of greater significance when ownership of the surface and minerals are being separated for the first time.

7. Moveables. It is not necessary to contract in writing for the purchase of moveables, but it is sometimes advisable to do so to avoid any disputes and doubt as to what is being transferred, eg the sort of disputes referred to in chapter 6 as to whether or not an item is a fixture and is, therefore, transferred with the land. In some cases, for example where stock is being purchased along with a business, a list of moveable property being purchased will be particularly important, as will a statement of the basis for valuing the stock if the value is not already agreed.

8. Implementation of notices. This condition is designed to protect the purchaser against the existence and effect of notices served by local authorities.

Local authorities have the power under a variety of statutory provisions to serve notices requiring action by property owners, some of the most common being notices requiring repairs to be carried out, particularly affecting tenement properties.[2] The significance of such notices is twofold. First, the purchaser will be bound by them in so far as they have not been complied with. Secondly, if, as is common, repair works have been undertaken by the local authority following service of a notice on the property owner requiring repairs, the person liable to pay for these works is the owner at the time the demand is made, not the owner at the time the notice was served. The purchaser might, therefore, find himself having to pay for repairs carried out when the property was owned by the seller.[3]

In order to ensure that there are no such notices the purchaser

---

1 Literally, this means from the heavens to the centre (of the earth).
2 For example, under s108 of the Housing (Scotland) Act 1987.
3 *Howard v Hamilton District Council* 1985 SLT (Sh Ct) 42; *Purves v City of Edinburgh District Council* 1987 SLT 366.

will normally require the seller to produce a Property Enquiry Certificate prepared by the relevant local authority. This Certificate will also contain information about any planning or other proposals likely to adversely affect the property.

9. Implementation of title conditions. Because of the nature of feudal tenure the purchaser as vassal may be held liable for failures to comply with real conditions affecting the property which occurred prior to his ownership of the property. In order to guard against this a condition in the missives will normally seek the sellers warranty that all such real conditions have been complied with, or even a certificate from the superior to that effect.

The other side of the coin is that after the purchaser takes entry to the property the seller remains liable to the superior for performance of all of the obligations of the feu until the superior is served with a notice of change of ownership.[1] This is not often done in practice, partly due to the difficulty, following the progressive redemption of feuduties, of identifying the superior, but, as a matter of strict law, it is still necessary.

10. Damage to/destruction of property. Following the decision in *Sloans Dairies v Glasgow Corporation*[2] it is clear that the risk of damage to or destruction of the property not caused by the seller passes to the purchaser immediately on conclusion of the missives, even although the purchaser has no control over the premises until after the date of entry. The standard condition disapplies this rule of law and provides that the risk of accidental damage or destruction remains with the seller until the date of entry. Usually this will not impose too substantial a burden on the seller as he will have the property insured anyway, since a requirement to insure is one of the standard conditions affecting heritable securities.[3] In addition, many solicitors operate block policies which provide cover for their purchasing clients between conclusion of missives and date of entry.

The Scottish Law Commission has made proposals for changes in the law in this area. The effect of these proposals, if implemented, would be that risk of damage would pass on what was the effective date of entry.[4]

It is also normal to include, either in this condition or as a separate

1 Conveyancing (Scotland) Act 1874, s4.
2 1976 SLT 147.
3 See ch 11, pt 3.
4 *Report on the Passing of Risk in Contracts for the Sale of Heritable Property* HC 628 1989–90.

condition, an obligation for the seller to maintain the property in substantially the same condition between the date of the missives and the date of entry.

11. Repairs. This condition will simply repeat the common law rule that repairs instructed by the seller must be paid for by the seller.

12. Maintenance of roads and sewers. For older properties this condition will specify that the roads, footpaths and sewers *ex adverso* (ie opposite) the property have been taken over and are maintained by the local authority. In urban areas this will normally be the case and means that the cost of repair will be borne by the local authority.

In uncompleted houses where there is accompanying road building the condition should ensure that a sufficient guarantee has been lodged with the local authority to ensure completion of the roads to the standard required by the local authority. Lodging of such a guarantee is a statutory requirement and once the roads have been completed to the required standard they must be taken over by the authority.[1]

If the local authority has not assumed responsibility for maintenance this could result in considerable expense for the purchaser.

13. Alterations to the property. Any major and some minor alterations to a property will require some form of consent. The main consents likely to be required are planning consent, building warrant and completion certificate,[2] and superior's consent. The importance of these is that if work is done without consent there is the possibility of enforcement action being taken against the owner of the property for the time being. There are limits on the power of authorities to take action under the planning legislation. These include a four year limitation on action against unauthorised building operations and an immunity from enforcement for material changes of use of property.[3] There is no such limitation on action under the Building (Scotland) Acts 1959 and 1970 against building works carried out without a building warrant or in breach of the terms of such a warrant, though in some cases local authorities will grant

1 Roads (Scotland) Act 1984, s16(2).
2 See ch 12, pts 2 and 3.
3 See ch 12, pt 2.

letters of comfort indicating that they will not take any action in respect of the breach.

In the case of works undertaken without the superior's consent there is the possibility of action being taken by the superior, with the ultimate possibility of his irritating the feu. In practice, however, the superior is usually willing, for a small fee, to grant a retrospective consent.

To protect the purchaser against the possibility of such action it is usual to include a condition requiring exhibition of any relevant consents and certificates, preferably before the date of entry. If breach of this condition comes to light after the date of entry it is very unlikely that the purchaser would be able to rely on it to raise an action against the seller. This last point will be considered more fully in the section below on non-supersession clauses.

Problems in this area are common in practice. It is almost universal practice for homeowners to alter their property with complete disregard for the need to obtain local authority or other consents.[1] In light of this it may be tempting for the purchaser's solicitor not to insist on production of the relevant certificates and consents; this, however, could lead to problems when the purchaser tries to sell the property, and may also lead to problems with the fabric of a building as a result of failure to comply with statutory requirements. In such a situation the purchaser may have no recourse against the seller.[2]

14. Matrimonial Homes (Family Protection) (Scotland) Act 1981. This legislation is considered more fully above in chapter 10, part 8. The relevant point here is that, subject to the exceptions noted below, a non-entitled spouse has an occupancy right preferable to the rights of a purchaser purchasing from the entitled spouse. A purchaser is only protected against an occupancy right if he has acted in good faith and has had produced to him either: (1) an affidavit by the seller to the effect that the property is not a matrimonial home to which a spouse has occupancy rights; or (2) a form of consent to the sale of the property; or (3) a renunciation of occupancy rights. The form of consent or renunciation must bear to have been properly made or given by the non-entitled spouse.[3] Where the non-entitled spouse is unable or, without reasonable cause,

---

1 See D A Johnstone 'Planning and Building Control Warranties' (1989) 34 JLSS 206 for some of the problems that can arise.
2 As happened in *Winston v Patrick* 1981 SLT 41; see also the sections on non-supersession clauses and NHBC Insurance below.
3 Matrimonial Homes (Family Protection) (Scotland) Act 1981, s6(3)(e).

unprepared to give consent, an application may be made to court for an order dispensing with her consent.[1] There is authority for the view that there must be a specific offer for the property before such an application can be made.[2] In other words, the entitled spouse cannot apply for what is effectively a blanket permission to sell on any terms if the non-entitled spouse is unwilling to consent.

Missives will therefore contain a condition requiring production of one of the documents referred to in the last paragraph to ensure that the purchaser is protected against possible occupancy rights. Formerly in the case of a sale this had to be done before the delivery of the conveyance of the property to the purchaser; that restriction no longer applies.[3]

15. Condition of services.   Here provision is made that any central heating or other services (for example, lifts or swimming pools) will be in good working order at the date of entry. It is desirable to include this requirement as to the date of entry otherwise the condition may simply be regarded as a statement of the state of affairs at the date of the missives. Such conditions also commonly include a time limit within which notification of any defects must be made and should, for reasons examined below, include an explicit undertaking by the seller to pay for repair works.[4]

16. Specialist treatment.   This condition will simply require that any guarantees obtained by the seller in relation to any specialist work carried out on the property will be transferred to the purchaser. The most common example relates to treatment of woodwork for rot.

17. Closing date.   To avoid the offer lying open for an unlimited period it is usual to specify a closing date and time for acceptance of the offer. It is common in practice for the actual acceptance to arrive after this time and the offeror to waive the condition. It does, however, prevent the prospective purchaser from being in the position of having an offer lying open for an unspecified period of time with the possibility of it still being accepted. In order to avoid doubt the condition will normally provide for the acceptance to be received in the solicitor's hands by a certain time.

1   Matrimonial Homes (Family Protection) (Scotland) Act 1981, s7.
2   *Fyfe v Fyfe* 1987 SLT (Sh Ct) 38.
3   Ibid, s6(3)(e) (as amended by Law Reform (Miscellaneous Provisions) (Scotland) Act 1990, s74 and Sch 8).
4   *Jamieson v Stewart* 1989 SLT (Sh Ct) 13; *Taylor v McLeod* 1990 SLT 194.

18. Non-supersession clause.[1]   This clause provides for the missives to continue in effect even after the disposition has been delivered. The clause may take a variety of forms. It may provide that all of the missive conditions are to remain in force with no limit of time, apart from that imposed by prescription; it may be time-limited, with the conditions stated to remain in force for a specified period after delivery of the disposition;[2] finally, it may provide that only certain of the conditions are to remain in force, with or without limit of time. The clause may also provide for the non-supersession condition to be repeated in the disposition, either as a matter of course or at the option of the purchaser.

Prior to 1981, the view of the legal profession was that conditions in missives which were not directly covered in the disposition would continue in effect notwithstanding the delivery of the disposition. This assumption was challenged by the case of *Winston v Patrick*.[3] In this case the Inner House is generally regarded as having taken the view that conditions in missives would only survive the delivery of the disposition in three circumstances:

(a)   where the obligation contained in the condition was collateral to the principal obligation contained in the missives, ie the obligation to convey the heritage;
(b)   where the condition related to moveables;
(c)   'where there was an agreement in writing either in the missives or in a separate document or in the disposition itself that a personal obligation would subsist and remain in force even if it was not included in the terms of the disposition.'[4]

The condition under dispute in *Winston* was 'that the seller warrants that all statutory and local authority requirements in connection with ... additions, extensions and alterations [to the property] have been fulfilled'. In fact they had not, which led to problems with a kitchen extension and brought about the court action. It was held that the condition was simply a statement of the state of affairs at the time of the missives and therefore not a collateral obligation. It therefore could not be founded on after the disposition

1   This area of law has been productive of a number of articles. Of these K G C Reid 'Prior Communings and Conveyancing Practice' (1981) 26 JLSS 414 gives an overview of the legal background, and D J Cusine '*Winston v Patrick* and Their Heirs and Assignees' (1988) 33 JLSS 102 with a response by Reid is concerned with the practical consequences of developments in the law.
2   For example, three months; *Pena v Ray* 1987 SLT 609.
3   1981 SLT 41.
4   1981 SLT at 49.

had been delivered. Lord Wheatley further seemed to suggest that since the condition did not impose a personal or collateral obligation on the seller it could not be extended even by a separate agreement to continue the condition in force.[1]

The decision in *Winston* gave rise to the practice of including non-supersession clauses in missives, and, following the decision in *Finlayson v McRobb*,[2] in the disposition itself.[3] Subsequent litigation has left the legal position as regards the effectiveness of non-supersession clauses in missives alone rather unclear, but on the basis of the cases decided so far the following propositions can be advanced:

(a) Regardless of the existence of a non-supersession clause a collateral obligation will always continue in existence after the granting of the disposition. Examples of such collateral obligations include an obligation to complete the property[4] or complete the renovation of the property[5] and a provision that the purchasers would be relieved of all responsibility for works carried out under a repairs notice.[6]

There is greater doubt, however, surrounding another common clause guaranteeing that central heating and other systems will be in good working order at the date of entry. It seems clear that if such a condition is coupled with an obligation undertaken by the seller to compensate the purchaser for the cost of any necessary repairs that a collateral obligation is created.[7] Where no such additional obligation is undertaken by the seller the position is less clear and there are conflicting sheriff court decisions.[8] The safest course, in practice, would therefore seem to be to include such an additional undertaking by the seller.

(b) It now seems quite clear that conditions relating to compliance with planning and other requirements similar to that in *Winston*

---

1 1981 SLT at 49, a view given some support in *Greaves v Abercromby* 1989 SCLR 11 at 15.
2 1987 SLT (Sh Ct) 150.
3 *Halliday* (para 15-118) suggests that a non-supersession clause should only be accepted in special circumstances.
4 *Hoey v Butler* 1975 SC 87; *Black v Gibson* 1991 GWD 15-938.
5 *Pena v Ray* 1987 SLT 609; *Hardwick v Gebbie* 1991 SLT 258.
6 *Central Govan Housing Association v R Maguire Cook & Co* 1988 SLT 386.
7 *Wood v Edwards* 1988 SLT (Sh Ct) 17; *Bourton v Claydon* 1990 SLT (Sh Ct) 7; *Taylor v McLeod* 1990 SLT 194.
8 *Wood v Edwards* 1988 SLT (Sh Ct) 17; *Jamieson v Stewart* 1989 SLT (Sh Ct) 13 (no collateral obligation); *Jones v Heenan* 1988 SLT (Sh Ct) 53 (collateral obligation).

v Patrick are not to be regarded as collateral obligations which survive the granting of the disposition by the seller.[1] The reason for this is that the courts appear to take the view that such conditions when they are expressed as in *Winston v Patrick* or, as is also common, when they are prefaced by the words 'it is understood that', are essentially retrospective, and refer to the situation at the time of the missives and do not impose an obligation which the seller can implement at some time in the future. For this reason also the general view appears to be that such conditions cannot be continued by non-supersession clauses, wherever they appear.[2] Further it now seems clear that imposing an obligation on the seller to produce evidence of compliance will not be sufficient to convert the condition into one which is capable of continuing past the granting of the disposition.[3] For such conditions to continue and to be available to the purchaser after entry some form of undertaking by the seller to pay the costs of compliance, similar to that used in the case of warranties about services, would seem to be required. The other alternative, which will often not be practical, is for the purchaser's solicitor to refuse to settle the transaction until all of the evidence has been produced, and even this would be ineffective in the situation where the purchaser was unaware that any alterations requiring consent had taken place.[4]

(c)   There is disagreement about the effect of a non-supersession clause appearing solely in missives. A number of cases suggest that such a clause is effective;[5] others suggest that it is not and that to be effective it must be repeated in the disposition.[6] In addition one case seems to suggest both that the condition must be repeated in the disposition and that a condition in

1   *Winston v Patrick* 1981 SLT 41; *Wood v Edwards* 1988 SLT (Sh Ct)17; *Finlayson v McRobb* 1987 SLT (Sh Ct) 150; *Greaves v Abercromby* 1989 SCLR 11; *Porch v MacLeod* 1991 GWD 18-1108.
2   See the cases cited in the previous footnote. The only dissenting voice from this view is *Finlayson v McRobb*.
3   *Greaves v Abercromby* 1989 SCLR 11; *Porch v MacLeod* 1991 GWD 18-1108.
4   See 'The Warranty Lingers On' (1982) 27 JLSS 37 at 38.
5   *Pena v Ray* 1987 SLT 609 (by implication – a time limit on a non-supersession clause was found to be effective); *Fetherston v McDonald (No 2)* 1988 SLT (Sh Ct) 39; *Jones v Heenan* 1988 SLT (Sh Ct) 53 (*obiter*); *Jamieson v Stewart* 1989 SLT (Sh Ct) 13; *Taylor v McLeod* 1990 SLT 194.
6   *Finlayson v McRobb* 1987 SLT (Sh Ct) 150; *Wood v Edwards* 1988 SLT (Sh Ct) 17.

missives may be effective if it is limited as to time and/or limited as to the conditions which are to remain in force.[1]

Although the law remains unclear, with the Scottish Law Commission promising a discussion paper, a tentative suggestion can be made that the second group of cases really concerns conditions of a type which could not anyway be continued by an agreement in missives (or, indeed, any other document)[2] and that the first group really concerns collateral obligations which do not need a separate agreement to remain in force after granting of the disposition.

(d) It is not clear what sorts of obligations could be maintained in force by a separate agreement or reference in the disposition. In *Winston* the reference was to personal obligations and in the judgement the distinction between personal and collateral obligations was blurred. Collateral obligations, as we have already seen, continue in existence after the granting of the disposition without separate agreement, so are there any conditions which can be continued by agreement or incorporation in the disposition which would not continue anyway? There seems to be some doubt about this, shared by the courts.[3]

(e) Any agreement in the missives regarding their remaining in force for a particular period may, regardless of whether or not it does continue conditions, have the effect of imposing a time limit on the continuation of any conditions which do endure because they are collateral obligations.[4] Thus the effect of this is to reduce the period during which the purchaser can rely on the obligation and raise an action for enforcement from the twenty years it would otherwise be.[5]

19. Actio quanti minoris.   At common law the *actio quanti minoris* is not available to purchasers of heritable property in case of breach of contract by the seller. This form of action allows a purchaser to retain defective property and claim damages measured by reference to the reduction in the value of the property caused by the seller's

---

1 *Greaves v Abercromby* 1989 SCLR 11 at 15.
2 See K G C Reid's note to *Greaves v Abercromby* 1989 SCLR at 17.
3 *Greaves v Abercromby* 1989 SCLR 11 at 14–15 and Reid's note; *Taylor v McLeod* 1990 SLT (Sh Ct) 194 at 199 B–C.
4 *Pena v Ray* 1987 SLT 609.
5 K G C Reid 'Five Years On: Living with *Winston v Patrick*' (1986) 31 JLSS 316 at 316–7; see also his comment in 'The Law of the Tenement' (1990) 35 JLSS 368 at 370.

breach of contract. There are, however, a number of exceptions to this rule, including cases where there is a collateral obligation and cases where there is an express agreement that this remedy will be available. Such an express provision is now common in missives.

The benefits of such a provision are, however, limited. If the claim concerns breach of a collateral obligation then that collateral obligation is a separate agreement from the agreement regarding conveyance of the property and the action should be based on breach of this separate agreement, not on the provision in missives.[1] Damages claimed in such an action would not be restricted to the difference in value, as they would be under the *actio quanti minoris*, but could be for the whole cost of rectifying the position caused by the seller's breach of contract. Secondly, *McDonald* suggests[2] that non-collateral obligations can be kept alive by a non-supersession clause inserted both in the missives and in the disposition and 'by including the additional *quanti minoris* clause, the purchaser can still retain the subjects and claim damages for breach of these obligations.' However if, as suggested above, it is not clear what non-collateral obligations might survive the disposition, even with appropriate non-supersession provisions, this benefit is illusory.

Other conditions

1. NHBC Insurance/Buildmark. Most new houses will be built by builders who participate in the schemes run by the National House Building Council, an organisation to which most builders belong, which provides insurance against certain defects affecting the property. The current scheme is Buildmark, introduced in 1988. This insurance lasts for ten years, and any purchase of a property less than ten years old should include a condition that the property is covered by this type of insurance, and for the transfer of the insurance to the purchaser.[3]

The existence of this insurance cover is particularly important as otherwise the only recourse the owner will have is against the builder if a defect in construction causes death or personal injuries, but not for the cost of any repair work;[4] otherwise they may have

---

1 See *McDonald* para 28-24.
2 Para 28-64.
3 For further details of the Buildmark scheme see D Calder 'Buildmark' (1990) 35 JLSS 151; see also 'NHBC Half Century' by the same author (1987) 32 JLSS 301.
4 *Murphy v Brentwood District Council* [1990] 2 All ER 908.

a claim against the surveyor who surveyed the property prior to purchase.[1]

2. *Tenement properties.* Offers to purchase flats in tenemental properties should include a condition to the effect that the costs of repair and maintenance are equally shared. The point of this condition is to confirm that, as is almost universal practice, the common law of the tenement has been varied by express provision in the titles to the property.[2] Offers should also provide for apportionment of common charges and *cumulo* feuduty at the date of entry.

3. *Apportionment of price.* It is common to apportion the price paid between the heritage and any moveables also being purchased. In some cases this apportionment will reflect the fact that moveables of substantial value are being purchased, in others the apportionment will be made to reduce the amount of stamp duty payable. This is particularly relevant when the price paid is only slightly over the threshold for paying stamp duty which is currently £30,000. There must be a real basis for any apportionment.

4. *Development.* In cases where the purchaser intends to develop the property purchased, this development will normally require some consents to allow it to proceed, the principle ones being planning consent, superiors' consent and building warrant. In order to protect the purchaser and ensure that the planned development can take place a condition will usually be inserted in the missives to the effect that all necessary consents are to be obtained before entry and allowing the purchaser to withdraw if they are not forthcoming. Normally there will be a time limit requiring consents to be obtained within a specified time, this being necessary to protect the seller's interests, otherwise he could be bound by missives without limit of time while the purchaser unsuccessfully attempts to purify the condition relating to consents.

Such conditions are often framed in terms that the consents obtained have to be to the satisfaction of the purchaser, and where this is the case he must generally act reasonably in deciding on the adequacy of the consents actually obtained.[3]

One question that has arisen in a number of cases is what happens

---

1   See *Martin v Bell-Ingram* 1986 SLT 575.
2   See also ch 7, pt 5.
3   *Gordon District Council v Wimpey Homes Holdings Ltd* 1988 SLT 141; *John H Wyllie v Ryan Industrial Fuels Ltd* 1989 SLT 302.

if the consents are not obtained, or are not obtained by the specified date. Can the purchaser then waive the condition and proceed with the purchase? The answer to this depends on the precise terms of the condition and its relationship with the other terms of the missives. For the purchaser to be able to waive the condition it must have been conceived solely in his interest and be separable from the other conditions in the missives.[1] In one of the leading cases neither of these requirements was satisfied; both parties were given the right to withdraw from the bargain if the consents were not obtained and the last possible date of entry was fixed by reference to the date on which consent was obtained.[2] If it is desired to give the purchaser the right to waive this type of condition the missives must be carefully drawn to ensure that this can happen, perhaps with an express provision to this effect.[3]

Law Society of Scotland standard clauses

In September 1991 the Law Society of Scotland produced a set of standard clauses for missives, the intention being in the long term to enable the more rapid conclusion of missives. The standard clauses are divided into three parts. Part A clauses are unalterable, Part B clauses will apply unless contracted out of or varied by agreement, and Part C clauses are effectively optional.

The clauses in Part A effectively correspond to standard conditions 1 and 14, 6, 4, 10, 8, and 3 considered above. Part B includes standard conditions 9, 8, 12, 13, 18, and 19 as well as other conditions 2 and 11. Part C includes standard conditions 2, 15 and 16.

In addition, Part B imposes a time limit for the production of evidence to satisfy the purchaser that the missive conditions have been complied with and deals with overriding interests. Part C includes conditions providing for a retention on the purchase price if the property is affected by a repairs notice, that there are no adverse proposals by neighbours known to the seller, and for transactions with limited companies.[4]

The extent to which these standard clauses will be used in practice remains to be seen. Certainly the provision requiring the production of evidence that the missive conditions have been complied with prior to entry, though desirable in principle, may cause problems

---

1 *Zebmoon Ltd v Akinbrook Investment Developments Ltd* 1988 SLT 146.
2 *Imry Property Holdings Ltd v Glasgow YMCA* 1979 SLT 261.
3 *McDonald* para 28–30; *Halliday* para 15–106.
4 See ch 16, pt 1.

in practice. In addition, it is not clear that the non-supersession clause and other clauses have taken full account of the developments in the law in this area.

2. CONVEYANCE OF THE PROPERTY

Missives merely constitute a binding contract to transfer heritage at some future date in exchange for payment of the price or other consideration. The actual transfer of the property is effected by a further document, referred to generally as a conveyance. At this stage, as we have already noted, the purchaser still has only a personal right in the property.

The fundamental requirement for a conveyance is that it must be in writing. More particularly it will take the form of a probative deed, ie one which 'complies with the statutory solemnities for the execution of formal deeds'.[1] In most cases this means that it is signed by the party(ies) in the presence of two witnesses who will also sign as evidence of their having witnessed the signature.[2]

The same requirements as to contractual capacity apply to conveyances as apply to missives, with the additional requirement that the granter of the conveyance must have title to the interest in land being transferred. That is, the granter's interest in the property must be extensive enough to allow him to sell it so that, for example, a tenant could not grant a valid conveyance of the property he leases.

The particular form of the conveyance will depend on the precise nature of the transaction. The three main categories are:

a. *Feu contract, feu charter or feu disposition.* One of these deeds will be appropriate where a new feudal estate is being created, ie where the consequence of the deed will be the creation of a new relationship of superior and vassal. The last two deeds are unilateral, that is, signed only by the granter; the feu contract is signed by both parties.

b. *Disposition.*[3] This type of deed is appropriate where a straight sale of an interest in land is involved with the seller retaining no interest in the land. Thus it will be the form of deed used in most sales of the *dominium utile* or in the sale of the *dominium directum*. This is sometimes referred to as a special disposition as it conveys a particular piece of the seller's property, as opposed

---

1 *Halliday* para 3-01.
2 See also ch 1, pt 3, and ch 17, pt 1.
3 See Appendix for a specimen disposition.

to a will, for example, which operates as a general disposition of all of a person's property.

c. *Contract of excambion.* This will be appropriate where the consideration for the purchase of a piece of land comprises in whole or in part another piece of heritage. The contract of excambion takes the form of a document signed by both parties which has the effect of a reciprocal transfer of the pieces of land involved so that only one document is needed rather than two separate dispositions.

The various clauses of these deeds and their effect will be discussed in chapter 17.

3. COMPLETION OF TITLE

Once the purchaser has received delivery of the conveyance of the property by the seller he has a right in the property which is still in the nature of a personal right.[1] A personal right in property in this context means one which can only be defended against a challenge by the granter of the deed and is therefore open to successful challenge by others who claim an interest in the land. In order to transform this right into one which is defensible against challenge by any other person the purchaser must convert it into a real right by the process of taking infeftment, also known as completing title. Title is completed either by recording the deed of transfer of the property in the General Register of Sasines, or by registration of the purchaser's title to the property in the Land Register for Scotland.

The importance of this distinction between real and personal rights and of the process of infeftment is illustrated by the case of *Ceres School Board v Macfarlane.*[2] In 1833 the proprietor of a piece of land on which a school had been built granted a feu disposition of that land to the body then responsible for the running of the school. The grantees of this deed did not take the necessary steps by way of recording the disposition in the Register of Sasines to complete title and make them infeft proprietors. In 1883 the estate of which the land formed part was sold and the plot of land was inadvertently included in the description of the property contained in the conveyance granted to the purchaser. The purchaser recorded his title in the Register of Sasines, thus becoming infeft and acquiring a real right in the property. The new proprietor advised the pursuers,

1   See ch 1, pt 1.
2   (1895) 23 R 279.

who had by now inherited the running of the school, that they had no right to the property and offered them a new feu contract at an increased feuduty. The pursuers then raised an action for declarator that they had full legal right and title to the property. Their action failed. In the words of Lord Adam 'The defender is infeft in the land with a regular feudal title, and the proposal of the pursuers is to oust him from that land ... on the ground that they have a personal right thereto. I have certainly never heard of any real title yielding to the personal in such a competition.'[1]

On the other hand, if the person challenging their right had been the original granter of the deed conveying the plot to them the pursuers in this case would have been entitled to succeed, as a personal right in property would be good as against that person.

The process of completion of title

The process of infeftment or completion of title originally involved the superior and vassal going on to the land to be conveyed. The vassal would then pay the price and the superior would hand over a symbol of the land. In time this ceremony came to be carried out on the land by agents of the parties[2] and by the nineteenth century a system of recording documents had taken the place of, and by statute been made equivalent in effect to, the ceremony of infeftment.[3]

Infeftment may now be taken in two ways:

(a) By recording the deed of conveyance in the General Register of Sasines; and

(b) by registering the purchaser's title in the Land Register for Scotland.[4]

(a) Recording in the Register of Sasines. In areas not yet covered by the Land Register for Scotland all deeds creating, transferring or extinguishing rights in land are to be recorded in the appropriate volume of the Register of Sasines.

The procedure involved in recording a deed in the Register of Sasines is as follows:

---

1 At 282-3.
2 For an account of such proceedings see 'Infeftment' (1980) 25 JLSS 90.
3 Titles to Land (Scotland) Act 1858; see *Halliday* ch 16 for a fuller discussion of these developments.
4 For matters relating to the Register of Sasines and Land Register see also chs 3 and 14.

(i)   The deed creating or transferring the rights in land will be received by the purchaser or, more likely, the purchaser's solicitor. The solicitor will endorse a warrant for registration of the deed. This warrant is an instruction to the Keeper of the Register of Sasines (who administers the register) to record the document in the register on behalf of the grantee.

(ii) The deed is then forwarded to the register in Edinburgh. On arrival it will be checked for errors or omissions. The particular purposes of this inspection are to ensure that the deed has been properly signed and witnessed; that the deed deals with an interest in land and so is eligible for recording in the register; that the property affected by the deed is properly, accurately and sufficiently described so that it can be identified without any difficulty or dispute; and that the deed contains a warrant for registration.

   If any mistake or defect is discovered the deed will be returned to the grantee's solicitor for correction. If no defects are found it will proceed on the way to recording.

(iii) A copy of the deed is made for retention in the appropriate volume of the register. As we saw in chapter 3, the register is divided geographically into thirty-three divisions representing the former counties of Scotland. Separate volumes are kept for each county, and the individual deeds are entered in chronological order into the volume applicable to the county where the land to which they relate is situated.

   By 'recording in the Register of Sasines' is meant the placing of a full copy of the deed in the appropriate volume of the register.

(iv) The original deed is then returned to the person who submitted it for recording. It will be endorsed with a note of the date of recording (usually the date of initial presentation of the deed) and of the register volume and page on which a copy of the deed can be found.

Once this procedure has been gone through the grantee of the deed is infeft and has a real right to the property. Under the system of recording in the Register of Sasines, however, this real right is not guaranteed. If challenged by a third party the title of the infeft proprietor to the land is not established simply by the possession of a recorded deed, nor is it guaranteed by such a deed. The title of the proprietor, rather, is established by the production of a valid progress of title.[1]

---

1   For a full discussion see ch 1, pt 4; ch 16, pt 1.

(b)   The Land Register for Scotland.[1]   The procedure for land registration depends on whether the application for registration is the first application relating to the property or the property is already registered.

(i)   *First registration.* On first registration the document of transfer is sent to the Keeper together with a completed application form, a prescriptive progress of title,[2] any deeds containing real burdens or conditions affecting the property and any other relevant documentation (eg feuduty redemption receipt). From this documentation are extracted: a description of the property which is transferred onto a title plan taken from Ordnance Survey maps, the owner(s) of the property and the price paid, details of any securities or other charges affecting the property and any real burdens and conditions affecting the property. These details are transferred to the Land Register and used to create a title sheet. Once a title sheet is created it forms the basis for a land certificate which is issued to the proprietor.

(ii)   *Transactions subsequent to first registration.* Here all that is really required is the document of transfer of the interest concerned and an application form, as all the details of the property will be stored in the register. In addition any documents or deeds which affect the land and have come into being since the register was last updated, eg a deed creating a servitude right affecting the property, must be forwarded so that the register can be altered to reflect the actual situation relating to the land. Aside from such alterations all that is involved is the substitution on the register of the new proprietor(s) in place of the seller(s).

Once the registration process is completed a land certificate will be issued to the applicant.

4. SALES OF PUBLIC SECTOR HOUSING[3]

Since 1980 tenants of certain public sector houses have had the right to buy their homes. The current provisions are contained in the Housing (Scotland) Act 1987.

To be entitled to purchase, the tenant must be a secure tenant

---

1   For a general account of registration of title, see ch 14.
2   See ch 1, pt 4; ch 16, pt 1.
3   *Halliday* paras 15-120 to 15-129; *McDonald* paras 28-79 to 28-88; *Sinclair* ch 19; C Himsworth *Public Sector Housing Law in Scotland* (3rd edn) ch 8; A McAllister *Scottish Law of Leases* (1989) 224-230.

of a public sector landlord; these are principally local authorities, Scottish Homes, and certain housing associations (though it should be noted that since January 1989 most new tenancies of housing association properties have not been secure tenancies).[1] The purchaser must also have been a public sector tenant for two years, either in his present house or in a house provided by another public landlord. There are certain exclusions from the right to buy for sheltered housing and amenity housing.

As an inducement to tenants to buy they are entitled to a discount on the price of the house. For houses the minimum discount is 32 per cent after two years tenancy rising by 1 per cent for each additional year of tenancy up to a maximum of 60 per cent. For flats the minimum discount is 44 per cent rising by 2 per cent per year to a maximum of 70 per cent.

There is a penalty if the house is sold within three years; this requires repayment of 100 per cent of the discount if the house is sold within one year, 66 per cent within two years and 33 per cent within 3 years. The penalty is secured by a standard security in favour of the landlord.

The conditions which the landlord can attach to the sale are regulated by the legislation. They must include conditions which will, for example, ensure that the tenant obtains a marketable title and that the tenant will get as full enjoyment of the property as owner as he had as tenant. Retention by the seller of a right of pre-emption (ie an option to buy back the property on first sale by the new owner)[2] is excluded except in certain restricted circumstances. If the tenant objects to any conditions proposed by the landlord he may request a change in the terms within one month. If the landlord refuses the tenant may appeal to the Lands Tribunal.

The procedure for exercise of the right to buy is that the tenant serves an application to purchase on the landlord. There is a statutory form for this. On receipt of the application the landlord may, within one month, issue a notice of refusal if the house falls into one of the categories excluded from sale or it disputes the tenant's right to buy. If the ground for refusal is that the information supplied by the tenant is incorrect the period for service of the notice of refusal is two months. If the landlord does not refuse to sell it must issue an offer to sell within two months. This offer will contain details of the market value of the house, the discount available and the price as well as the conditions attaching to the sale. A tenant

1   Housing (Scotland) Act 1988, s43.
2   See also ch 17, pt 1.

who wishes to accept the offer to sell must do so within two months, and once the offer is accepted the sale will proceed in the same way as any other sale. Disputes arising during the sale process are generally to be resolved by application to the Lands Tribunal.

As a further incentive to exercise the right to buy, a tenant is entitled to a loan from a local authority or Scottish Homes to assist with the purchase of his house. A loan is obtainable where the tenant cannot secure a loan from a building society; however it may not exceed the price of the property or the relevant multiple of the applicant's income. Application for a loan must be made within one month of receipt of the offer to sell.

5. PUBLIC SALES[1]

Although it is now the case that virtually all sale transactions take the form of sales by private bargain, it is still possible to sell heritable property by auction at a public sale. This method of sale was formerly of importance in that heritable creditors under a bond and disposition in security or bond of cash credit selling security subjects had to proceed in this way. The rationale for this was that the creditor had a duty to obtain the highest possible price for the property, and a public sale was thought to be the best way of safeguarding this. However, the virtual disappearance of public sales in other contexts meant that this was no longer necessarily so, and this was recognised in the Conveyancing and Feudal Reform (Scotland) Act 1970 which allowed such creditors to exercise their power of sale by private bargain.[2] There are still some cases where a public sale is necessary, eg as a precursor to raising an action of foreclosure over security subjects,[3] and in the 1980s it was briefly popular as a means for the British Railways Board to sell off surplus property; this was probably a policy imported from their English headquarters, as auction sales of real property (as it is called there) are still quite common south of the Border.

Public sales will generally proceed under articles of roup. This is a probative document which is in the form of an offer to sell by the seller. It will typically contain, among other things, the following:

1. A description of the property being offered for sale. This will

---

1 *Halliday* paras 15-141 to 15-148.
2 See ch 11, pt 2.
3 Conveyancing and Feudal Reform (Scotland) Act 1970, s28(1).

normally be fuller than a description in missives. The exposer (seller) will also be identified.

2. An upset price.
3. A date of entry when possession will be given and the price will be payable.
4. An undertaking by the exposer to grant a valid conveyance of the property in exchange for payment of the agreed price.
5. A statement that the purchaser will be bound to take the title to the property as it stands. The effect of this is that the purchaser will be obliged to accept a title which is subject to minor deficiencies and to bear the cost of rectifying or curing these deficiencies. This is in contrast to the normal position in sales under missives where the seller is bound to produce a marketable title.[1]

    The obligation to accept the title as it stands only requires the acceptance of minor deficiencies in title; the purchaser is not obliged to accept a title which is radically defective.
6. A requirement for the successful bidder to produce caution or a deposit within a short time of the sale, and provision for what is to happen if this is not done. Such a deposit will not generally be recoverable by the purchaser if he does not proceed with the sale.[2]
7. An arbitration clause referring disputes arising under the contract to arbitration.
8. A judge of roup will be appointed who will act as auctioneer and conduct the sale.

Once the articles of roup have been executed the sale will be held at the place and time advertised, with the property being sold to the highest bidder.

After the sale is completed a minute of enactment and preference will be endorsed on the articles of roup. This will identify the highest bidder and will be signed by him and the judge of roup.

Once the minute of enactment and preference has been endorsed on the articles of roup, a binding contract of sale has been concluded. From this stage on the sale proceeds in the same way as a sale by private bargain.

1 See ch 16, pt 1.
2 *Zemhunt Holdings Ltd v Control Securities plc* 1991 GWD 40-2482.

16. Examination of title: obligations of the parties

Following conclusion of missives the next stage of a conveyancing transaction is the examination of title.[1] The purposes of examination of title are to ensure that the seller has legal title to sell the property, that he is under no legal incapacity (eg bankruptcy) and that all of the conditions contained in the missives are complied with. Essentially, then, examination of title is a means of ensuring that the seller complies with his obligations under the contract of sale. These obligations and the reciprocal obligations of the purchaser are the subject of this chapter.

The physical process of examination of title involves the inspection of relevant title deeds relating to the property. In Sasine and first registration transactions the relevant deeds will be those needed to establish a marketable title and those deeds which contain burdens and conditions affecting the property. In the case of property which is already in the Land Register the relevant deeds will be the land certificate and any deeds affecting the property after the date of the certificate. As well as examining the deeds the purchaser's solicitor will also need to see searches affecting the property and other documents which are relevant to ensure that the seller is fulfilling his obligations. Examples of this latter category would be planning and other consents, completion certificates for building work, and feuduty redemption receipts. At the stage of examination, drafts of the various deeds needed to complete the transaction will be adjusted and finalised between the two solicitors.

The actual structure of the main types of title deed will be the subject matter of the next chapter.

---

1 For a fuller discussion see McDonald *Conveyancing Manual* (4th edn, 1989) ch 33; Halliday *Conveyancing Law and Practice* ch 21; Sinclair *Handbook of Conveyancing Practice in Scotland* (2nd edn, 1990) ch 7.

1. OBLIGATIONS OF THE SELLER

At common law the obligations of the seller are to deliver or exhibit a marketable title, to deliver or exhibit clear searches, to deliver a valid conveyance of the property, to give possession, and to comply with any other conditions of the contract. As we noted in chapter 15, part 1, these obligations are usually expressly stated, often with some modifications, in the missives.

(a) Marketable title[1]

This is sometimes expressed as an obligation to deliver a good and marketable title, although it is not clear what the addition of 'good' to 'marketable' achieves or if there is any conceptual difference between the two types of title.[2] The basic obligation is that the seller should give the purchaser an unchallengeable right to the property which is not affected by any real conditions, servitudes or reservations which would materially diminish the value of that property. The precise content of the obligation will depend on whether the sale is a Sasine transaction, will induce first registration in the Land Register, or involves a dealing in a property already registered, although some of the same principles apply in all three. Regardless of the nature of the transaction, the seller's obligation is to deliver or exhibit a marketable title within a reasonable time. In practice missives usually require this to be done before the date of entry.

Sasine transactions.   Production of a marketable title in this context means essentially three things.
(i) The seller must possess a title to the property which is sufficient to enable him to sell the property interest which he has undertaken to sell. This means, for example, that if he has undertaken to sell the ownership interest in the *dominium utile*, production of a title in the form of a lease, even for 999 years, will not be adequate.[3] He must also be in a position, if no qualification has been made in the missives regarding this, to convey the minerals lying under the property.[4]
(ii) The seller must be able to produce a prescriptive or valid progress of title to the property. As has already been discussed,[5] possession

---

1   See K Reid 'Good and Marketable Title' (1988) 33 JLSS 162; *Halliday* paras 21–01 to 21–72; *McDonald* paras 28–42 to 28–48 and 33–3 to 33–5.
2   Compare Reid's article referred to above at p162 with the view expressed by Gretton in *The Law of Inhibition and Adjudication* (1987) at 143.
3   *McConnell v Chassels* (1903) 10 SLT 790.
4   *Campbell v McCutcheon* 1963 SC 505, 1963 SLT 290.
5   See ch 1, pt 4.

of property for the prescriptive period of ten years cures any latent defects (ie defects not apparent merely from perusal of the title deeds) in the title to that property and effectively gives the owner a guaranteed title which is not open to challenge by any third party.

Prescription, however, will not cure patent defects in the foundation writ (see below). Patent defects are those which are obvious from looking at the title deeds. Examples of such defects would be the omission of necessary clauses from the deed, defects in signature by the parties, or defects in witnessing. There is provision for rectification of deeds either under the Conveyancing (Scotland) Act 1874, s39 or the Law Reform (Miscellaneous Provisions) (Scotland) Act 1985, s8(1). The former relates to informalities in execution, the latter allows rectification where the deed fails to reflect the intention of the parties as would arguably be the case if a necessary clause was left out of a deed rendering it ineffective contrary to the parties intentions.[1] Defects which cannot be rectified or overlooked will vitiate a deed and hence the proprietor's title.

To show that he has an unchallengeable title to pass on to the purchaser the seller must be able to demonstrate possession for the prescriptive period. In practice it is common for properties to change hands every few years so the title offered to the purchaser is unlikely to be a title possessed by the seller alone for ten years or more; more likely it will take the form of a number or progress of titles culminating in the deed in favour of the seller. In order to establish a good progress of title in such circumstances the seller must exhibit the first title deed outwith the ten year period. This deed must be *ex facie* valid (ie free from patent defects) and sufficient in its terms to include the interest being sold to the purchaser.[2] Following on this deed (referred to as the foundation writ) all of the transfers of the interest must be in the form of deeds, each of which is *ex facie* valid and granted by someone having the legal capacity to do so. These deeds must be clearly linked together. Linking may be evident from the grantor of one deed being the grantee of the previous deed, or it may be evidenced by some other document linking two recorded deeds together, or linking the right of the seller to sell back to a recorded deed. This linking (where it appears in a deed it is referred to as deduction of title)[3] is necessary where the granter of a deed is uninfeft; his right to grant the deed is linked back to the last recorded deed through a deed or document, for example a confirmation of an executor or an unrecorded disposition.[4]

1 See also ch 17, pt 4.
2 Prescription and Limitation (Scotland) Act 1973, s1.
3 See also ch 17, pt 1.
4 See *Halliday* paras 22–06 to 22–11.

To take a simple example, suppose that in 1967 Whippy Developments sold a house to Frank Smith. Following that the following transactions have taken place:

1971   Disposition by Frank Smith to Philip Marlowe
1976   Disposition by Philip Marlowe to Philo Vance
1983   Disposition by Philo Vance to Sam Spade
1986   Disposition by Sam Spade to Miles Archer
1989   Disposition by the Executor of Miles Archer to
       Steve Carella (the seller)

In this example the foundation writ (assuming the sale took place in 1991) would be the 1976 disposition by Marlowe to Vance, and the progress of title would include that deed, all the subsequent dispositions, and the confirmation of Miles Archer's executor.

In practice, the only check on the capacity of the parties to grant the deeds in the progress of title is through the searches in the Personal Register which are examined by the purchaser's solicitor. These searches are discussed below, but for the moment it is worth noting that checking the searches alone is not a perfect check as these will not reveal some forms of incapacity, for example, insanity.

The final element in establishing a prescriptive title is, of course, possession. In practice it is normally assumed that the property has been possessed consecutively by those appearing to be its owners over the period of the prescriptive progress. The reason for simply assuming this is that 'demanding evidence of possession would be a real menace for everyday conveyancing'.[1] In virtually every case the assumption will be justified.

(iii) Finally, the 'seller is bound to convey the subjects free from burdens that were unknown to the purchaser at the date of the missives if these burdens materially diminish the value of the subjects'.[2] In the past the following have all been held to be breaches of the seller's obligation entitling the purchaser to rescind: the existence of a servitude right of access preventing redevelopment along the entire frontage of a property,[3] a prohibition on building,[4] a right of access and prohibition on rear windows on the second floor of a two storey building,[5] a servitude right of way through

---

1   G Gretton 'Searches' (1989) 34 JLSS at p85; see also *McDonald* para 33–19.
2   *Armia Ltd v Daejan Developments Ltd* 1979 SLT 147 at 161 per Lord Fraser.
3   *Armia, supra.*
4   *Louttit's Trs v Highland Railway Company* (1892) 19 R 791.
5   *Smith v Soeder* (1895) 23 R 60, although this decision seemed to turn, at least in part, on the fact that the purchaser was foreign and did not have legal assistance in the early stages of the transaction.

a small garden,[1] and a prohibition on selling alcohol.[2] It is only fair to say however that the law in this area is not entirely clear with some of the older cases, when deciding in favour of the purchaser, failing to distinguish clearly between conditions which are commonplace and those which are restrictive. One example is *Smith v Soeder*.[3] In this case a condition that only dwellinghouses should be built on the land, and a condition requiring a passage to be left for access by the superior were both regarded, on appeal, as being objectionable. Conditions such as the former are, however, commonplace in dispositions of land for building. In this case, also, the Lord Ordinary had taken the view that the conditions were unobjectionable.

In cases where the purchaser has actual knowledge of the restriction or such knowledge can be imputed to him then, at common law, he will be barred from resiling from the contract.[4] Reid, in his article 'Good and Marketable Title'[5] suggests that the normal missives provision that 'There are no unusual, unduly onerous or restrictive conditions of title affecting the subjects', may, because it makes no mention of the purchaser's state of knowledge, allow him to resile even if he had prior knowledge of the restriction.

In view of the lack of clarity of the law and the lack of modern precedent it is advisable that where a use of the property (eg sale of alcohol) is contemplated which might fall foul of a title restriction this should be specifically dealt with in the missives. Any such specific term will add to the seller's common law obligation.[6]

In order to discover what burdens and conditions affect the property the purchaser's solicitor will have to examine any deeds outwith the progress of title which impose burdens or conditions.

First registration. Where a transaction will induce registration of the property in the Land Register for the first time the seller will have to supply such material as will enable the Keeper to register the purchaser's title without exclusion of indemnity. This will involve production of a good progress of title, prior writs containing burdens, any feuduty redemption receipt and also documentation which would not normally be required in a Sasine transaction, such as a plan

1 *Welsh v Russell* (1894) 21 R 769.
2 *Umar v Murtaza* 1983 SLT (Sh Ct) 79; although this decision has been criticised, see K Reid 'Good and Marketable Title' (1988) 33 JLSS 162 at 163.
3 (1895) 23 R 60.
4 *Crofts v Stewart's Trs* 1926 SLT 577.
5 (1988) 33 JLSS 162 at 163.
6 *Armia Ltd v Daejan Developments Ltd* 1979 SLT 147 at 161.

of the property or a description accurate enough to identify the property clearly on the Ordnance Survey plan.

Dealing in registered property. Where a property is already registered there should be no problem about the marketability of the seller's title because of the state indemnity given by the Keeper. The documentation that the seller will have to produce is his land certificate with no exclusion of indemnity, and any deeds relating to subsequent dealings in the property. The existence of any adverse real conditions can be easily ascertained from the certificate. The only relevance of prescription here is that possession for ten years on a registered title involving an exclusion of indemnity cures that defect.[1]

Occupancy rights. Where the seller's title is in the name of an individual (rather than joint names of husband and wife) it is possible that there may be a non-entitled spouse having occupancy rights to the property. In order to protect the purchaser against the claim of a non-entitled spouse having such rights it is necessary, first of all, to see all the relevant documentation (ie form of consent, renunciation, affidavit or decree dispensing with consent)[2] for the current transaction. Secondly, since occupancy rights last for five years from the date of last occupation by the non-entitled spouse[3] it is necessary also to see this documentation for any transaction within the last five years in which a question of occupancy rights may arise, ie basically those where the seller had sole title to the property. In the case of dealings in registered land this second check may be unnecessary as the Keeper may have certified on the title sheet (copied on the land certificate) that no occupancy rights exist in respect of prior proprietors.[4]

(b) Clear searches

The obligation of the seller is to deliver or exhibit clear searches.[5] The searches required in any transaction will depend on whether the transaction will result in the purchaser's title being recorded in the Register of Sasines or registered in the Land Register, and

---

1 Prescription and Limitation (Scotland) Act 1973, s1(1)(b)(ii).
2 See ch 10, pt 8.
3 Matrimonial Homes (Family Protection)(Scotland) Act 1981, s6(f).
4 See *Registration of Title Practice Book* H.4.
5 See *Halliday* paras 21–73 to 21–94; *McDonald* paras 33–21 to 33–44; *Sinclair* ch 8; G Gretton 'Searches' (1989) 34 JLSS 50 and 85.

in the latter case, whether the title is already registered or will be registered for the first time. The main forms of search will be discussed below, with separate consideration of transactions involving companies.

(i) Search in the Property Register. This is a search in the Register of Sasines and is generally only required in Sasine transactions or transactions inducing first registration. The object of the search is to disclose all of the deeds affecting the property. This acts as a check that there are no undisclosed securities affecting the property and that the seller has produced all of the deeds necessary to give a marketable title. There is no clear period required by law for such a search, so this must be specified in the missives, and is usually forty years. The reason for the search being for forty years rather than the ten year period specified by law for positive prescription is to guard against the existence of old securities affecting the property. It is assumed that if such a security did exist some deed would have been recorded referring to it within the forty year period.[1] This length of search does not usually cause a problem as most searches are continuations of existing searches over the property which will stretch back over this period. The search in the property register and that in the Personal Register have to be continued down to the date of recording of the deed transferring ownership to the purchaser.

(ii) Search in the Personal Register.[2] A search in the Personal Register is a search in the Register of Inhibitions and Adjudications where certain types of notice which in practice prevent an individual from dealing with his property must be registered if they are to be effective. The main types of notice are notices of litigiosity, inhibitions and awards of sequestration.

A notice of litigiosity is a notice that an action affecting land has been started. This may take the form of an action of adjudication, an action for reduction of the deed conferring the right to the land, or an action for rectification of a deed affecting the land under the terms of the Law Reform (Miscellaneous Provisions)(Scotland) Act 1985.

An inhibition is available as a form of diligence in execution of a court decree; on the dependence of a court action, to preserve the defender's property pending the outcome of the action; or, very

---

1 See *Halliday* para 21–73; *McDonald* para 33–24.
2 See G Gretton *The Law of Inhibition and Adjudication* ch 12.

unusually, as a remedy for a creditor proceeding on a document of debt. For these purposes a document of debt has been defined as 'any probative document whereby a debtor binds himself to pay'.[1]

Finally, an award of sequestration against a bankrupt must be forwarded by the clerk of court for registration in this register.[2]

The effect of a notice of litigiosity is that the title of any person acquiring the property after this has been registered can be set aside. Inhibitions and notices of award of sequestration have similar consequences. They both operate to prevent future voluntary transactions relating to the property of the debtor or bankrupt, with the result that any such transaction can be set aside. The important qualification is that **future voluntary** transactions are struck at. This means that if missives are concluded before an inhibition is registered against the seller, that inhibition will not prevent the effective transfer of the property to the purchaser. Such a transfer is not a **voluntary** act by the seller as the purchaser can go to court and secure an order for implement requiring the seller to fulfil his obligations undertaken in the missives. Registration of an inhibition in such circumstance will, however, as noted below, mean that the seller cannot exhibit a clear search.

Notices of litigiosity prescribe in five years or six months after final decree in the court action, whichever is earlier,[3] inhibitions prescribe in five years,[4] and notices of award of sequestration last for three years, but may be renewed for further three year periods.[5] Because of these time limits the search in the personal register is normally against everyone having an interest in the property within the ten year prescriptive period for a period of five years immediately prior to their disposal of the property.[6]

(iii) Interim report. As a matter of practicality it is impossible for the seller to deliver or exhibit a clear search at the time of settlement of the sale. This is partly because of the backlog at the Register of Sasines,[7] but, more fundamentally, because at the date of settlement the seller cannot possibly fulfil an obligation to produce a search which is clear right down to the date of recording of the

1 G Maher & D Cusine *The Law and Practice of Diligence* (1990) para 9.10; see generally paras 9.01–9.36 on inhibitions.
2 Bankruptcy (Scotland) Act 1985, s14.
3 Conveyancing (Scotland) Act 1924, s44(3)(a)
4 Ibid.
5 Bankruptcy (Scotland) Act 1985, s14(4).
6 For the reasoning behind this see *McDonald* para 33–37 and Gretton 'Searches' (1989) 34 JLSS 50 and 85 at 86.
7 See, for example, 1990 SLT (News) 202.

purchaser's disposition. This is so, simply because this deed will not be sent for recording until after settlement.

In order to get round this problem two devices are used. The first of these is the Interim Report on the search which is completed in the property register to the date when that register is complete and in the personal register up to the midnight before the report. This provides an interim indication that the search is clear. The second device is the letter of obligation in which the seller's solicitor gives his personal undertaking that there will be no adverse entries on the registers that will appear prior to the deed transferring ownership to the purchaser.

(iv) Form 10 and 11 Reports.   These reports are appropriate where the transaction will result in first registration of the property. In effect they are similar to the Interim Report in Sasines transactions covering the Property and Personal Registers as explained above. The normal practice is to instruct a Form 10 Report at an early stage in the transaction and have it brought up to date by a Form 11 Report nearer the date of entry. There is no necessity for the search to be continued as in a Sasine transaction. The reason is that the Keeper will have to be satisfied that there are no adverse entries before registering the purchaser's title. If anything does appear to prevent the Keeper registering the purchaser's title without indemnity, the seller will be in breach of his obligation to produce a marketable title.

(v) Form P16 Report.   This is also relevant in first registration, and takes the form of a request to the Keeper to compare the boundaries of the property as disclosed by the title deeds with those appearing on the Ordnance Survey plan which forms the basis of the register. The importance of this is that a serious discrepancy between the two will require remedial action or may result in indemnity being excluded or partially excluded by the Keeper.[1]

(vi) Form 12 and 13 Reports.   These reports are appropriate in dealing with a registered interest. The Form 13 Report is simply an update of the Form 12. They serve the same purpose as an Interim Report.[2] For the reasons stated in (iv) above there is no need for a search to be continued beyond the date of the later of the reports.

---

1   See *Registration of Title Practice Book* E.16 and E.33–35.
2   Ibid, F.11–13.

Transactions with companies.[1]   Transactions with companies are, of course, quite common, as a result of the growth in home ownership and the number of new private dwellings sold by housebuilding companies. Where the seller of property is a company, additional searches are necessary. This is so for two reasons. In the first place the company may have granted floating charges affecting the whole of their property, including their heritable property.[2] Such charges, even though they affect heritage, need not be registered in the Register of Sasines, and so will not be disclosed by a search there. A floating charge may contain conditions prohibiting the sale of property without the consent of the creditor, or it may have crystallised as a result of the appointment of a receiver or the commencement of liquidation. On crystallisation the floating charge becomes a fixed charge over the company's property which effectively prevents its sale. In order to check for the existence of floating charges or the appointment of a receiver a search must be made in the Register of Charges.

Secondly, even if the company has not granted floating charges which might affect the sale the company may have gone into administration (a process designed to rescue ailing companies)[3] or liquidation. This will only be revealed by a further search in the company file maintained by the Registrar of Companies. The significance of the appointment of an administrator or liquidator is that he becomes the only person entitled to enter into transactions on behalf of the company, and in the case of a liquidator can disclaim contracts entered into before his appointment.

These additional searches must therefore be instructed when purchasing from a company both in Sasine and land registration transactions. In relation to the latter it should be noted that Form 10, 11, 12 and 13 Reports only involve searches in the Property and Personal Registers, so a separate search must be instructed against the company. In addition to obtaining these searches further steps are usually taken to protect the purchaser against crystallisation of a floating charge, administration or liquidation. These include obtaining a personal undertaking from directors of the company that it is not insolvent and a deed of release from the creditor in a floating charge releasing the property being sold from the charge.[4]

---

1   See *McDonald* ch 35; *Halliday* para 21-87; G Gretton 'Searches' (1989) 34 JLSS 50.
2   See ch 11, pt 4.
3   Insolvency Act 1986, Pt 2.
4   *McDonald* para 35-18; G Gretton 'Searches' (1989) 34 JLSS 50 at 52.

What is a clear search?   A clear search is one which indicates that the seller has a marketable title; in other words there is nothing on the face of the search, apart from entries which the operation of statute renders ineffective, which would appear to prevent or limit the granting of a good title to the purchaser. Examples of entries which are rendered ineffective by the operation of statute are inhibitions more than five years old which have prescribed in terms of the Conveyancing (Scotland) Act 1924, s44, and inhibitions lodged against a debtor in a standard security after the grant of the security where the property is being sold by the creditor in exercise of his right of sale.[1] An example of an entry which would prevent a clear search, though not prevent the granting of a good title, is an inhibition lodged after the conclusion of missives. In this case, as noted above, the granting of a disposition is not a future voluntary act which is struck at by the inhibition as it can be compelled by court action. The search is, nonetheless, not clear, as to establish that this is the case would involve reference to material extrinsic to the search, in this instance the missives.[2]

There is one type of entry commonly found on a search which means that, in law, the search is not clear. This is the grant of a security over the property to a bank or building society to secure the loan used for its purchase. In practice this is not usually a problem as the loan will be repaid on sale of the property and a discharge of the security will be handed over to the purchaser's solicitor at settlement of the transaction or will be dealt with in the letter of obligation.

Letter of obligation.[3]   As has been explained above it is not possible for the seller to deliver or exhibit a clear search at the time when the price is paid and the transaction settled. In order to get over this problem the seller's solicitor grants a letter of obligation, which in effect is his personal guarantee.[4] The precise terms of the guarantee depend on the nature of the transaction, but in essence the basic guarantee is to the effect that no deeds or diligence will be recorded by or against the seller between the date of the search exhibited at settlement and the date of recording or registration of the

---

1   *Newcastle Building Society v White* 1987 SLT (Sh Ct) 81, referring to s26(1) of the Conveyancing and Feudal Reform (Scotland) Act 1970.
2   See *Henderson v Dawson* (1895) 22 R 895 at 902 per Lord McLaren.
3   See *Halliday* paras 23–09 to 23–11, 23–21 to 23–24 and 23–30 to 23–32; *McDonald* paras 33–44 to 33–51 and 35–17; *Sinclair* para 8.11; D J Cusine 'Letters of Obligation' (1991) 36 JLSS 349.
4   *Johnston v Little* 1960 SLT 129.

purchaser's title which will prevent him obtaining a good title to the property. In order to protect the solicitor some time limit is usually placed on the length of this guarantee. Letters of obligation in Sasines transactions will usually require recording of the conveyance to the purchaser within a set period. In registration transactions the guarantee takes the form of an undertaking to clear the registers of any entry which would lead to exclusion of indemnity, provided that such an entry is registered between the date of the Form 10 or 11 Report and a second date, usually fourteen days after settlement.

As well as this basic obligation, letters of obligation commonly contain other obligations, eg to deliver a duly recorded discharge of a loan. There are dangers in doing this, particularly in respect of items which are not within the control of the seller or his solicitor.[1]

(c) Delivery of valid conveyance

This involves the seller in delivering a conveyance of the property which meets the contractual requirements and is adequate to convey the interest in land being purchased. In most cases this will be a disposition, but it is common for housebuilders to feu new houses by way of a feu disposition.

(d) Possession

The obligation of the seller at common law is only to give possession of the subjects of sale within a reasonable time of the date of entry. What is a reasonable time will depend on the circumstances of the particular case. It is usual, however, as noted in chapter 15, part 1, to specify in the missives for actual vacant possession of the property to be given on the date of entry. The effect of this is that if the seller does not give possession on the due date the purchaser can resile.

(e) Other terms of the contract

As noted in chapter 15, part 1, missives of sale can contain a variety of provisions which are not covered by the obligations examined above. Examples would be the exhibition of a completion certificate for work undertaken on the property, or a warranty relating to central

1   *McDonald* paras 33–47 to 33–51; *Sinclair* para 8–11.

heating. The final obligation of the seller, then, is to comply with any terms of the missives not covered above.

2. OBLIGATIONS OF THE PURCHASER

The principal obligation of the purchaser is to pay the purchase price and as a matter of general law that is the only obligation which is incumbent on him. It should be recalled that unless there is express provision to the contrary in the missives the purchaser's obligation is to pay within a reasonable time.[1]

It is, of course, possible that the purchaser will undertake other obligations in the missives, eg to pay interest on late payment of the price or to apply for planning permission, and if this is done the purchaser must fulfil these additional obligations.

3. THE PURCHASER'S TITLE FOLLOWING EXAMINATION OF TITLE

Although examination of title involving the examination of the relevant deeds relating to the property and searches will disclose some of the possible defects in the seller's title, not all defects will be brought to light by this process. Thus, for example, naturally occurring incapacities affecting the seller (or one of the owners in the prescriptive progress), such as insanity or incapacity due to age, servitude rights over the property, latent defects in prior title, and occupancy rights under the Matrimonial Homes (Family Protection) (Scotland) Act 1981 will not necessarily be disclosed by examination of title.

Clearly, to establish a complete absence of any such defects in title would require an extremely long and exhaustive investigation. In practice, then, armed with searches or reports, having closely examined the titles to the property and ancillary documents (eg feuduty redemption receipt), having placed suitable protective conditions in the missives (eg relating to occupancy rights), and having received a letter of obligation, an assumption will be made by the purchaser's solicitor (and by the Keeper in land registration cases) that, if all of these are satisfactory, it is safe to accept the title as one not affected by any incapacity of the seller or subject

1 See ch 15, pt 1.

to any defect.[1] The result will be that the purchaser, on recording or registration of his title, will get a good unchallengeable title to the property purchased.

There is one exception to this that should be noted. Where a purchaser knows of a prior sale to another person who has not completed title his right to the property may be successfully challenged by that third party. This happened in *Rodger (Builders) Ltd v Fawdry*.[2] In this case the defenders entered into missives to sell property to the pursuers. There was a delay in the payment of the price and the sellers purported to withdraw from the contract and subsequently sold the same property to a Mr Bell who completed title to it. The pursuers raised an action against the sellers arguing that their purported withdrawal had been unlawful and asking for Bell's title to be reduced. The court accepted that the withdrawal was ineffective and granted the reduction sought. The reason for this was that Bell knew of the sale to the pursuers and of all the circumstances surrounding the seller's withdrawal. He was therefore not acting in good faith in relying on the seller's assurances that the previous agreement was at an end and in failing to make proper enquiries of his own to establish that this was indeed the case.

4. BREACH OF OBLIGATIONS[3]

Where one of the parties is in breach of any of his obligations prior to settlement of the transaction, the normal remedies are rescission or an action for implement of the obligation not complied with. In the case of rescission it may be necessary to issue an ultimatum to the party in default requiring compliance by a certain date before rescission takes place. The reason for this is that many of the obligations involved need only be fulfilled within a reasonable time, unless clear provision is made in the missives that time is of the essence. Examples include the obligation to exhibit a good title, and the obligation to pay the price. Any time limit fixed must be reasonable, and what is reasonable will depend on the circumstances of each case.[4]

After settlement, provided that *restitutio in integrum* (ie restoration of the parties to their pre-contract positions) is still possible the

---

1 Further protection is offered by warrandice; see ch 17, pt 1.
2 1950 SLT 345.
3 *McDonald* paras 28–92 to 28–101.
4 See *Rodger (Builders) Ltd v Fawdry* 1950 SLT 345 at 350.

appropriate remedy is rescission. Where *restitutio* is no longer possible the remedy is either action for specific implement or damages. The special case of the *actio quanti minoris* is considered in chapter 15, part 1. Where the breach relates to a collateral obligation a claim for damages is always possible.

In cases of rescission, either before or after settlement, the party withdrawing is entitled to claim damages for any loss resulting from the breach.

17. Examination of title: clauses in deeds

As indicated in chapter 14, a large part of examination of title consists in the examination of prior deeds affecting the property. This chapter will deal with the structure of dispositions, feu grants and deeds of conditions. The structure of standard societies is considered in chapter 11 and of the title sheet/land certificate in chapter 14.[1] The points made in relation to the structure of deeds are, of course, also relevant in the context of drafting such deeds.

1. DISPOSITIONS AND FEUDAL GRANTS

Dispositions and feudal grants of property have a large number of common clauses; the additional clauses found in a feu grant will be considered at the end of this section.

(i) Narrative clause[2]

The narrative clause is the introductory clause in the deed and will contain details of the grantor, the consideration, and the grantee.

The grantor must be described in such a way as to identify him clearly. In most cases all this involves is his name and address, though where the grantor has moved since the transfer in his favour was granted the new address will be given and the grantor linked to the previous deed by the phrase 'previously residing at'. Similarly, if the grantor's name has changed, for example on marriage, the new name will be linked to the old. If the grantor is acting in any special capacity (eg as a trustee) this will also be mentioned here.

In the case of feu grants the grantor must be infeft; in the case

---

1 See also the Appendix for specimens of a disposition, land certificate and standard security.
2 Halliday *Conveyancing Law and Practice* (1986) paras 17–01 to 17–07; McDonald *Conveyancing Manual* (4th edn, 1989) paras 7–2 to 7–5, 29–16; Sinclair *Handbook of Conveyancing Practice in Scotland* (2nd edn, 1990) paras 9.3–9.4.

of a disposition this is not essential and an uninfeft grantor can deduce title[1] from a previous owner who was infeft by a deduction of title clause.[2] This clause will normally appear after the clause of entry, and involves linking the title of the uninfeft proprietor back to the last infeft proprietor by reference to any intermediate document or documents which transfer ownership, but for one reason or another (perhaps because it is not appropriate) have not themselves been recorded. Examples would be where an uninfeft executor links title back to the deceased via the confirmation, or the holder of an unrecorded disposition uses this as a link back to the infeft grantor of that deed.

The consideration involved will, in most cases, be the payment of money, though it may involve some other consideration or, indeed, no consideration at all. In this last case it may be expressed to be for 'love, favour and affection'.In the case of feu grants the usual consideration included payment of a feuduty. Since 1 September 1974 it has no longer been possible to create new feuduties, so that payment of a feuduty will no longer be a consideration for transfer of an interest in land, although other conditions may be imposed on the vassal.[3]

If there is an agreement in the missives to apportion the price between heritage and moveables the consideration appearing in the disposition or feu grant will be the amount apportioned to heritage.

Finally, the narrative clause will identify the grantee of the deed. Normally this will be done in the same way as identification of the grantor.

(ii) Dispositive clause[4]

The dispositive clause is often described as the ruling clause in any grant or disposition. The reason for this is that this clause is the one which determines the nature and extent of the rights in property transferred by the deed. This clause must therefore contain a description of the property, details of any reservations in favour of the grantor and any real burdens and conditions affecting the property. Restrictions on the use of the property, or any other statement affecting the interest transferred found elsewhere in the

---

1 Conveyancing (Scotland) Act 1924, s3.
2 Conveyancing (Scotland) Act 1924, Sch A, Form 1; see *Halliday* paras 22-06 to 22-11; *Sinclair* para 9.7.
3 Land Tenure Reform (Scotland) Act 1974, s1; see also ch 2, pt 2.
4 *Halliday* paras 17-08 to 17-13; *McDonald* paras 7-7 to 7-19; *Sinclair* paras 9.5-9.6.

deed will be ineffective. There are four main elements found in the dispositive clause:
(a) words of conveyance;
(b) designation of the grantee;
(c) description of the property;
(d) qualifications of the grant or transfer.

Words of conveyance.   No special word or form of words is necessary as long as what is said indicates a clear present intention on the part of the grantor to transfer the property to the grantee.[1] The precise form of words will depend on the nature of the deed. In dispositions the word 'dispone' is normally used, whereas 'in feu farm dispone' is common in feu grants.

The grantee.   The grantee will already have been identified in the narrative clause. This section of the dispositive clause will, however, contain additional details relating to the grantee and the rights in property he is obtaining. It will indicate whether the property is being transferred to the grantee acting in any special capacity, eg as a trustee, and, in the case of there being more than one grantee, it will indicate whether the right in property being obtained by each is joint or common property.[2] It will also usually contain a destination to the 'executors and assignees' of the grantee, though this is unnecessary as it would be implied by law in any event. A destination is essentially a mechanism to determine what will happen to the property on the death of the grantee. Apart from the one mentioned here they are now rare.[3]

Description of the property.[4]   As the dispositive clause is conclusive as to the extent of the property obtained by the grantee, it is clearly of great importance that the description of the property is accurate and that it reflects the prior agreement between the grantor and grantee. There are a variety of ways of describing property, though it should be noted that whichever of these is used it will normally be preceded by the address of the property, and, in the case of flats, the position of the flat.

1. **General description**. A general description simply refers to the general name by which a property is or was known. The problem

1   Conveyancing (Scotland) Act 1874, s27.
2   See ch 7, pts 2 and 3.
3   See *McDonald* paras 31-10 to 31-17.
4   *Halliday* ch 18; *McDonald* ch 8.

with this type of description, which is often found in older deeds, is that as time passes it becomes increasingly difficult to establish precisely the area of land, and especially the boundaries, which the general name includes. For example, it may now be very difficult, if not impossible, to define accurately the boundaries of a piece of land described by a general name in the eighteenth century. For this reason this type of description is rarely used in modern deeds.

2. **Particular description**. This consists of a precise description of the property by reference to its boundaries and for this reason it is sometimes referred to as a bounding title. There are a number of elements which can be found in particular descriptions. These include:

(a)   Reference to any physical feature forming part or all of the boundaries to the property, for instance, a road or a fence. Measurements for the boundaries may or may not be given, and if they are will usually be expressed in such a way as to leave a little leeway (generally by the addition of the words 'or thereby' after each measurement).

(b)   The area of the property may be referred to. As this is of little use on its own it will usually be combined with one of the other elements.

(c)   The clause may refer to a plan annexed to the deed which shows the boundaries. Historically there was a problem in identifying property in this way. Until 1934 no record of plans annexed to deeds was kept in the Register of Sasines so that if the principal deed was lost, and this was the only form of description used, problems could arise. From 1924 this problem could be overcome by lodging a duplicate plan in the register.[1] Now plans attached to deeds are copied along with the deed.

In practice it is common in framing a particular description to use more than one of these elements, and, in some cases, all three. This, in turn, can give rise to problems if there are inconsistencies between different elements of the description. For example there may be inconsistency between the boundaries and measurements stated in the deed and the attached plan, or a boundary may be expressed to run for a certain distance along a feature, but the actual distance differs from that in the deed. Where such disagreements arise the courts will attempt to give effect to the intentions of the parties. There are some general rules used in cases of conflict[2], and applying these to the examples above would suggest that the

1   Conveyancing (Scotland) Act 1924, s48.
2   *Halliday* para 18-13; *McDonald* para 8-15.

measurements stated in the deed would be preferred in the first example[1] and the actual physical boundary in the second. Difficulties can also arise as to interpretation where a physical feature is stated to be a boundary. For example, if the boundary is stated to be a road, does the property end at the near side of the road, the middle of the road, or the far side of the road? Again, the courts have developed a series of presumptions,[2] and these would mean that the road was excluded from the property unless it was a public road, in which case the boundary would be the middle of the road.

Because of these problems great care is necessary in framing particular descriptions. Even the use of a measured boundary referring to physical features, statement of area, and reference to a plan may still leave room for doubt over the precise location of a boundary.[3]

3. Description by reference at common law. At common law it is possible to describe subjects by simply referring to an earlier deed in which they are fully described. The precise requirements for this are unclear,[4] though the basic requirement seems to be that the deed referred to for the full description is sufficiently identified. In one case this was held to be achieved by inclusion of the family name of the grantor, the full name of the grantee, and the date of recording.[5]

4. Description by reference to a general name. There is a statutory provision[6] which allows a general name to be created for a particular piece of land. Once this is done the property is in future referred to simply by the general name. In practice this type of description is uncommon.

5. Statutory description by reference. This is the type of description which is most commonly encountered in practice, and consists of a reference to an earlier deed which contains a particular description of the property. As this is a procedure regulated by statute,[7] the requirements set out there must be fulfilled to have

---

1 *Anderson v Harrold* 1991 SCLR 135.
2 *Halliday* para 18–11.
3 *Suttie v Baird* 1991 GWD 5–272.
4 *Halliday* para 18–14; *McDonald* para 8–17.
5 *Matheson v Gemmell* (1903) 5 F 448 at 451 per Lord McLaren. In this case the description of the prior deed was considered adequate even though the wife of the grantor was, in error, described as being the grantor.
6 Titles to Land Consolidation (Scotland) Act 1868, s13.
7 Conveyancing (Scotland) Act 1874, s61; Conveyancing (Scotland) Act 1924, s8 and Sch D.

a valid statutory description by reference. It should be noted that even if the precise terms of the statutory provisions are not met the description given may be adequate as a description by reference at common law or as a general description (eg for the purposes of the latter, the address of the property may be sufficient).

The principal requirements for a statutory description by reference are, firstly, a statement of the county, or if appropriate, the burgh and county in which the property is situated. This refers to the county in which the property is situated for the purposes of registration, reflecting historical local authority boundaries. The second requirement is reference to a deed containing a full particular description of the property. It is not adequate to refer to another deed which contains only a description by reference. The deed must be clearly identified and this will involve stating the type of deed, the parties, the date of recording, the division of the Register of Sasines in which it is recorded and, if necessary to avoid possible confusion, the volume in which the deed is recorded and the folio number. This last would be necessary if there were two deeds of the same type involving the same parties recorded on the same date, although failure to include it would not vitiate the description by reference, provided that the rest of the information given was sufficient to identify the prior deed.[1]

6. **Description in registration of title.** In transactions inducing first registration the property will usually be described in the same way as it would be in a Sasines transaction, ie in most cases simply by reference to a previous deed, or, in new houses, with a particular description or plan. However, in applying for registration the applicant must provide the Keeper with sufficient information to allow the property to be identified by reference to the Ordnance Survey map.[2] This information need not be contained wholly in the disposition in favour of the applicant, and deficiencies may be made good from other sources. In transactions involving property which is already registered all that is necessary is a reference to the number of the title sheet for that property,[3] though the postal address should also be included.[4]

7. **Conclusion.** However it is done, the description of the property should include the whole rights of property which are being transferred. This is true not only of the description in the disposition

1   Conveyancing (Scotland) Act 1924, s8(3).
2   Land Registration (Scotland) Act 1979, s4(2)(a).
3   Ibid, s15(1).
4   *Registration of Title Practice Book* C.95.

in favour of a purchaser, but also of the description in any prior titles affecting the property, particularly those in the progress of title. This means that if the transfer is to include any interests in land which need to be specifically mentioned to effect a transfer (for example salmon fishings), the description should expressly include these. It should also be borne in mind that if a tenement flat is being purchased and the understanding is that there will be a right of common property in the roof, solum, walls etc, this should also be expressly provided for, otherwise the law of the tenement will apply.[1]

Qualifications of the grant or transfer. Qualifications of the grant or transfer can take a variety of forms. The main examples are reservations of rights in favour of the grantor, real burdens and conditions, and servitudes. These can all be created both in feu grants and in dispositions. Only the first two are considered here; servitudes, which of course do not have to be created by a formal deed, are considered in chapter 9.

Reservations. Common reservations are:

1. **Reservation of minerals.**[2] Minerals lying under land are a separate tenement in land and are therefore capable of separate ownership. It is common to find that ownership of the surface and ownership of the underlying minerals has been split. This is usually achieved by way of a reservation of minerals inserted into a disposition or feu grant. The effect of this is to reserve ownership of the minerals to the grantor of the deed, usually the superior since most reservations are found in feu grants, though he may then transfer them to a third party. If there is no express reservation of the minerals the person owning the surface will also, subject to statutory provisions mentioned below, own the minerals.

The nature of the right reserved will depend on the precise terms of the reservation. Normally this will reserve a right of property in the minerals and a right to work them, though the latter is implied in the former. Where a right to work the minerals is reserved this implies a right only to work them underground; a right to enter onto the property to work and/or transport the minerals over it must be specifically created.

Even if minerals are reserved the owner of the surface will still

1 See ch 7, pt 5.
2 *Halliday* paras 19–01 to 19–12; *McDonald* ch 9; see also ch 4, pt 2.

enjoy a right of support[1] and a right of compensation for any damage caused to the surface property. The reservation may go into more detail regarding the means of assessing compensation, providing, for example, for arbitration in the event of disagreement, though if there is no mention of compensation a right to compensation is presumed. Very occasionally, a reservation of minerals will exclude liability for compensation.

Questions of rights of support and compensation in relation to coal and coal workings are also regulated by statute. The Coal Act 1938 and the Coal Industry Act 1975 confer on British Coal a right to withdraw support and regulate the payment of compensation. The Coal Mining (Subsidence) Act 1991 makes British Coal responsible for compensating for subsidence damage caused by coal workings, even though they were not responsible for them[2].

The final, and perhaps most important, point relating to reservations of minerals is what such reservations cover; in other words, what are minerals? What is included in the minerals is often more specifically defined in the reservation, but in general minerals must be something distinct from the normal subsoil of the property. If this were not the case the surface proprietor would have a right which, despite rights to compensation, was effectively worthless, as the mineral proprietor could remove the whole of the subsoil. In the case of dispute, notice will also be taken of whether or not the substance in question was referred to as a mineral in the vernacular of the mining world, commercial world, and landowners at the time of the reservation.[3] Regardless of the terms of any reservation, the ownership of certain minerals is governed by statute. Thus, coal is vested in British Coal[4] and gold and silver[5] and petroleum and natural gas[6] in the Crown.

2. **Right of pre-emption.**[7] A right of pre-emption requires the owner of the property, before selling it, first to offer it to the person (usually the superior) in whose favour the right is reserved.

Normally the property will be offered back on the same terms and conditions as those offered by the prospective purchaser of the property, but the terms of the reservation may make a different provision. If no response to the offer is made within twenty-one

---

1 See ch 4, pt 2.
2 See ch 4, pt 2.
3 *North British Railway Co v Budhill* (1909) 2 SLT 331, especially at pp334–5.
4 Coal Industry Nationalisation Act 1946; Coal Industry Act 1987.
5 Royal Mines Act 1424.
6 Petroleum (Production) Act 1934.
7 *Halliday* paras 17–68 to 17–89; *McDonald* 33–13; *Sinclair* paras 7.28.

days, the right of pre-emption lapses and will not affect any future sale of the property.[1] Failure to offer the property to someone having a right of pre-emption before completing a sale means that any disposition granted by the seller can be reduced at the instance of the person holding the right.[2] A right of pre-emption is a land obligation in terms of the Conveyancing and Feudal Reform (Scotland) Act 1970, and so application may be made to the Lands Tribunal for discharge.[3]

3. **Right of redemption.**[4] A right of redemption is a right on the part of the person to whom it is reserved (again probably the superior) to reacquire the property, either on the happening of a specified event or at his own discretion. The reservation of the right will also normally specify the price (if any) to be paid, or a formula for ascertaining the price, eg by arbitration. Rights of redemption created before 1 September 1974 exist in perpetuity; rights created after that date, which are exercisable either on the happening of an event which is bound to happen or at the option of the holder, prescribe in twenty years[5]. Rights of redemption are also land obligations which may be varied by the Lands Tribunal. Though rights of redemption are rare, they have potentially serious consequences for the prospective purchaser, who should ensure that any such right will be waived prior to his purchase.

Real Burdens and Conditions.   Most of the material relating to these will be found in chapter 10. Once real burdens and conditions have been created they must be repeated or referred to in subsequent deeds relating to the property. It is no longer necessary to repeat them at length in such deeds; all that is necessary is reference to a recorded deed which does describe them at length, and this is achieved in the same way as in a statutory description by reference.[6] Once the property has been registered in the Land Register, a reference in a deed to the title number, as well as sufficing to describe

---

1 Conveyancing Amendment (Scotland) Act 1938, s9 (amended by the Conveyancing and Feudal Reform (Scotland) Act 1970, s46) (reservations in feu grants); Conveyancing Amendment (Scotland) Act 1938, s9(3) added by the Land Tenure Reform (Scotland) Act 1974, s14 (reservations in dispositions).
2 *Matheson v Tinney* 1989 SLT 535; see also *Roebuck v Edmunds* 1991 GWD 27–1624.
3 See, for example, *Banff and Buchan DC v Earl of Seafield's Estate* 1988 SLT (Lands Tr) 21; see also ch 10, pt 6.
4 *Halliday* para 17–80; *McDonald* para 33–14; *Sinclair* para 7–29.
5 Land Tenure Reform (Scotland) Act 1974, s12.
6 Conveyancing (Scotland) Act 1874, s32; Conveyancing (Scotland) Act 1924, s9; Conveyancing Amendment (Scotland) Act 1938, s2(1).

the property, is sufficient to incorporate real burdens and conditions noted on the title sheet.[1]

The creation of real conditions is usually accompanied by an irritant and resolutive clause which allows the superior or grantor to start proceedings for declarator of irritancy if the conditions are breached.

(iii) Clause of entry

This clause simply states the date when the grantee obtains entry to the property. If no clause of entry is stated in the deed entry will be at the first term of Whitsunday (28 May) or Martinmas (28 November) following the date or last date of the conveyance, unless there is a clear contrary intention in the deed.[2]

(iv) Assignation of writs[3]

The assignation of writs clause made explicit the right of the grantee to call upon the grantor or his predecessors for production of any deeds necessary to defend his interest in the property. Production of such deeds might, of course, be necessary to enable the grantee to demonstrate a prescriptive and unchallengeable right to the property, for example in the event of sale or challenge to his title by a third party. Since 4 April 1979 it is no longer necessary to include a clause of assignation of writs, as the Land Registration (Scotland) Act 1979 imposes statutory obligations on the grantors of deeds. In the case of dispositions these are mainly to deliver all deeds and searches relating exclusively to the property and to make available as necessary deeds and searches relating in part to the property.[4] Where a feu grant is involved the obligation is to make available the deeds and searches necessary to enable the grantee to defend his right in the feu.[5] Both of these obligations can be expressly varied by the terms of a clause inserted in the deed.

---

1 Land Registration (Scotland) Act 1979, ss15(2), 17.
2 Conveyancing (Scotland) Act 1874, s28; Term and Quarter Days (Scotland) Act 1990, s1(1)(a).
3 *Halliday* paras 17-64, 22-12; *McDonald* paras 12-5, 29-27.
4 Section 16(1).
5 Section 16(2).

(v) Assignation of rents[1]

The effect of this clause was to transfer the right to receive any rents payable on the property to the grantee. Such a clause is no longer necessary as a result of s16(3)(a) of the Land Registration (Scotland) Act 1979, which, as with assignation of writs and obligations of relief, imports an implied term into the deed.

(vi) Obligation of relief[2]

The effect of the obligation of relief was to relieve the grantee of all feuduties and local and public burdens (eg rates) payable in respect of the land prior to the date of entry. This effect is now achieved by s16(3)(b) of the Land Registration (Scotland) Act 1979 and a specific clause is no longer necessary.

(vii) Warrandice[3]

Warrandice is a personal guarantee on the part of the grantor of the deed to the effect that:

(1) The grantee will not be evicted from the whole or any part of the subjects conveyed because of any defect in title. In this context mere lack of title is insufficient to found a claim based on warrandice; there must also be eviction in the form of a court decree against the grantee, or a court action to which the grantee has no defence.[4]

(2) There exist no real rights affecting the subjects conveyed which are adverse to the interests of the grantee and of which the grantee was unaware at the date of delivery of the deed in his favour. Such a situation might arise, for example, where a right of way which substantially interfered with the grantee's use or enjoyment of the property was discovered.[5]

The effect of the guarantee is that the grantor is bound to indemnify the grantee if either of these situations arises. The practical value

1 *Halliday* paras 17-65 and 22-13; *McDonald* para 12-6.
2 *Halliday* paras 17-66 and 22-14; *McDonald* para 12-7.
3 *Halliday* paras 4-28 to 4-52; *McDonald* paras 12-8 to 12-20; K Reid 'Warrandice in the Sale of Land' in D Cusine (ed) *A Scots Conveyancing Miscellany*, 152.
4 Reid op cit 157; *Watson v Swift & Co's JF* 1986 SLT 217 at 220H.
5 *Welsh v Russell* (1894) 21 R 769.

of warrandice therefore depends on the ability of the grantor to pay compensation, and, perhaps more fundamentally, the ability of the grantee to find the grantor at the time when the claim arises. The grantee's position will be strengthened if the defect is something which should have been discovered by his solicitor, in which case a claim may lie against him for professional negligence.

How far and in what circumstances the grantee is protected by warrandice depends on the degree of warrandice involved. There are three degrees of warrandice: absolute, fact and deed, and simple.

Absolute warrandice is an absolute guarantee that nothing will happen to interfere with the grantee's property rights. Therefore, if any interference does take place, whether or not arising from a cause under the control of the grantor, the grantee will be entitled to compensation. This form of warrandice is implied in all transfers of land for valuable consideration (and, therefore, all sales), and is the form of warrandice implied by statute to be conferred by the normal warrandice clause found in deeds which takes the form: 'I/We grant warrandice'.[1]

Warrandice from fact and deed is a guarantee against any loss caused by or arising out of any action by the grantor, whether the action is past, present or future. This is the form of warrandice usually granted by trustees.

Simple warrandice provides the lowest form of protection for the grantee. It merely guarantees that the grantee will not suffer loss as a result of a future voluntary act by the grantor. Simple warrandice would be appropriate in a gratuitous transaction.

Where no warrandice is provided for in the deed the appropriate degree will be implied. So in a sale absolute warrandice would be implied. On the other hand an express statement of a certain degree of warrandice supersedes any implied degree, so that a provision for simple warrandice in a sale would supersede absolute warrandice.

(viii) Certificate of value[2]

This certificate is included for the purpose of assessment of Inland Revenue stamp duty. Stamp duty is currently payable at the rate of 1 per cent on conveyances of land over £30,000. The duty is payable on the whole consideration, not merely the excess over £30,000.

---

1 Titles to Land Consolidation (Scotland) Act 1868, s5 and Sch B1.
2 *McDonald* paras 5–1 to 5–7 and 5–9 to 5–12; *Sinclair* para 9.7.

(ix) Testing Clause[1]

The testing clause simply records details of the execution of a probative deed, in this case a disposition or feu grant. Thus it contains details of the place and date of signature by the grantor(s) and details sufficient to identify the witnesses to these signatures. The inclusion of the designations of witnesses is not strictly essential although it is common practice, at least in dispositions and feu grants. All that is strictly necessary is that the designation of each witness should be appended to or follow his signature.[2]

A natural individual (as opposed to a corporate body), even if acting in a special capacity such as trustee, will normally simply sign the deed himself in the presence of two witnesses, who then also sign the deed, each adding the word 'witness' after his signature. It is not essential that the witness actually sees the signing, as long as the person signing acknowledges the signature before the witness signs. Certain categories of people cannot act as witnesses; these include the blind, corporate bodies, and children under sixteen.[3] It is in general no objection to a witness's competence that he is a beneficiary in terms of the deed witnessed.

Dispositions and feu grants are now commonly made by companies and local authorities and there are special provisions regarding the execution of deeds by these bodies.

As far as companies are concerned there are now three main ways in which they may execute a deed. These are signature by two directors, signature by one director and the company secretary, and signature by two persons authorised by the company.[4] The law as to execution by companies changed twice in the course of 1990,[5] but essentially all deeds granted since 30 July 1990 which are executed in one of these ways will be valid.[6] Deeds granted prior to that date could be executed either by signature by two directors, or by one director and the company secretary; in both cases the common seal of the company would have to be affixed.[7]

Local authorities execute deeds by affixing their seal and having

---

1   *McDonald* paras 2–28 to 2–30; *Sinclair* paras 9.9 to 9.10.
2   Conveyancing (Scotland) Act 1874, s38.
3   Age of Legal Capacity (Scotland) Act 1991, ss1, 9; see also K Norrie 'Age of Legal Capacity (Scotland) Act 1991', (1991) 36 JLSS 434 at 438.
4   Companies Act 1985, s36B, inserted by s72(1) of the Law Reform (Miscellaneous Provisions) (Scotland) Act 1990.
5   See K Reid 'Execution of Deeds by Companies' 1990 SLT (News) 369.
6   A variety of other methods are also valid for the period from 31 July to 30 November 1990; see K Reid, *supra* at 374.
7   Companies Act 1985, s36(3).

them signed by a responsible officer and two members of the council, witnesses not being essential[1].

Normally the testing clause will specify the number of pages in the deed, the place(s) of execution, the date(s) of execution, the name(s) of those signing, the names and designations of the witnesses, and contain details of any obvious alterations made to the deed prior to execution.

(x) Warrant for registration

This is only necessary where the deed is going to be recorded in the Register of Sasines. It takes the form of a warrant endorsed on the deed, usually signed by the grantee's solicitor, instructing the Keeper to record the deed in the appropriate division of the register.

(xi) Tenendas and reddendo clauses

These are peculiar to feu grants. The tenendas clause sets out the feudal nature of the holding, and the reddendo clause sets out the return in exchange for the vassal's holding. With the prohibition on creation of new feuduties the latter clause is now normally omitted from feu grants, though from the point of view of examination of title the terms of such clauses in older deeds may be important.

2. DEEDS OF CONDITIONS

A deed of conditions provides a means whereby real conditions affecting a number of properties can be created in a single document. They are commonly used where a number of properties are to be sold off, eg in a block of flats or even in a complete housing estate. The advantage of a deed of conditions is that once it is recorded the conditions it contains can be imported into any conveyance by reference to the deed without having to repeat them at length in each conveyance.[2]

A deed of conditions will normally contain a description of the property to be affected, followed by a list of the conditions applying

---

1 Local Government (Scotland) Act 1973, s194. This section also empowers local authorities to make their own arrangements as to execution of deeds.
2 Conveyancing (Scotland) Act 1874, s32.

to the property, and concluding with a clause constituting the conditions as real conditions. Conditions so created become effective from the date of recording or registration unless the contrary is specified in the deed.[1]

3. RECTIFICATION OF DEEDS

There is provision for application to court for the correction or rectification of deeds either under the Conveyancing (Scotland) Act 1874, s39 or the Law Reform (Miscellaneous Provisions)(Scotland) Act 1985, s8(1). The former relates to informalities in execution and all of the more recently reported cases have, in fact, been concerned with wills.[2] The latter allows rectification where the deed fails to reflect the intention of the parties. It has been suggested that before the court can order rectification under this provision six matters must be established:

'(1) that there is a document to be rectified; (2) that the document was intended to express or give effect to an already existing agreement arrived at between two (or more) parties; (3) that there was, when the document was executed such a pre-existing agreement – whether or not enforceable;[3] (4) that the agreement itself embodied and was an expression of one or more intentions common to (that is, shared by) the parties; (5) that the intentions were actual (not deemed) intentions; (6) that the agreement itself must have been reached at a definite point in time.'[4]

Cases where this provision has been invoked have involved: the erroneous inclusion of an additional piece of land in a disposition,[5] an error in numbering a unit in an industrial estate in a disposition of that unit,[6] and omissions in filling in a pro forma security document.[7]

1   Land Registration (Scotland) Act 1979, s17.
2   eg *Walker v Whitwell* (1916) 1 SLT 2.
3   On the necessity for a prior agreement see *George Thompson Services Ltd v Moore* 1992 GWD 3-149.
4   *Shaw v William Grant (Minerals) Ltd* 1989 SLT 121 at 121.
5   *Oliver v Gaughan* 1990 GWD 22-1247.
6   *MAC Electrical and Heating Engineers Ltd v Calscot Electrical (Distributors) Ltd* 1989 SCLR 498.
7   *Bank of Scotland v Graham* 1991 SLT 879.

18. Compulsory purchase[1]

1. INTRODUCTION

It is often necessary in the public interest for land to be purchased by bodies (such as local authorities) who have the duty to carry out developments necessary for the community at large, eg roads, airports, schools, hospitals etc. As the sites earmarked for such projects may have a number of existing owners, it is inevitable that some of those owners will be unwilling to sell. A number of public bodies, therefore, have statutory powers of compulsory purchase.

Where property is acquired compulsorily, the end result is the same as in a voluntary sale: the new owner becomes infeft by recording a title in the Register of Sasines (or registering it in the Land Register). However, the route by which that end is achieved is somewhat different. Our first task in this chapter, therefore, will be to outline the procedure by which title is transferred in a compulsory purchase. There is also a complex set of statutory rules for determining the price and other compensation due to the possibly unwilling seller; these too will be looked at briefly, but it is beyond the scope of this book to deal with them in a comprehensive fashion.

The main statutes covering compulsory purchase procedure are the Lands Clauses Consolidation (Scotland) Act 1845 and the Acquisition of Land (Authorisation Procedure) (Scotland) Act 1947. Parallel Acts for England were consolidated in the Compulsory Purchase Act 1965, but the Scottish legislation has not so far been similarly consolidated. The compensation principles are mainly contained in the Land Compensation (Scotland) Act 1963 and the Land Compensation (Scotland) Act 1973 (both as amended by the Planning and Compensation Act 1991). These acts also have English counterparts, containing substantially identical provisions.

The above legislation provides the statutory framework for all compulsory acquisitions. However, before any particular body can

---

1 For an up to date treatment of this subject from its Scottish point of view, see Rowan-Robinson *Compulsory Purchase and Compensation*.

carry out a compulsory purchase, there must be a statute (generally known as the 'special act'), not only conferring compulsory purchase powers on that body, but giving it powers to acquire land for the particular purpose it has in mind.

2. ACQUISITION PROCEDURE

Purchase by agreement

The special act usually gives power to an acquiring authority to purchase land by agreement as well as compulsorily. This can be done either before a compulsory purchase order has been confirmed by the Secretary of State (if the seller is willing), or after an order has been confirmed (where the seller may not have been willing, but is now prepared to bow to the inevitable). The acquiring authority may also use this power to purchase property which has come on the market anyway, either because it will need that land some time in the future and is taking the present opportunity to buy in advance of its requirements, or because its proposed scheme does not require a particular site and it is convenient to take the first suitable one that becomes available for sale.

The procedure in such a case is the same as for any voluntary sale. However, the purchaser should be careful to negotiate a price that is no less than he would have been statutorily entitled to had the sale been compulsory; otherwise, his co-operation might cost him financially.

Even although the sale is voluntary, the acquiring authority may take title by schedule conveyance (see below) in order to clear the site of any real conditions in the title.

Compulsory purchase procedure

Compulsory purchase order.   When a public body with compulsory purchase powers decides that it requires a particular piece of land, its first step (if it cannot negotiate a purchase by agreement) is to draw up a compulsory purchase order. This document is in statutory form and includes a description of the property and a plan. The CPO does not become effective, however, until it has been confirmed by the Secretary of State; and before it has been submitted to the latter for confirmation, an advert announcing the order must be published on two successive weeks in one or more local newspaper. Notice of the order must also be served on every owner, lessee or occupier within the site (apart from tenants for a month or less).

Before the Secretary of State makes his decision on the CPO, there is a period within which persons with an interest in the land, or any other members of the public, may lodge objections with the acquiring authority. If the objections are sufficiently extensive, the Secretary of State may hold a public local enquiry (which will be advertised in the press) before a reporter appointed by him.

There are three possible decisions by the Secretary of State: he may confirm the order, he may refuse it entirely, or he may confirm it with modifications; in the last case, the modifications may originate from objections lodged and/or the findings of any enquiry, or they may originate from the Secretary of State himself or his advisers.

If a CPO is confirmed, with or without modifications, the acquiring authority cannot proceed further without first advertising the fact in a local newspaper; this advert can be combined with an announcement that title is to be taken by means of a general vesting declaration (see below).

Appeal to Court of Session. The Secretary of State's decision is final on the merits of the CPO. However, any person aggrieved by the order may appeal within six weeks of the order being made on certain legal grounds, ie (a) that the order is *ultra vires* or (b) that there has been a procedural irregularity.

Taking title: notice to treat procedure

After a compulsory purchase order has been confirmed by the Secretary of State, and the required advertisement has appeared in the press, the acquiring authority has set the scene to proceed with the actual acquisition of property from individual owners. The traditional method is by sending each owner a **notice to treat**, notifying the owner that his land is to be acquired and inviting him to submit a compensation claim. A minimum of six weeks must pass after the confirmation of the order before a notice to treat can be sent; at the other end of the scale, the right to serve a notice to treat expires three years after the confirmation of the CPO, and an acquiring authority who still wanted to proceed after the lapse of such a period would have to submit a fresh CPO to the Secretary of State. After the service of a notice to treat, it was formerly the case that there was no time limit imposed upon the acquiring authority for proceeding with the purchase. It is now provided in the Planning and Compensation Act 1991[1] that a notice to treat will cease to have effect at the end of a period of three years unless a specified event has occurred which demonstrates the authority's intention to implement the rights given by the notice.

Settlement of compensation. The compensation claim of each owner will initially be negotiated with the acquiring authority. If any of them cannot agree, their claim will be remitted to the Lands Tribunal for Scotland.

Notice of entry. Where a notice to treat has been served and the acquiring authority requires entry to the land prior to the amount of compensation being settled, it can serve a notice of entry on the owner concerned. At least fourteen days notice must be given, after which the acquiring authority may take possession of the land.

Schedule conveyance. The acquiring authority may take title in the same way as in a voluntary sale, ie by recording in the Register of Sasines or registering in the Land Register a disposition in its favour signed by each owner. The 1845 Act[2] provides a special form of disposition (generally known as a schedule conveyance) which may be used when bodies with compulsory purchase powers are taking title. There is some uncertainty about the exact legal effect of recording such a conveyance, but the weight of judicial opinion favours the view that it gives the acquiring authority a title that is free of any relationship with the superior, and clear of any real conditions, imposed by the superior or otherwise.[3] This does **not** include any feuduty, which must be redeemed by the acquiring authority making the requisite capital payment to the superior;[4] this contrasts with the case in voluntary sales where of course it is the **seller's** obligation to redeem the feuduty, and is a recognition of the fact that in the present context the seller may have been unwilling to sell.

Notarial instrument. If the seller is unwilling to sign a conveyance, or he cannot be traced, or there is some problem with his title, the acquiring authority may instead become infeft by recording a

1 Section 78
2 Lands Clauses Consolidation (Scotland) Act 1845, s80 and Sch A.
3 See *Rowan-Robinson* (1990) pp 69–71.
4 See chs 2 and 10 above.

notarial instrument (signed by a Notary Public) in the Register of Sasines (or registering it in the Land Register).[1] This has the same legal effect as recording a schedule conveyance. The acquiring authority must first deposit the compensation due to the seller in a bank account in his name.

General vesting declaration

The notice to treat method is the traditional way by which an acquiring authority takes title. However, this method has obvious disadvantages; this is particularly true if the acquiring authority is purchasing a site where there are a number of owners involved, with the consequent necessity of a number of individual conveyances (or notarial instruments). Using a general vesting declaration allows an acquiring authority to take title to the entire site comprised in the CPO by recording a single document signed only by themselves.[2] Because of this, it is the commonest method used nowadays.

If the acquiring authority wants to use a general vesting declaration, it must advertise the fact in a local newspaper; this advert may be combined (and usually is) with the advert announcing the confirmation of the CPO by the Secretary of State. Then, although strictly speaking a notice to treat as such is not required, it must give written notification to each person having a legal interest in the land in a similar way, inviting them to submit their compensation claims.

The general vesting declaration (which is in statutory form and contains a conveyancing description of the lands) cannot be recorded until two months have passed since the confirmation of the CPO. It must also contain a date of vesting (at least twenty-eight days after the recording of the GVD), which is the date when title passes to the acquiring authority; it is also entitled to take entry at this point, without the necessity of sending a notice of entry.

The above time limits effectively mean that a minimum period of three months must pass between the confirmation of the CPO and the acquiring authority being able to take entry. If the acquiring authority requires early entry, therefore, the notice to treat procedure can cut this period by up to a month; otherwise the general vesting procedure is a far easier way to complete title.

1 Lands Clauses Consolidation (Scotland) Act 1845, ss 75, 76.
2 Town and Country Planning (Scotland) Act 1972, s278 and Sch 24.

Date of entry

The date of entry is normally the date when the acquiring authority actually takes possession of the land; however, where title is taken by means of a general vesting declaration, the date of entry is taken to be the date of vesting (even if the claimant is still in possession), as that is the date when ownership passes.[1] As in the case of voluntary sales, interest is paid on the price (in this case the compensation) for the period from entry until settlement; the rate of interest is prescribed in regulations made by the Treasury from time to time.[2]

The date of entry will also be the date of valuation of the claimant's interest, except in cases where the amount of the compensation claim is fixed (either by agreement or by the Lands Tribunal) at an earlier date; in the latter case, the date of valuation is the date when the amount of compensation was determined.[3]

3. ASSESSMENT OF COMPENSATION

Introduction

The statutory rules regarding the assessment of compensation payable to owners (as well as tenants and others with a legal interest that has been compulsorily acquired), are extremely complex, and a detailed exposition of them is well outwith the scope of this book. In the pages that follow therefore, we will be attempting only to provide an overview, so that the reader new to these concepts can establish some basic landmarks as an aid to further exploration.

Although the detailed rules may be complex, the rationale behind compulsory purchase compensation is straightforward: its purpose is to put the owner (or other claimant), so far as money can achieve it, in the same position as if the compulsory purchase had not taken place. The overall measure of his compensation is therefore the loss he has incurred due to the compulsory acquisition of his interest, and in this respect it is not dissimilar to the measure of damages for delict or breach of contract. And so (confining ourselves for

---

1 *Birrell Ltd v Edinburgh District Council* 1982 SC (HL) 75, 1982 SLT 363.
2 Land Compensation (Scotland) Act 1963, s40.
3 *Birmingham Corporation v West Midland Baptist (Trust) Association Inc* [1970] AC 874.

the moment, for the sake of simplicity, to the situation where the interest being acquired is that of an owner-occupier) although the major element of his compensation is likely to be the market value of the land taken, his loss will generally extend beyond that. If only part of his land has been taken, he may be due a sum for **injurious affection,** representing the drop in value to the part remaining in his ownership. And (whether all or only part of his land is taken), he will certainly incur other losses (removal expenses, loss of business etc) which he can claim under the heading of **disturbance.**

An essential concept in calculating a claimant's loss is the adoption of a fiction generally known as the **no scheme world.** By this is meant an imaginary world in which the acquiring authority never obtained their CPO and the development scheme for which the land was acquired never took place, or was ever even proposed. The reason for this is that the completion of the acquiring authority's scheme (or even the announcement of it) will change the value, not only of the land developed, but in the surrounding area; in the latter case, sometimes the value will be increased (eg if the scheme provides better amenities) and sometimes it will be decreased (if a new road, for example, creates a nuisance to immediate neighbours). If the purpose of compensation, therefore, is to put the claimant as far as possible in the position in which he would have been had the scheme not taken place and his interest not been acquired, it follows that this position belongs in the no scheme world; it is in the context of that world, therefore, rather than the real one where the scheme exists, in which his compensation should be calculated.

When studying (and sometimes getting lost in) the detail of the statutory rules for working out compulsory purchase compensation, it is useful to fix one's sights on the concept of the no scheme world as one's guiding star; for the re-creation of this imaginary world is the end purpose of all these rules.

Compensation for land taken

Whether all or only part of a claimant's land has been taken, three main elements are taken into account in working out its value in the no scheme world. These are (1) the market value rules (2) the statutory planning assumptions and (3) the effect of betterment and worsenment. Most of this derives from the Land Compensation (Scotland) Act 1963.

Market value rules. These are derived from s12 of the 1963 Act and are as follows:

(1) No allowance is to be made on account of the acquisition being compulsory. Prior to 1919, the law allowed an additional payment as a 'sweetener' to take account of the fact that the seller was unwilling; the rationale was that, without their compulsory purchase powers, the acquiring authority would probably have had to pay over the odds to get him to move, and that at least part of this should be recognised in the compensation payment. Such a payment no longer forms part of the current philosophy as represented in the 1963 Act. A partial exception to this is the entitlement to a home loss payment of a person displaced from his home (including an owner-occupier) as the result of a compulsory purchase scheme.[1]

(2) The value is to be the amount which the land if sold in the open market by a willing seller might be expected to realise.[2] This rule is the main yardstick by which compensation for land taken is calculated; in special circumstances, as we will see below, rule 5 may be used instead.

(3) No allowance is to be made for the special suitability of the land to a particular purchaser. This special suitability is to be discounted in two[3] particular situations: (a) where the acquiring authority's purpose could be applied only in pursuance of statutory powers and (b) where there is no market apart from the requirement of any authority possessing compulsory purchase powers.

The purpose of rule 3 is to discount any special value which the land has to the acquiring authority (because of its nature or location) which would not apply to other potential purchasers and so would not form part of the market value in the no scheme world. However, part (a), though superficially effective, turns out on closer examination to have very little application: very few of the usual purposes for which an acquiring authority purchases land can **only** be pursued with statutory powers. Bodies with compulsory purchase powers may be the **normal** developers of roads, airports, hospitals, schools and the like,

---

1 Land Compensation (Scotland) Act 1973, ss27–30 (as amended by the Planning and Compensation Act 1991, s71).
2 For an analysis of this see *Inland Revenue Commissioners v Clay and Buchanan* [1914] 3 KB 466, (1914–15 All ER 882).
3 Formally three; see the Planning and Compensation Act 1991, s79.

but all of these, and others, may also be undertaken by private developers.

(4) No allowance is to be made for any use of the land that is illegal or contrary to public health. This, for example, would exclude any value resulting from a development that did not have planning consent (even if it was immune from enforcement). Also discounted would be any value resulting from a use that amounted to overcrowding in terms of the housing legislation or was in breach of fire regulations etc.

(5) In special cases, the Lands Tribunal may allow the basis of compensation to be, instead of the market value in terms of rule 2, the cost of equivalent reinstatement. This means the cost of purchasing, building or adapting other property for the particular purpose for which the claimant had used the acquired land. This rule is used to cover cases where the market value of the property for its existing use would be insufficient to provide the claimant with the means to set up similarly elsewhere. The most common example of a rule 5 valuation is where the property being acquired is a church. Rule 5 valuations can only be applied at the discretion of the Lands Tribunal, where they are satisfied that certain conditions apply: (a) that the land is devoted to a purpose, and but for the acquisition would continue to be so devoted (b) that the purpose is one for which there is no general demand or market for the property and (c) there is a *bona fide* intention to reinstate on another site.

(6) The provisions of rule 2 are not to affect compensation for disturbance or any other matter not directly based on the value of the land. This is simply to make it clear that the market value rules are only designed for working out the value of the heritable property element in a compensation claim, and do not apply to other pre-existing heads of compensation, such as disturbance.

Statutory planning assumptions.[1] In a no scheme world, it is not necessarily the case that an owner selling his land would sell it at a value reflecting only its existing use; sometimes the land will be worth more because of its potential for being developed for a different purpose, ie it has development value. For example, an owner of farmland may sell the land to a house builder and achieve a higher

---

1 Land Compensation (Scotland) Act 1963, ss22–25.

price than is normally paid for farmland because of its potential as building land.

However, this farmland would only have development value as building land for houses if planning permission had been obtained for the new purpose or, at the very least, there was a strong likelihood of planning permission being granted. The best way of determining the latter possibility is to check how the land is classified in the development plan (ie the structure and local plans);[1] only if the farmland in question was earmarked for possible residential development would there be any reasonable certainty of planning permission being granted, and of the land's development value being realised.

If such land is being compulsorily purchased, it seems only fair that the price paid should include any such potential development value which the owner could have realised by a sale in the no scheme world. This is done by applying the statutory planning assumptions (eight in all) which are designed to cover all possible types of development for which planning permission might be granted. For example, in assessing the market value, any existing planning permission can be taken into account (assumption 1); also, planning permission can be assumed for a development where the land is allocated primarily for a use specified in the current development plan (assumption 5), eg if the land is allocated for housing purposes, planning permission may be assumed for any development for the purpose of housing. The remaining assumptions allow planning permission to be assumed in a number of other situations, designed to include all possibilities of development value.

Effects of betterment or worsenment. Betterment and worsenment refer respectively to situations where land values in an area have either been increased or decreased by the acquiring authority's scheme, or the prospect of it. In the no scheme world such effects would not exist, and so should be disregarded in assessing the market value of the land being acquired. For example, local land values might increase if the scheme had the effect of improving amenity, eg by the provision of a new shopping centre, but no account should be taken of such an increase in assessing the market value; conversely, if the scheme involved the building of an industrial estate, any decreases in local land values should similarly be disregarded.

1 See ch 12, pt 2 above.

The best formulation of this rule is to be found in case law, where it is embodied in the *Pointe Gourde Principle*:[1]

'Compensation for the compulsory acquisition of land cannot include an increase [or decrease] in value which is entirely due to the scheme underlying the acquisition.'

The *Pointe Gourde* case itself was a case of betterment; however subsequent case law has extended the principle to cover cases of worsenment also.[2]

Section 13 of the Land Compensation (Scotland) Act 1963, in two and a half pages of obscure and tortured prose, appears to be attempting to give statutory formulation to basically the same principle, though less comprehensively and much less elegantly. Strictly speaking, of course, the statutory formulation should take precedence as a legal source over the case law version; suffice it to say, in a work at this level, that the two read together operate to discount any betterment or worsenment caused by the acquiring authority's scheme.

Even before a scheme is proposed and the required land made the subject of a CPO, there may be an indication in the development plan or elsewhere that compulsory purchase is a future possibility. This may deter potential purchasers, with the result that the market value of the land decreases because of the prospect of compulsory purchase. Section 16 of the 1963 Act provides that, if and when the land is acquired, such depreciation (unknown of course in the no scheme world) should be disregarded.

It may be that an owner wants to sell ahead of the time when the land might be required by the acquiring authority which, if it happens at all, might not occur for several years. Meanwhile the prospect of the compulsory acquisition may be preventing him from being able to sell at the expected value, or at all. In this situation (known as **planning blight**) the owner is entitled to serve a notice on the acquiring authority (known as a blight notice), requiring it to purchase ahead of its requirements, so that he can sell when he needs to and obtain his full entitlement to compensation, including the market value in a no scheme world.[3] This right is not enjoyed

---

1 *Pointe Gourde Quarrying & Transport Co Ltd v Sub-Intendant of Crown Lands* [1947] AC 565, 63 TLR 486.
2 *Jelson Ltd v Blaby District Council* [1978] 1 All ER 548, [1977] 1 WLR 1020; *Melwood Units Property Ltd v Commissioner of Main Roads* [1979] AC 426, [1979] 1 All ER 161.
3 Town and Country Planning (Scotland) Act 1972, Part IX.

by all possible claimants, but only owner-occupiers of dwelling-houses, of agricultural units and of certain small businesses.

Injurious affection[1]

If only part of a person's land is taken, it is likely that the part remaining in his ownership will drop in value as a result. This may be due to nuisance value caused by the new development on the acquired land (eg if the remaining land is now up against a new main road), or it may be that the land left is less economically viable when not part of a larger site. The latter result is particularly likely if the land taken intersects the site, leaving the claimant's land in two separate parts, eg where a new road cuts across farmland, separating the farm buildings from some of the fields. Injurious affection caused by the physical separation of the acquired land from that remaining (as opposed to depreciation caused by the operation of the scheme) is known as **severance**.

In addition, therefore, to the market value of the land taken, a claimant is entitled to an additional payment in respect of injurious affection for the land remaining in his ownership. The amount payable is the drop in value to the claimant's interest in the remaining land. This of course is in keeping with the general principle which we discussed above, ie that the overall basis of a claim should be the loss incurred by a claimant as a result of the compulsory purchase.

Material detriment.[2] When part of a person's land is acquired, it may be such a substantial portion that the owner feels he has no use for what is left, ie that the remaining part is unviable on its own. In certain cases he is entitled to serve a notice on the acquiring authority claiming that there has been material detriment to his interest and requiring it to acquire all of that interest. The acquiring authority may accept the notice or dispute it, and in the latter case the matter will be decided by the Lands Tribunal. If material detriment is confirmed, the claimant will of course not get injurious affection, but will instead be entitled to the market value for the whole of his land.

Set off. The principles discussed above apply to situations where the compulsory acquisition of part of a site lowers the value of the part remaining. There could, however, be cases where it has the

1 See *Rowan-Robinson* pp 239–257.
2 See *Rowan-Robinson* pp 62–67.

opposite effect. The arrival of the acquiring authority's scheme, if it adds new amenities, may actually add to the value of the claimant's remaining land. In such a case there is applied the principle of set off, which is basically the principle of injurious affection in reverse. Instead of the drop in value of the remaining land being added to the compensation for the land taken, the **increase** in value to the land remaining is **subtracted** from the compensation for the land being acquired, and the claimant receives the net amount.[1]

There could of course be cases where the increase in value of what he has left exceeds the market value of what is being taken. In such a case the claimant simply gets nothing at all. There cannot be a situation where he has to pay money to the acquiring authority for the privilege of having part of his land taken.

Compensation for disturbance[2]

Any loss resulting from the compulsory acquisition which is additional to the market value for land taken and injurious affection can be claimed under the general heading of disturbance.

Typical items in a disturbance claim would include goodwill, temporary loss of profits, the cost of new premises, removal expenses, legal fees, bank interest for bridging loans etc.

A tenant who has no compensatable interest (eg a residential tenant with statutory security of tenure)[3] has a more limited disturbance claim (eg for removal expenses) under statute.[4]

---

1   Land Compensation (Scotland) Act 1963, s14.
2   See *Rowan-Robinson* ch 10.
3   See ch 8, pt 4 above.
4   Land Compensation (Scotland) Act 1973, ss34, 35.

Appendix

There follow specimens of a disposition, land certificate and charge certificate, all in respect of the same fictitious property. The burdens section of the land certificate includes conditions typical of those normally inserted by a superior in a feu charter or feu contract, and the charge certificate includes a specimen standard security of the type used by a building society.

These specimen documents are not intended as legal styles, but only by way of illustration, in view of the many references to such deeds throughout the book.

The specimen charge certificate and land certificate are reproduced by kind permission of the Keeper of the Registers of Scotland.

1 Specimen disposition

(1) I COLIN ANDREW MACPHERSON, residing formerly at Twenty-three Firpark Crescent Paisley and now at Fifteen Park Avenue Paisley heritable proprietor of the subjects hereinafter disponed IN CONSIDERATION of the sum of NINE THOUSAND POUNDS (£9,000) STERLING paid to me by MICHAEL FRANCIS DONOGHUE residing at One Wellmeadow Street Paisley of which sum I hereby acknowledge
(2) receipt and discharge him Have Sold and Do Hereby DISPONE to and in favour of the said Michael Francis Donoghue and to his executors and assignees whomsoever
(3) heritably and irredeemably (First) ALL and WHOLE that plot or area of ground within the Parish of Paisley and Shire of Renfrew extending to Four hundred and fifty-two square yards or thereby Imperial Measure being the plot or area of ground more particularly described in, disponed by and delineated blue on the plan annexed and subscribed as relative to Feu Contract containing Feu Disposition by Sir Gabriel

245

Walker in favour of Joseph Smith dated the Fifteenth and Twenty-first and recorded in the Division of the General Register of Sasines for the County of Renfrew on the Twenty-seventh all days of November in the year Nineteen hundred and eight and (Two) that plot or area of ground within the said Parish and County extending to One hundred and three square yards or thereby Imperial Measure being the plot or area of ground more particularly described in, disponed by and delineated pink on the plan annexed and subscribed as relative to Feu Charter by the said Sir Gabriel Walker in favour of Marion Wilson or Bennett dated Twenty-second and Twenty-fifth November and recorded in the said Division of the General Register of Sasines on Third December all in the year Nineteen hundred and twenty-seven; Together with (One) the dwelling house erected on the said plot or area of ground first above disponed known as Fifteen Park Avenue Paisley (Two) the heritable fittings and fixtures in the said dwellinghouse (Three) the whole parts privileges and pertinents of the subjects hereby disponed and (Four) my whole right

(4) title and interest present and future therein; But the subjects hereby disponed are so disponed always with and under the burdens stipulations conditions provisions declarations and others specified and contained in the said Feu Contract and in the said Feu Charter dated and recorded as aforesaid;

(5) WITH ENTRY as at the Fourteenth day of February Nineteen
(6) hundred and seventy-three; And I assign the writs and have delivered those specified in the Inventory thereof annexed and subscribed as relative hereto being the only writs in my possession; and I assign all right competent to me quoad the subjects hereby disponed to demand exhibition or delivery of

(7) all other and prior writs and searches; And I assign the rents; And I bind myself and my successors to free and

(8) relieve my said disponee and his foresaids of all feuduties and
(9) public burdens; And I grant warrandice; And I certify that
(10) the transaction hereby effected does not form part of a larger transaction or of a series of transactions in respect of which the amount or value or the aggregate amount or value of the consideration exceeds ten thousand pounds:

(11) IN WITNESS WHEREOF these presents typewritten on this and the two preceding pages are subscribed by me at Paisley on the Fourth day of January Nineteen hundred and seventy-

three before these witnesses Flora MacDonald, Secretary and Charles Edward Stewart, Law Apprentice, both in the employment of Gilmour and Moss, Solicitors, Paisley.

(sgd) Flora MacDonald, Witness

(sgd) Colin A MacPherson

(sgd) Chas E Stewart, Witness

(12) REGISTER on behalf of the within named MICHAEL FRANCIS DONOGHUE in the REGISTER of the COUNTY of RENFREW.

(sgd) Gilmour and Moss
Solicitors, Paisley,
Agents.

KEY TO CLAUSES (See ch 17)

(1) Narrative clause
(2) Dispositive clause
(3) Statutory description by reference
(4) Reference to burdens
(5) Clause of entry
(6) Assignation of writs (no longer required in dispositions signed
       after 4 April 1979)
(7) Assignation of rents ("   "   )
(8) Obligation of relief ("   "   )
(9) Warrandice clause
(10) Certificate of value
(11) Testing clause
(12) Warrant of registration

2   SPECIMEN LAND CERTIFICATE

(Land Registration (Scotland) Rules 1980 Rule 14)

LAND REGISTER OF SCOTLAND

LAND CERTIFICATE

TITLE NUMBER: REN   4701

SUBJECTS: 15 PARK AVENUE, PAISLEY

This Land Certificate, issued pursuant to Section 5(2) of the Land Registration (Scotland) Act 1979, is a copy of the Title Sheet relating to the above subjects.

Statement of Indemnity

Subject to any specific qualifications entered in the Title Sheet of which this Land Certificate is a copy, a person who suffers loss as a result of any of the events specified in section 12(1) of the above Act shall be entitled to be indemnified in respect of that loss by the Keeper of the Registers of Scotland in terms of that Act.

ATTENTION IS DRAWN TO THE NOTICE AND GENERAL INFORMATION OVERLEAF.

NOTICE

This Land Certificate was made to agree with the Title Sheet of which it is a copy on the most recent date entered below.

14 APR. 1981	20 AUG. 1983			

This Land Certificate may be made to agree with the Title Sheet at any time without payment. Application should be made on Form 8.

GENERAL INFORMATION

1.   OVERRIDING INTERESTS. A registered interest in land is in terms of section 3(1) of the Land Registration (Scotland) Act 1979 subject to overriding interests defined in section 28 of that Act (hereinafter referred to as 'the 1979 Act') as:

in relation to any interest in land, the right or interest over it of

(a) the lessee under a lease which is not a long lease;

(b) the lessee under a long lease who, prior to the commencement of the 1979 Act, has acquired a real right to the subjects of the lease by virtue of possession of them;

(c) a crofter or cottar within the meaning of section 3 or 28(4) respectively of the Crofters (Scotland) Act 1955, or a landholder or statutory small tenant within the meaning of section 2(2) or 32(1) respectively of the Small Landholders (Scotland) Act 1911;

(d) the proprietor of the dominant tenement in a servitude;

(e) the Crown or any Government or other public department, or any public or local authority, under any enactment or rule of law, other than an enactment or rule of law authorising or requiring the recording of a deed in the Register of Sasines or registration in order to complete the right or interest;

(f) the holder of a floating charge whether or not the charge has attached to the interest;

(g) a member of the public in respect of any public right of way or in respect of any right held inalienably by the Crown in trust for the public;

(h) any person, being a right which has been made real, otherwise than by the recording of a deed in the Register of Sasines or by registration; or

(i) any other person under any rule of law relating to common interest or joint or common property, not being a right or interest constituting a real right, burden or condition entered in the title sheet of the interest in land under section 6(1)(e) of the 1979 Act or having effect by virtue of a deed recorded in the Register of Sasines,

but does not include any subsisting burden or condition enforceable against the interest in land and entered in its title sheet under section 6(1) of the 1979 Act.

General Information continued on inside back cover.

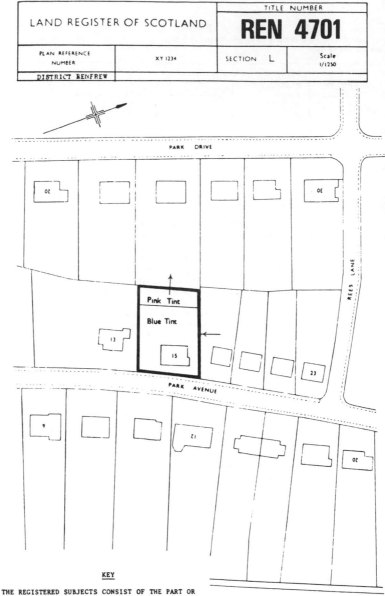

	TITLE NUMBER
LAND REGISTER OF SCOTLAND	**REN 4701**

PLAN REFERENCE NUMBER	XY 1234	SECTION L	Scale 1/1250
DISTRICT RENFREW			

KEY

THE REGISTERED SUBJECTS CONSIST OF THE PART OR
PARTS EDGED WITH A THICK LINE REPRESENTING THE
RED EDGING ON THE TITLE PLAN, MORE PARTICULARLY
DESCRIBED IN THE PROPERTY SECTION.

1.

LAND REGISTER OF SCOTLAND

Date of First
Registration
14 Apr. 1981   TITLE NUMBER REN 4701

A. PROPERTY SECTION

INTEREST   MAP REFERENCE
Proprietor   XY 1234L

DESCRIPTION
Subjects 15 PARK AVENUE PAISLEY, edged red on the Title Plan.

Note: The minerals are excepted. The conditions under which the minerals are
       held are set out in the Feu Contract in Entry 1 and the Feu Charter in
       Entry 2 of the Burdens Section.

2.

TITLE NUMBER REN 4701

B. PROPRIETORSHIP SECTION

Entry Number	Proprietor	Date of Registration	
1.	GEORGE BERNARD McDONALD and MARY ISABELLA HALL or MORRIS or McDONALD, spouses, 45 North Road, Paisley, equally between them and the survivor of them	20 AUG. 1983	Consideration £27,500 Entry 12 AUG. 1983

Note: There are in respect of the subjects in this title no subsisting occupancy rights, in terms of the Matrimonial Homes (Family Protection) (Scotland) Act 1981, of spouses of persons who were formerly entitled to the said subjects.

3.

TITLE NUMBER REN 4701

C. CHARGES SECTION

Entry Number	Specification	Date of Registration
1.	Standard Security for £20,750 and further sums by said George Bernard McDonald and Mary Isabella Hall or Morris or McDonald to FOUNDATION BUILDING SOCIETY, having its Chief Office at New Malden House, Cardiff	20 AUG. 1983

4.

TITLE NUMBER REN 4701

D. BURDENS SECTION

Entry
Number   Specification

1.   Feu Contract containing Feu Disposition by Sir Gabriel Walker (first
          party) to Joseph Smith (second party) and his heirs and assignees,
          recorded G. R. S. (Renfrew) 27 NOV. 1908 of the plot of ground tinted
          blue on the Title Plan, contains the following burdens:

          (First) The first party reserves to himself and his successors in the
          Estate of Superiority hereby created the whole coal, shale, ironstone,
          limestone, freestone, whinstone, fireclay and whole other stones,
          metals, minerals, fossils and other substances whatsoever in and under
          the said plot or area of ground hereby disponed with full power to
          search for, work, win and carry away the same by such mode or
          process either by complete or partial excavation as he or they may
          consider expedient, and also right to carry underground from one
          adjacent subjects to another the metals, minerals and others therein
          and for these or any of these purposes to sink pits and carry on all
          other operations necessary but so as not to enter upon the surface of
          the said plot or area of ground being always bound to pay to the
          second party or his foresaids the damages that may be occasioned to
          the said plot or area of ground or the buildings thereon by any of the
          said operations as such damages shall be ascertained failing mutual
          agreement by two arbiters to be mutually chosen or by an oversman to
          be named by such arbiters in the event of their differing in opinion;
          (Second) The second party and his foresaids shall be bound within
          twelve months from Whitsunday 1908 to erect and thereafter maintain
          in good order and repair on the said plot or area of ground hereby
          disponed a self-contained dwelling house and relative
          offices; /

5.

TITLE NUMBER REN 4701

D. BURDENS SECTION

Entry
Number   Specifications

offices; Declaring that the said self-contained dwelling-house and
relative offices and any renewals thereof shall be erected in conformity
with plans and elevations and of materials approved of by the first
party or his foresaids and shall be capable of yielding in all time coming
a yearly rental of at least triple the amount of the feuduty of £5. 5s and
shall not at any time be occupied by more than one tenant; (Third) The
second party or his foresaids shall be bound forthwith to erect and
thereafter maintain in good repair and when necessary renew on the
East a parapet wall and railing and on the West an iron bar fence to be
approved of by the first party or his foresaids, and to erect on the
remaining boundaries suitable fences to be approved of by the first
party or his foresaids, which fences shall be mutual and shall be
maintained in good repair and if necessary renewed at the joint expense
of the second party or his foresaids and the adjoining feuars to the
satisfaction of the first party or his foresaids; (Fourth) The first party
and his foresaids shall not be bound to adhere to the existing feuing or
road plans of the Lands of which the said plot or area of ground forms
a part, but he may alter or vary the same as he may think proper;
(Fifth) The second party and his foresaids shall provide for the drainage
of the said plot or area of ground and the buildings thereon to the
satisfaction of the Local Authorities regulating such matters from time
to time; (Sixth) It shall not be lawful to the second party or his
foresaids to excavate the said plot or area of ground excepting
only/

6.

TITLE NUMBER REN 4701

D. BURDENS SECTION

only for the purpose of building thereon or to carry on upon the said plot or area of ground any business whatever, or to do anything on the ground that can be deemed a nuisance, or to erect any buildings except of the description before specified, the said plot or area of ground being feued for the erection thereon of a self-contained dwelling house and relative offices as before specified and for no other purpose whatever; and (Seventh) The second party and his foresaids shall be bound to keep the said self-contained dwelling house and relative offices to be erected on the said plot or area of ground constantly insured against loss by fire with a responsible Insurance Company to the full value thereof and regularly to pay the premiums of insurance thereon and to exhibit the receipts therefor if and when required by the first party or his foresaids; And in the event of the said self-contained dwelling house and offices being destroyed or damaged by fire the second party or his foresaids shall be bound to restore them to the stipulated value aforesaid within one year after such destruction or damage, and the whole sum to be received from the Insurance Company shall be expended in the re-erection of said buildings or the repair of such damage; Declaring that if the second party or his foresaids shall contravene or fail to implement any of the burdens,/

7.

TITLE NUMBER REN 4701

D. BURDENS SECTION

Entry
Number   Specification

burdens, conditions declarations and others herein written, this feu
right and all that may have followed hereon shall at the option of the
first party or his foresaids become null and void, and the second party
and his foresaids shall forfeit his or their whole right and title to the
feu, which with all buildings erected thereon shall revert and belong to
the firsty party or his foresaids free and disencumbered of all burdens
whatsoever as if this feu right had never been granted.

2.   Feu Charter by Sir Gabriel Walker (who and whose successors are
          referred to as 'The Superior') to Marion Wilson or Bennett (who and
          whose heirs and assignees are referred to as 'The feuars'), recorded G.
          R. S. (Renfrew) 3 DEC. 1927, of the plot of ground tinted pink on the
          Title Plan contains the following burdens:
          (First) there are expressly reserved from this Conveyance the mines,
          metals and minerals and all quarries of stone of all kinds within the said
          plot or area of ground hereby disponed with right to search for, work,
          win and carry away the same on payment to the feuar of such
          damages as may be thereby occasioned to the surface of the lands, as
          the same shall be ascertained by two Arbiters, one to be chosen by
          each of the Superior and the feuar or in the event of their differing in
          Opinion by an Oversman to be appointed by such Arbiters: (Second)
          the said plot or area of ground being in addition to the plot or area of
          ground already held in Feu by the feuar in terms of the Feu Contract in
          Entry 1 it is hereby expressly declared that the said areas shall be
          regarded as one indivisible feu and that the feuar shall not be allowed
          at any time to erect any buildings of any kind whatsoever unless of a
          temporary nature and design on the said plot or area of ground
          and/

8.

TITLE NUMBER REN 4701

D. BURDENS SECTION

Entry Number	Specification

and that with the written consent of the Superior: (Third) The feuar shall so far as not already done enclose except on the South the said plot or area of ground with a boundary wall or other sufficient fence to the satisfaction of the Superior (Fourth) As regards all unfeued portions of the lands of which the said plot or area of ground forms part, the Superior is at liberty to deviate from, alter or abandon the feuing plan of his lands as he may think fit: and (Fifth) the feuar shall not be entitled to sub-divide the said plot or area of ground not to quarry stone or sand thereon not to use the said plot or area of ground for any purpose which might be deemed a nuisance or in any way which might be to the injury of the amenity of the neighbourhood or locality.

3.   Minute of Waiver by Trustees of Alan Smith, registered 6 NOV. 1976, waives the conditions in the Feu Contract in Entry 1 to the extent of allowing a Garage to be built on the plot of ground thereby disponed.

2.   THE USE OF ARROWS ON TITLE PLANS

(a) Where a deed states the line of a boundary in relation to a physical object, e.g. the centre line, that line is indicated on the Title Plan, either by means of a black arrow or verbally.

(b) An arrow across the object indicates that the boundary is stated to be the centre line.

(c) An arrow pointing to the object indicates that the boundary is stated to be the face of the object to which the arrow points.

(d) The physical object presently shown on the Plan may not be the one referred to in the deed. Indemnity is therefore excluded in respect of information as to the line of the boundary.

(e) Lineal measurements shown in figures on Title Plans are subject to the qualification "or thereby". Indemnity is excluded in respect of such measurements.

3.   SUBMISSION OF LAND CERTIFICATE WITH SUBSEQUENT APPLICATIONS FOR REGISTRATION.
In terms of Rule 9(3), this Land Certificate should be submitted to the Keeper of the Registers of Scotland with any application for registration.

4.   CAUTION. No unauthorised alteration to this Land Certificate should be made.

3 SPECIMEN CHARGE CERTIFICATE

(Land Registration (Scotland) Rules 1980 Rule 15)

LAND REGISTER OF SCOTLAND

CHARGE CERTIFICATE

TITLE NUMBER: REN 4701

SUBJECTS: 15 PARK AVENUE, PAISLEY

The within-mentioned Charge has been registered against the subjects in the above Title.

Statement of Indemnity

Subject to any specific qualifications entered in the Title Sheet to which the Charge Certificate relates a person who suffers loss as a result of any of the events specified in Section 12(1) of the Land Registration (Scotland) Act 1979 shall be entitled to be indemnified in respect of that loss by the Keeper of the Registers of Scotland in terms of that Act.

NOTICE

1. This Certificate must be presented to the Keeper on every transaction affecting the interest of the within-mentioned Registered Creditor.

2. The relative Title Sheet contains a specification of the reservations and burdens affecting the subjects in the above title.
    An Office Copy of the Title Sheet may be obtained on application to the Keeper.

3. No unauthorised alterations to this Charge Certificate should be made.

NOTICE

This Charge Certificate was made to agree with the Title Sheet to which it relates on the most recent date entered below.

20 AUG. 1983				

This Charge Certificate may be made to agree with the Title Sheet at any time without payment. Application should be made on Form 8.

LAND REGISTER OF SCOTLAND

CHARGE CERTIFICATE

TITLE NO. REN 4701

SUBJECTS: 15 PARK AVENUE, PAISLEY

Registered Proprietor of subjects: GEORGE BERNARD McDONALD and MARY
ISABELLA HALL or MORRIS or McDONALD,
spouses, 45 North Road, Paisley.

THIS IS TO CERTIFY that   FOUNDATION BUILDING SOCIETY, having its Chief
Office at New Malden House, Cardiff

is the Registered Creditor in the heritable security attached

registered on 20 AUG. 1983

NOTE

There are no heritable securities ranking prior to or *pari passu* with the above mentioned
heritable security appearing on the Register affecting the subjects

WE, GEORGE BERNARD McDONALD and MRS MARY ISABELLA HALL or MORRIS or McDONALD, spouses, both residing at 45 North Road, Paisley

WHEREAS the expressions set out below shall have the meanings and effect respectively set opposite them, namely

THE SOCIETY	FOUNDATION BUILDING SOCIETY, having its Chief Office at New Malden House, Cardiff
THE ADVANCE	Words TWENTY THOUSAND SEVEN HUNDRED AND FIFTY POUNDS Figures £20,750
THE REPAYMENT TABLE	The Society's Twenty (20) year Repayment Table
THE MONTHLY INSTALMENT	Words TWO HUNDRED AND EIGHTY POUNDS AND THIRTY FIVE PENCE Figures £280.35 or other amount fixed from time to time by the Society
THE INTEREST RATE	Fifteen and one half (15.50) per centum per annum or other rate fixed from time to time by the Society
THE SUBJECTS	The Property known as 15 PARK AVENUE, PAISLEY described below

If there shall be more than one granter hereof words in the singular shall include the plural and the obligations of the granter are undertaken jointly and severally

HEREBY UNDERTAKE TO PAY to the Society all sums due and that may become due by me to the Society in respect of (a) the Advance made or about to be made by the Society to me upon the terms of the Repayment Table with interest from the date of advance computed in accordance with the practice of the Society at the Interest Rate by equal calendar monthly payments of the Monthly Repayment commencing on the date specified for such purpose in the Notice of Completion issued by the Society and each subsequent payment at successive intervals of one calendar month and (b) any re-advance or any further or other advance or payment whether made or arising prior to or after delivery hereof which may be due by me to the Society with and including interest as certified by the Society, declaring that the amount or any part of the amount due to the Society hereunder at any time shall be sufficiently ascertained by a notice in writing signed by a duly authorised official of the Society: FOR WHICH I GRANT A STANDARD SECURITY in favour of the Society over the subjects registered under Title Number REN 4701:

The/

The Standard Conditions specified in Schedule 3 to the Conveyancing and Feudal
Reform (Scotland) Act 1970 as varied by the Deed of Variations made by the Society
dated and registered in the Books of Council and Session on the twentieth day of
November, Nineteen hundred and seventy, receipt of a copy of which deed, together
with a copy of the Society's Rules, is hereby acknowledged by me and any lawful
variations thereof operative for the time being shall apply: and I grant warrandice; and I
consent to registration hereof and of any said notice in writing for execution: IN
WITNESS WHEREOF these presents partly printed and partly typewritten on this and the
preceding page are subscribed by us the said George Bernard McDonald and Mrs Mary
Isabella Hall or Morris or McDonald at Paisley on the seventeenth day of July Nineteen
hundred and eighty three before these witnesses Alan John Bowden, Law Apprentice
and Mary Dow Gibb, Typist, both of eight Hall Street, Paisley,

A J Bowden (Witness)   *George B. McDonald*

M D. Gibb (witness)   *Mary I. McDonald*

Index

Sasines, Register of—*continued*
record in—*continued*
  heritable securites, 125
  lease, 7–8, 73, 74–5
  marketable title, and, 203, 206–7
  real right created by, 6, 125, 195
  title deed, real right created by, 4
registration for publication, 29
replacement by Land Register for
    Scotland, 530
searches, 29–30, 208
Sea
Crown rights, 50, 51
territorial waters, 50
Seabed
Crown rights, 50
Searches
company, transaction with, 211
Form 10 and 11 Reports, 210
Form 12 and 13 Reports, 210
Form P16 Report, 210
Interim Report, 209–10
letter of obligation, 212–13
Personal Register, 208–9
Property Register, 208
Register of Sasines, 29–30
registers, of, generally, 28–9
seller's obligation to deliver or
    exhibit clear, 207–13
Secretary of State for Scotland
town and country planning, 148
Securities
heritable. *See* HERITABLE SECURITIES
Seller
examination of title, obligations as to,
    203–14, 215–6
fixtures, dispute over, 53
Services
condition of, missives standard
    conditions, 186
Servitudes
aquaehaustus, 89
aqueduct, 89
civiliter, must be exercised, 86
classification, 86–7
creation of—
  documents creating need not be
      recorded or registered, 89
  express grant, 90–1
  express reservation , 92
  generally, 89–90
  implied grant, 91–2
  implied reservation, 92–3

Servitudes—*continued*
creation of—*continued*
  prescription, 94
definition, 85
dominant tenement, 85
eavesdrop, 88
extinction—
  acquiescence, 95–6
  change of circumstances, following,
      95
  confusione, 95
  generally, 94
  Lands Tribunal for Scotland,
      variation or extinction by, 96–
      7
  prescription, 95
  renunciation, 95
fuel, feal and divot, 89
grant of, 4
light or prospect, right of, 88
nature of, 85–7
negative, 86–7
  creation, 90
pasturage, 89
personal, 86, 87
positive, 86–7
  creation, 90
praedial, 86, 87
real conditions compared, 89–90
real right, as, 6, 85
right of way compared, 97
running with land, 6, 85–6
rural, 86, 87
scope, 90
servient tenement, 85
stillicide, 88
support, right of, 44, 88
title deeds, need not appear in, 89
types of, 87–9
urban, 86, 87
variation or discharge by Lands
    Tribunal for Scotland, 109
way, 88–9
Sewerage
statutory control, 161
Sewers
maintenance of, conditions in
    missives, 184
Shetland
allodial land, 8–9
Singular successor
meaning, 85